P

"[*Bailout*] is an interesting behind-the-scenes account of how Washington tried to save the economy . . . [and] an enjoyable tale of how a prosecutor of Colombian drug gangs got drafted for the thankless task of policing a $700 billion bailout from a dank basement office of the Treasury."

—*Fortune*

"A damning new insider's account . . . [*Bailout*] portrays in stunning detail the Bush and Obama administrations' unwillingness at every turn to deal with a spiraling housing crisis"

—Chris Hayes, host of *Up with Chris Hayes*

"[One] of our favorite business books so far this year . . . The former special inspector general policing the $700 billion Troubled Asset Relief Program lifts the lid on the U.S. Treasury and settles scores . . . [an] illuminating memoir."

—*Bloomberg Businessweek*

"A quick, intense read . . . [Barofsky] gave up a great career and his life to move to D.C. and, up against extreme adversity, stuck his neck out to help protect taxpayers and the American people . . . Read [*Bailout*], it's beyond illuminating, and will surely make you question government and what those in it tell you."

—*Business Insider*

"[An] explosive account of the mishandling of the Troubled Asset Relief Program funds."

—*Fort Worth Star-Telegram*

"Scathing."

—Andrew Ross Sorkin, *New York Times DealBook*

"[Anyone who wants] to call out the Obama administration for being too friendly to Wall Street and the banks at the expense of Main Street [should] be using *Bailout* as the cheat sheet that keeps on giving . . . [a] detailed and convincing indictment."

—Steven Brill, Reuters

"A very honest, detailed, entertaining and insightful addition to the existing roster of financial blockbusters."

—*American Banker*

"This book is essential reading . . . as it goes deeper than any of the hundred or so books covering the 2007–2012 period, when financial debacles plunged the real economy into recession."

—*Seeking Alpha*

"[An] everyman account of the pervasive cynicism and insider-dealing of the D.C. establishment."

—*The American Spectator*

"A damning indictment of the Obama administration's execution of the TARP program."

—*Washington Examiner*

"Blistering in its assessment of the Treasury Department's handling of the bailouts."

—*Huffington Post*

"A compelling critique of how the bailout was handled . . . as Mr. Barofsky makes clear, there is almost nothing about these bailout measures that should make you feel good."

—Simon Johnson, *New York Times* Economix Blog

"[Barofsky] unleashes a blistering attack on President Barack Obama's Treasury Department and its management of government bailout programs."

—*Politico*

"In *Bailout*, [Barofsky] gives a detailed account of just how far-reaching, and how much, the corruption spread."

—*Publishers Weekly*

"We're all falling in love with Neil Barofsky for the memoir of his days as the Special Inspector General for TARP bailout programs."

—*Alternative Banking*

"A very important story about what happened after the financial crisis . . . *Bailout* is a fabulous book, and it rings true . . . finally, someone who was there in a pivotal role has a book telling this story."

—Matt Stoller, *Naked Capitalism*

"Barofsky tells all in a fluid narrative that's as laden with damning facts as it is eminently readable. If you're still mad that we saved the *BANKS* and *THE BANKERS* as opposed to saving the *BANKING SYSTEM*, then this is the book for you."

—*The Reformed Broker*

"A terrific book . . . [with] a fascinating, well-told story."

—Lou Dobbs, *Lou Dobbs Tonight*

"An excellent read."

—Ali Velshi, *Your Money*

"Neil Barofsky . . . has written a juicy new book about the bailout and how it was handled—mishandled, rather, which is where the juicy parts come in."

—Mary Phillips-Sandy, *Comedy Central's Indecision*

"Barofsky proves that the Obama administration didn't give a damn about protecting taxpayer money or protecting homeowners, only shoveling dough at banks and AIG (the auto companies were treated like unwanted stepchildren). It's one thing to surmise that, another to deliver the goods."

—Yves Smith, *Naked Capitalism*

"Revelatory . . . It's well worth your time."

—David Dayen, *Fire Dog Lake*

"From December 2008 to March 2011, Barofsky served as the official watchdog for the Treasury Department's financial crisis response. (His official title was Special Inspector General for the Troubled Asset Relief Program, or TARP.) In that role, he made headlines with his scathing criticisms of the effort and its alleged deference to Wall Street interests. Now he's back with a new book on his experiences—entitled *Bailout*—and the criticisms are even louder."

—James O'Toole, CNNMoney

"Neil Barofsky, the former special inspector general for the TARP program, paints a thoroughly unflattering portrait of the Treasury secretary in his new book, *Bailout*. Barofsky may have an axe to grind, but he grinds it well."

—Darrell Delamaide, MarketWatch

"[One] of the best books . . . you should be reading this season."

—Mark Crumpton, Bloomberg TV's "Bottom Line"

"It's a great read."

—CNN, *Amanpour*

"A great book."

—Greta Van Susteren, host of *On the Record with Greta Van Susteren*

"[*Bailout*] should be mandatory reading for everyone in America. In fact, if it was . . . we'd be on our way toward recovery."

—Martin Andelman, host of the "Mandelman Matters" podcast

"[Neil Barofsky] peel[s] back the onion on the banking industry . . . a great book."

—Pimm Fox, Bloomberg TV's "Taking Stock"

"Barofsky's anecdotes about the Obama bailout team read much like a lost adult script for *Mean Girls*."

—Heidi N. Moore, *Marketplace*

*f*P

BAILOUT

How Washington Abandoned Main Street

While Rescuing Wall Street

NEIL BAROFSKY

FREE PRESS

New York London Toronto Sydney New Delhi

*f*P
Free Press
A Division of Simon & Schuster, Inc.
1230 Avenue of the Americas
New York, NY 10020

First Free Press trade paperback edition February 2013

FREE PRESS and colophon are trademarks of Simon & Schuster, Inc.

For information about special discounts for bulk purchases,
please contact Simon & Schuster Special Sales at 1-866-506-1949 or
business@simonandschuster.com.

The Simon & Schuster Speakers Bureau can bring authors to your
live event. For more information or to book an event contact the
Simon & Schuster Speakers Bureau at 1-866-248-3049 or
visit our website at www.simonspeakers.com.

Manufactured in the United States of America

1   3   5   7   9   10   8   6   4   2

The Library of Congress has catalogued the hardcover edition as follows:
Barofsky, Neil M.
Bailout : how Washington abandoned Main Street while rescuing
Wall Street / by Neil Barofsky.
p.   cm.
Includes bibliographical references and index.
1. Troubled Asset Relief Program (U.S.) 2. Finance—Subsidies—United
States. 3. Banks and banking—Subsidies—United States. 4. Corporate debt—
United States. 5. Global Financial Crisis, 2008–2009. 6. Rich people—
United States. I. Title.
HG181.B32 2012
338.973'02—dc23

ISBN 978-1-4516-8493-3
ISBN 978-1-4516-8495-7 (pbk)
ISBN 978-1-4516-8494-0 (ebook)

CAST OF CHARACTERS

At the Office of the Special Inspector General for the Troubled Assets Relief Program (SIGTARP)

Neil Barofsky: former special inspector general for TARP; former assistant U.S. attorney for the Southern District of New York

Kristine Belisle: former communications director, SIGTARP

Lori Hayman: director of legislative affairs, SIGTARP

Barry Holman: former deputy special inspector general for audits, SIGTARP

Geoff Moulton: former deputy special inspector general, SIGTARP

Kevin Puvalowski: former deputy special inspector general, SIGTARP; former assistant U.S. attorney for the Southern District of New York

Christopher Sharpley: former deputy special inspector general for investigations, SIGTARP

At the Treasury Department

Herbert Allison: former assistant secretary of the Treasury for financial stability, nominated by the Obama administration and confirmed by the Senate in June 2009; former president and CEO of Fannie Mae, former chairman and CEO of TIAA-CREF, former president of Merrill Lynch

Timothy Geithner: U.S. secretary of the Treasury; former president of the Federal Reserve Bank of New York

Timothy Massad: assistant secretary of the Treasury for financial stability, former chief counsel for the Office of Financial Stability

Robert Hoyt: former general counsel, Treasury Department

Neel Kashkari: former interim assistant secretary of the Treasury for financial stability.

Mark Patterson: chief of staff to Treasury Secretary Geithner

Henry Paulson: former U.S. secretary of the Treasury; former chief executive officer of Goldman Sachs

Eric Thorson: inspector general for the Treasury Department

Jim Wilkinson: former chief of staff to Treasury Secretary Paulson

At the Federal Reserve

Benjamin Bernanke: chairman of the Board of Governors of the Federal Reserve System

William Dudley: president of the Federal Reserve Bank of New York

Members of Congress

Max Baucus: senior U.S. senator from Montana; chairman of the Senate Committee on Finance, a Democrat

Elijah Cummings: the U.S. representative for Maryland's 7th District and ranking member of the House Committee on Oversight and Government Reform; a Democrat

Barney Frank: U.S. representative for Massachusetts's 4th Congressional District and ranking member and former chairman of the House Financial Services Committee; a Democrat

Chuck Grassley: senior U.S. senator for Iowa; former ranking member of the Senate Committee on Finance; a Republican

Darrell Issa: U.S. representative for California's 49th District; chairman and former ranking member of the House Oversight and Government Reform Committee; a Republican

Richard Shelby: senior U.S. senator from Alabama; ranking member and former chairman of the Senate Committee on Banking, Housing, and Urban Affairs; a Republican

Edolphus Towns: U.S. representative for New York's 10th district and former chairman of the House Oversight and Government Reform Committee; a Democrat

Other Characters

Preet Bharara: former chief counsel to Senator Charles E. Schumer; became U.S. attorney for the Southern District of New York in May, 2009

William Burck: former White House deputy counsel and former assistant U.S. attorney for the Southern District of New York

Michael Garcia: former U.S. attorney for the Southern District of New York

Lee Sachs: member of Obama administration transition team; former advisor to Treasury Secretary Timothy Geithner

Elizabeth Warren: former chair of the Congressional Oversight Panel created to oversee the Troubled Assets Relief Program; former assistant to the president and special advisor to the secretary of the Treasury on the Consumer Financial Protection Bureau; professor at Harvard University Law School

To Karen

CONTENTS

FOREWORD TO THE
PAPERBACK EDITION

I N WRITING *BAILOUT*, I was given the opportunity to relive the tumultuous twenty-seven months of my life that are recounted in the pages that follow. It was a harrowing time, both for me and for the country, but it was an experience I will always treasure. As a line prosecutor in Manhattan, I never dreamed I would have the opportunity to serve my country at such a crucial time, and while I certainly had more than my fair share of setbacks, I believe that the work we did at the Office of the Special Inspector General for the Troubled Asset Relief Program (SIGTARP) played an important role in protecting TARP from greater abuse and in bringing to justice those who sought to criminally profit from it.

Although I was initially reluctant to take the job in Washington, I felt it was my duty, and I felt a similar call to write this book, in order to bring attention to what I saw as a hijacking of both the bailouts and the government itself by a handful of Wall Street financial institutions and their executives. I saw how they were able to exert their power and influence to protect and reinforce a dangerous status quo that worked brilliantly for them but has left the rest of the country behind. In writing this book, I wanted to send a warning about what I see as a treacherous future given the banks' continued dominance.

Events that have happened since I finished the original hardcover version have unfortunately only further confirmed my fears about where we are headed as a country if we continue to ignore the dangers presented by banks deemed "too big to fail." Specifically, in the past several months we have seen a parade of banking scandals that have reflected just as poorly on the government and its captured regulators as on the banks themselves.

First, we learned of what appears to be a global conspiracy among several of the largest banks to manipulate one of the most important interest rate benchmarks in the world, the London InterBank Offered Rate (LIBOR), which is used to set interest rates for everything from complex derivative contracts to home and auto loans. A few banks are supposed to send in estimates of their borrowing costs each day to the British Bankers' Association, which then averages the reported numbers and issues the official LIBOR rate for that day. One of those reporting banks, Barclays, settled allegations that its employees had taken part in cooking the rate. The bank lied about its estimated costs in order to manipulate this number, originally so that its traders could rip off its counterparties and earn illicit profits, and then later to make it appear that the bank was in better financial shape than it actually was, thus potentially lowering its costs and fooling potential shareholders, regulators, and others.[1] A number of other banks are also apparent subjects of the ongoing investigation, including the all-too-familiar triumvirate in banking scandals: JPMorgan Chase, Bank of America, and Citigroup.[2]

As damning as the breathtaking arrogance, size, and scale of the alleged misconduct by the banks were the allegations indicating that one of the banks' primary regulators, the Federal Reserve Bank of New York, and its president at the time, Timothy Geithner, were made aware by Barclays by April 2008 both of the ongoing manipulation and that other banks were involved.[3] But rather than immediately alerting the Department of Justice or even calling in the banks subject to his jurisdiction and warning them that they needed to cease the manipulation immediately, Geithner took far more modest steps. He apparently did little more than send a memo to his regulatory counterparts in England, recommending that the rate-setting process be changed,[4] and call a meeting of U.S. regulators, during which the New York Fed generally reported that the LIBOR process was vulnerable to potential manipulation but reportedly did not cite the *actual* manipulation to which Barclays had confessed.[5]

This regulatory response was so remarkably tepid that Barclays actually *continued* to manipulate LIBOR for a full year after Geithner took the actions he later defended as "necessary and appropriate," which apparently included relying on the British regulators to "fix this."[6] Indeed, although at the time some suspicions were reported in the press that LIBOR was being manipulated,[7] rather than alerting the public, Geithner effectively endorsed the rate by baking it into several bailout programs, using it as a benchmark to determine the interest rate that taxpayers would receive from AIG and in certain TARP programs. According to news reports, it wasn't until 2010 that a referral was made to the Department of Justice, and even then it came from the U.S. Commodity Futures Trading Commission, not the New York Fed or Treasury.[8]

A number of other banking scandals have also broken since *Bailout's* completion. Standard Chartered joined JPMorgan Chase in settling charges that they illicitly processed monetary transactions for institutions in nations such as Iran and Cuba,[9] and a Senate Committee detailed HSBC's apparent facilitation of financial transactions for rogue organizations, including those potentially involved in terrorism or narcotics trafficking.[10] The Department of Justice has also brought civil charges against Wells Fargo and Bank of America for defrauding the government of more than a billion dollars in connection with fraudulent mortgage activity that continued through 2009, well after the banks had accepted TARP funds. These cases, brought in October 2012, followed the settlement of similar charges against Citigroup and Deutsche Bank. Also in October, the New York State attorney general brought a broad civil case against JPMorgan Chase for fraud committed by Bear Stearns in the assembling and sale of mortgage-related securities during the run-up to the financial crisis, and he filed a similar case against Credit Suisse the following month. The SEC also settled cases against both JPMorgan Chase and Credit Suisse over the packaging and sale of similar securities.[11]

To date, however, all of these cases and scandals have one thing in common. Not a single institution or senior executive has been criminally charged for the underlying conduct. And while there have been leaked news stories suggesting that some of the lower-level Barclays traders may in fact be charged criminally in the LIBOR case, it seems as if the likelihood of high-level criminal charges for cases related to the financial crisis or actions taken in its aftermath has diminished to close to zero. As the New York attorney general told reporters, he chose civil over criminal cases not necessarily because of a paucity of evidence, but because the authorities had waited too long to file criminal charges.[12] The five-year statute of limitations in New York for criminal cases (as opposed to the six-year statute for civil cases) had run its course. Similarly, it now appears to be too late for the president's Financial Fraud Enforcement Task Force, originally announced in October 2009, to do its promised job "to hold accountable those who helped bring about the last financial meltdown."[13]

There are a number of potential explanations for the failure to bring criminal cases, some of which are detailed in the pages that follow. After the terrorist attacks of September 11, 2001, federal law enforcement personnel and resources were understandably redirected toward counterterrorism efforts, creating a significant shortfall in white-collar criminal investigative expertise. As a result, as I saw firsthand, by 2008 the Department of Justice lacked sophistication when it came to investigating complex accounting fraud cases.

But there was another reason for the lack of cases: a staggering absence of referrals from regulators—such as Geithner's New York Fed—to the Department of Justice. As William K. Black, a banking regulator during the savings and loan crisis of the 1980s and 1990s, has explained, prosecutors back then leaned heavily on banking experts at the regulatory agencies to refer and shape the cases, with Black's agency making 30,000 referrals to the Department of Justice relating to frauds committed by the banks.[14] In contrast, Black reported that the Office of the Comptroller of the Currency and the Office of Thrift Supervision, the two bank regulators housed at Treasury, had made only a handful of referrals in connection with the current crisis.[15] Also, despite the promising announcement of the president's Financial Fraud Enforcement Task Force, there was never a significant commitment of investigative and prosecutorial resources to focus exclusively on sophisticated crisis-related crimes.

The absence of cases is likely also related to the power, influence, and control in Washington of the largest banks. The entire federal regulatory and political apparatus coalesced during the crisis and in the aftermath around one goal—to rescue the "too big to fail" banks by any means nec-essary, with trillions of taxpayer dollars flowing out the door with few conditions and little accountability. With Treasury having invested so much time, effort, and treasure into *saving* the big banks, it was simply inconceivable that the Department of Justice could have sought crimi-nal indictments against any of the largest banks or their top executives. Doing so would have risked causing them to fail, thereby undoing all of Treasury's and the Federal Reserve's efforts and putting the entire finan-cial system at risk once again.

These problems, of course, endure, with the largest banks now nearly 25 percent bigger than they were before the crisis. If they were too big to fail in 2008, they became too big to jail in 2009. Worst of all, Wall Street knows this to be true, and each settlement of a civil case on favor-able terms, and with no accountability for the individuals who committed the fraudulent acts, reinforces the most dangerous perception of all: for a select group of executives and institutions, crime pays. Why not risk crossing the line and continue to perpetrate fraud in the assembling and sale of mortgages if the penalty for getting caught is a fine that can be paid off with a few days or weeks of earnings? Why worry about violating sanctions in order to profit illegally by laundering money for terrorist-sponsoring states? Why not rip off investors by selling bonds that are designed to fail so that you can profit from your bet against them?[16] Why not spend ten years defrauding the Federal Housing Administration? You know you'll get to keep all of the ill-gotten profits if you go undetected, and on the off chance that you're caught, your shareholders will pay a minor fine that will not affect your bottom line. In other words, the com-plete lack of meaningful consequences—financial or penal—for those committing these frauds encourages future fraudulent conduct.

Ultimately, the financial crisis was a game of incentives gone wild, and the lack of accountability in the aftermath of the crisis only reinforced those bad incentives. We had a chance to bring real accountability to the system in 2009 with the announcement of the Financial Fraud Enforce-ment Task Force, but it was left underfunded and under-resourced. We had a second chance to fix the system in 2010 by breaking up the largest banks through regulatory reform, but the banks—with a healthy assist from Geithner and the Treasury Department—won that battle too. And we had an election in 2012 that could also have been an opportunity for meaningful change. But both candidates staunchly defended the status quo, which maintained the size and power of the banks, even as they made the incredible claim that they would never bail them out again. I fear that we may not have many more opportunities left before it is too late, and that meaningful reform will arise only out of the ashes of the next economic conflagration. That is a sequel I would prefer not to have to write.

ALTHOUGH it was only April, we were in the midst of a mini heat wave in Washington that foreshadowed what would turn out to be a scorching summer. I'd been in the city for almost a year and a half, but I just couldn't get used to the otherworldly heat, the swamplike humidity, and the complete absence of anything that might resemble a breeze. Even so, I decided to walk the ten minutes from our offices in Dupont Circle to Potenza restaurant, located on the first floor of a luxury rental building inhabited by the former banking executives and lawyers from New York who frequent the revolving door between Wall Street and Washington.

I was meeting that night with Herb Allison, who lived in the building and fit its profile perfectly. Allison was the former president of Merrill Lynch and chief executive officer of the financial services organization TIAA-CREF. He'd enjoyed an illustrious and highly profitable Wall Street career before retiring to his sprawling mansion in Connecticut. In late 2008, then Secretary of the Treasury Henry Paulson called the sixty-five-year-old while he was enjoying a vacation in the Caribbean and asked him to come to Washington immediately to run the recently failed and now government-owned mortgage behemoth Fannie Mae. Allison accepted and after a short stint was tapped by incoming Treasury Secretary Timothy Geithner to run the Troubled Asset Relief Program, or TARP, as the Treasury assistant secretary for financial stability. He became, in other words, the "TARP czar," and I quickly became one of his least favorite people on the planet.

I had initiated this meeting. As the special inspector general assigned to oversee the spending of the TARP money—my office was known as SIGTARP—it was my job to scrutinize just about every aspect of Allison's professional life in Washington. By April 2010, that had meant issuing a

series of highly critical reports that generated a stream of negative headlines for the Treasury Department and a seemingly unending series of
congressional hearings in which Allison, Geithner, and other Treasury
officials were subject to bipartisan roastings, occasionally punctuated by
one member of Congress or another calling for Geithner's resignation. I
offered to meet with Allison "offline" after yet another one of my weekly
meetings with him had devolved into a screaming match. I wanted to get
together away from the office, just the two of us, over a drink—or "over
shots," as Allison had joked when I'd invited him—to clear the air.

Never knowing how much longer I was going to be welcome in Washington, I hadn't invested in a new Washington-appropriate wardrobe and
was wearing the unseasonal dark gray wool suit that had become my uni-
form. I could feel the sweat pooling at the small of my back as I walked into
the restaurant. Because I'd told the hostess we were only having drinks,
she wanted to seat us up front, where it would have been difficult for us
to have a private conversation. After first asking politely to be seated in
the back and refused, Allison adopted a formidable "Do you know who I
am?" tone that he'd obviously perfected over his decades as a top executive
on Wall Street. The hostess was no match, and we were quickly ushered to
a quiet table in the back. We chatted cordially for a few minutes about our
families and nonwork lives, as people tend to do at these Washington ren-
dezvous. Allison said how tough his weekly commute from Connecticut
was, while I told him that my wife's regular commute from New York had
just ended because she had entered the final month of pregnancy with our
first child. I said I was excited about the imminent arrival of our daughter,
and he said how thrilled he'd been about the birth of his first son decades
before. He then got to the heart of things.

"Neil, you're obviously very talented, with a bright future," he started.
He talked about how clear the reports my office had submitted to Congress were and noted that the press was generally effusive in its praise
of me and my team. Always circumspect about being complimented in
Washington, I waited for the kicker.

"But you're really hurting yourself."

"In what way?" I asked, genuinely curious about where this might be
going.

"Well, you're a young man, just starting out with a family, and obviously this job isn't going to last forever. Have you thought at all about what you'll be doing next?"

It was not the first time I'd been asked that question in Washington. It's the question that everyone asks, always to themselves and sometimes to others. What's next? What's your angle? What's going to be the payout? How are you going to leverage your current position to get a better one with more power and a bigger payout? I gave Allison my standard answer, whether to a reporter, congressional staffer, senator, family member, friend, my wife, Karen, or myself.

"Herb, in my first Senate hearing, Shelby"—Richard Shelby, the top Republican on the Senate Banking, Housing, and Urban Affairs Committee and whose southern drawl I couldn't help affecting as I told this story—"told me, 'Mister Inspector General, you have a wonderful opportunity here. An opportunity not too many people get. The opportunity to make a real difference. An opportunity to serve the American people in a true and meaningful way. And if you do this job the right way, you'll never be able to get a job again. No one will hire you. And that would be a good thing.'"

I explained to Allison how meaningful that exchange had been to me.

"Shelby was trying to be funny," I said, "but there was an important point there too—that the only way to do this job was *not* to think about what I would be doing next. If I ever start thinking about a law firm job, or a job on Wall Street, or even another government job, those concerns will inevitably start creeping into my decision making."

Allison was unimpressed with my speech. Not that I can blame him— I'm sure it sounded like a sound bite devised for a press interview. He continued, "You have to think about it. And I'm telling you, you're doing yourself real harm. Out there in the market, there are consequences for some of the things that you're saying and the *way* that you're saying them."

I was impressed with Allison's approach. By that point I'd been in Washington long enough to know when I was being played, and Allison was essentially threatening me with lifelong unemployment. But, to his credit, his tone dripped with sincerity.

"Herb, I know that. I understand that. But like I just said, I really can't think that way. I wouldn't be doing my job if I started thinking that way."

Having failed to achieve the desired response by holding up the specter of homelessness for my wife, my soon-to-be-born daughter, and me, Allison shifted course.

"Well, it's not just that. On the Hill, I'm hearing a lot of things about you. Sure, during a hearing they may say some nice things, but there are a lot of members of Congress, particularly in the Senate, who think that you've gone too far, and you're losing credibility fast."

A much better play, Herb, I thought. Allison had struck a nerve. The relevance of my oversight depended on strong credibility with members of Congress. At SIGTARP we had limited authority, and without strong backers in Congress, our work would quickly recede into irrelevancy.

"I can't control that, Herb," I responded. "It's not as if we sit there and craft each word in our reports based on how we think some senator or congressman might react. We just tell the truth in the way that we see it."

Allison persisted, "It's not so much the content as it is the tone. Your *tone* is the problem."

My tone was part of my job, I explained. "Herb, when I first got here, a senior congressman took me aside and said, 'Neil, let me tell you how this town works. You can write the best and most important reports in the world, and Treasury will ignore you. The only way that you're going to be able to have an impact is to get us, Congress, involved. And the only way that we'll pay attention is if your reports are covered in the press. Then we'll embrace you. *And then* Treasury will pay attention.'" I explained to Allison that I had stuck with that advice and it had proven exactly right, and that my tone was necessary to penetrate all of the noise in Washington and get the attention of the press, Congress, and ultimately Treasury itself.

Allison changed gears. "Well, is it an appointment you might be looking for? Something else in government? A judgeship?"

I laughed. "Herb, obviously that would be amazing, but there is no way that this White House, after the things we've said, is going to nominate me for anything."

Allison paused. "Well, Neil, it doesn't have to be that way. It's not necessarily off the table. All you really have to do is change your tone, just a bit, and things can really change for you. Including with the White House."

It was my turn to pause, as I took a good sip of my wine. "Well, Herb, I certainly appreciate your advice," I said, not quite believing what I thought he was saying, and then tried desperately to turn our conversation back to more trivial matters.

But Allison wouldn't give up that easily. He stuck to his script for a good ten minutes more before I managed to steer the conversation back to beltway gossip and other banal niceties before wrapping up.

I was all of thirty seconds back out into the heat when I called my deputy and friend for nearly a decade, Kevin Puvalowski. Kevin and I had met as prosecutors in the United States Attorney's Office in Manhattan in 2001, and we worked closely together on cases against the world's biggest drug cartels as members of the international narcotics trafficking unit.

"How'd it go?" he asked. We had both been curious about how this encounter would play out.

I burst out laughing. "You are not going to believe it," I responded, and then recounted the conversation.

Kevin laughed. "It was the gold or the lead."

"Yeah, the bullet or the bribe, I think he totally Escobarred me." We were referring to the practice that, as former narcotics prosecutors, we both well knew. The most notorious method of persuasion used by the legendary Colombian cocaine kingpin Pablo Escobar to bend elected officials, police officers, or local judges to his will was to offer them one of two choices: a giant pile of pesos to do his bidding or a bullet in the head. I'd just received the Washington equivalent. Either I started playing ball and would then get either a plum appointment or a lucrative job on Wall Street, or I'd end up discredited and unemployed.

Kevin responded, "Unbelievable. Every trick in the book. He flattered you, insulted you, tried to scare you, and then effectively tried to bribe you. Welcome to Washington."

"Yeah, but what about what he said about the Hill?" I asked. "Do you think we have a problem there?" Allison's assertion that some members of Congress had become unhappy with me was a little unnerving.

But Kevin wasn't worried. "Don't give it a second thought," he said. "He's probably full of shit."

Looking back, I don't now think that Allison was in fact really threatening me, nor do I think that he was actually offering me a plum appointment if I played ball. I think he was, in a very Washington way, sincerely trying to be helpful, to educate me on how to survive and thrive, both in Washington and on Wall Street. They are both worlds where if you play by the rules of those in power, great things can follow, whether in the form of multimillion-dollar paydays in the private sector or escalating power and prestige in the government. The allure of those payoffs is a powerful and pernicious force in government service, especially, as I saw up close in my dealings with Treasury, in agencies that deal with Wall Street.

As an elder statesman now of both worlds, Allison was, I think, probably just trying to explain to me how the system worked. Although he was undoubtedly right, I hadn't left a job I had loved in New York to go down to Washington and play by its rules. I was still a prosecutor at heart, and for as long as I managed to hang on at SIGTARP, I was going to keep doing exactly what I'd been given the job to do: hold Treasury and the banks it had bailed out accountable for their management and use of hundreds of billions of taxpayer dollars.

1

Fraud 101

I WAS SITTING AT my desk after hours on Wednesday, October 15, 2008, when the phone rang. I'd been sifting through a pile of FBI reports about my newest case—a loathsome ring of predators who were stealing houses out from under home owners who had fallen behind in their mortgage payments. Looking down at the caller ID, I saw that it read US ATTORNEY. *Shit,* I thought. It was my boss, Mike Garcia, the U.S. attorney for the Southern District of New York, and I figured that either I was in trouble or he was going to dump something urgent on me.

"You got a minute?" he asked. "C'mon up."

As I headed out of my office, I tried to think of who I might have pissed off enough to warrant getting called to the principal's office. While I was waiting for Mike to get off the phone, he handed me a copy of a statute describing the creation of an inspector general's office for the Troubled Asset Relief Program, the $700 billion bank bailout Congress had passed less than two weeks earlier.

When he hung up, Mike asked, "Did you know that when they passed TARP, they also created a $50 million law enforcement agency to oversee it?"

"No, I had no idea," I replied.

He then started describing the new office in detail. It would have two roles. First, it was going to be a full-fledged law enforcement agency, a mini-FBI for the TARP, which would try to catch the inevitable criminal flies that would be drawn to the $700 billion in government honey. It would also have an audit function, providing Congress with regular reports on how the Treasury Department was carrying out the bailout. Relieved that I wasn't in trouble, I half listened while trying to figure out why Mike was telling *me* about this new agency. Rumors were swirling around the office that with the presidential election just a few weeks away, Mike, who was a Bush appointee, was about to step down. I thought maybe he was taking the inspector general job and that he might be trying to recruit me to go with him. I began planning my polite refusal.

"So, you think you'd be interested?" Mike asked, snapping my attention back.

"In what?" I responded, making a mental note to pay closer attention when the boss was talking.

"In the job," he said.

"What job?" I asked, still not understanding what he was getting at.

He looked exasperated and said, "The special inspector general job."

I was stunned. As a federal prosecutor I had been fortunate to investigate and try some remarkable cases, but I sucked at office politics. I had a hard time keeping my opinions to myself, and my aversion to bullshit and hypocrisy occasionally led to an Asperger's-like bluntness. That didn't always endear me to people, particularly some of my recent supervisors. (Months later, Mike explained that was partly why he had recommended me: "You can be kind of a dick at times, and they needed someone who could be kind of a dick.") And although Mike had recently promoted me to lead the office's newly created mortgage fraud group, he had also passed me over for a supervisory job a couple of years earlier.

Now, out of nowhere, he was asking me if I was interested in a job that he explained would require a nomination from President George W. Bush and confirmation by the U.S. Senate. Clearly this job would be a highly sought after political appointment for the type of person who aspires to such things. Did Mike not realize that I was a nobody? That I knew almost no one in Washington? More important, did he not realize that I was a lifelong Democrat who had recently contributed to the Barack Obama campaign? Me? A *Bush* appointee?

It wasn't just that I couldn't see how I could possibly get the nomination; I wasn't interested. I didn't even really know what an inspector general did. My experiences with IGs, as they were called, were largely limited to a handful of cases I'd handled back when I first started as a prosecutor in 2000. My friend and colleague Mike Purpura used to joke that the true sign a case was going to prove a colossal waste of time was if it involved what he referred to as "those three magic letters, O-I-G"—for Office of the Inspector General. I started thinking of excuses.

"Is the job in New York?" I asked.

"No, D.C., of course it's in D.C.," Mike responded in a tone that made clear he didn't subscribe to the old adage that there is no such thing as a stupid question.

I explained that the timing really wasn't right. I was getting married in a few months to my fiancée, Karen, for one thing, and I was preparing to try a big case against the lawyer Joseph Collins, who had been charged in a multibillion-dollar accounting fraud related to the collapsed giant commodities broker Refco. I'd worked like a rented mule to get the case indicted. It had become my "white whale," and I couldn't imagine walking away from it. Not only that, but I was also just getting the mortgage fraud group off the ground. These were some of the most appalling cases imaginable, with predators feasting on struggling borrowers and clueless banks while lining their own corrupt pockets. I was looking forward to bringing these criminals to justice. Mike's face told me that he wasn't buying any of my excuses, so I rolled out the big gun.

"And, Mike, you know that I'm a Democrat, right?" I said, pausing for a moment for effect, then delivering my coup de grâce. "And just last week I donated to Obama's campaign."

I was sure that would be a deal killer, but Mike persisted.

"I thought of you exactly because of Collins and the mortgage fraud group. Those cases are exactly the types of experiences that the White House is looking for. As for your politics, they won't care; this is a merit appointment."

I wondered for a moment where Mike had found the unicorns and fairies to hand out those "merit" Bush nominations to Obama-contributing Democrats.

Then Mike pulled out his "God and country" speech. The Southern District office stands just a few blocks from Ground Zero, and he reminded me of the sacrifices some of the recent legends of the office had

made after the terrorist attacks on September 11, 2001, dropping everything to work around the clock chasing down the terrorists.

"They had expertise in terrorism, and it was never a question that they
would step up. That is what this office does. Our people step up and sac-
rifice when they need to."

Now he had my full attention. On that perfect blue-skied morning
as I walked up the stairs out of the subway on my way to work, I saw a
woman crying hysterically and pointing at the smoking gash in the North
Tower. She told me that she had just seen an American Airlines plane
strike the building, and I stood next to her along with dozens of others as
we watched the rest of the terror unfold.

When what seemed like strange debris began falling from the towers,
I commented to a man next to me about it, uncomprehendingly, and he
responded simply, "Debris don't move like that." With horror I immediately realized we were watching people jumping to escape the raging fire.
I had tried hard to forget those images, along with the sound of the blast
and the heat of the fireball that burst from the guts of the South Tower
when the second plane struck. Every night for months when I tried to
close my eyes to sleep, I would relive those moments. It is still difficult to
look at 9/11 footage on television without breaking down.

"What we're going through now is the economic equivalent of 9/11,"
Mike continued. "It's time for you to step up. The American taxpayer has
paid a lot of money to train you and give you this unique set of skills.
Who else is going to protect the public from what could be a $700 billion
clusterfuck of fraud?"

It was a good speech.

There was no question that the country was in the midst of a true crisis.
The Dow Jones Industrial Average had plunged more than 5,500 points
over the past year, and once iconic New York firms such as Bear Stearns
and Lehman Brothers had melted down. Unprecedented sums of money
were being poured into the insurance giant AIG to keep it afloat. The
value of people's 401(k)s, including my own, would lose a third of their
value, $2.8 trillion in all, between September 2007 and December 2008.[1]
Foreclosures had also been exploding nationwide, with more than 2.3
million properties receiving filings in 2008 alone, an 81 percent increase
from 2007 and a 225 percent increase from the year before that.[2] As chief

of the mortgage fraud group, I had seen one of the causes: widespread fraud involving sophisticated rings of professionals who took advantage of the lenders' complete disregard of their underwriting standards as part of Wall Street's blind quest for profit and fees. I had seen the predatory practices of those criminals, which still had the capacity to shock me even after spending years prosecuting international narcotics kingpins. Though I knew in my heart that Mike was right, that it was my duty to put in for the job, I also couldn't imagine giving up the only job I'd ever wanted, disrupting my marriage before it even really began, and leaving the city that I loved.

THE OFFICE OF the U.S. Attorney for the Southern District of New York, known simply as "the Office," is just one of the ninety-four U.S. Attorney's Offices in the country. But the Office is different: it has long been the preeminent prosecutor's office in the country. In recent years, it has handled a string of high-profile cases, including landmark Wall Street prosecutions against executives like Michael Milken, Ivan Boesky, Bernie Ebbers, and Bernie Madoff, as well as those against the terrorists responsible for the 1993 World Trade Center attack and the bombings of the U.S. embassies in Tanzania and Kenya in 1998.

I got the bug to work in the Office while at law school at New York University, when Professor Andrew Schaffer regaled my criminal procedure class with war stories from his own time in the Office. I knew I needed experience at a law firm before I could get a job there, so after I graduated, I joined one of the large New York City firms before moving to a smaller litigation boutique to begin a three-and-a-half-year apprenticeship under two brilliant white-collar defense lawyers, Robert Morvillo and Elkan Abramowitz. They taught me both the nuts and bolts of being a lawyer and the necessity of following a strict ethical code while doing so. They had both served as former chiefs of the Criminal Division of the Office, and I hoped that by working my tail off I could gain their support for my application.

I distinctly remember sitting in my office in the spring of 2000 when the call came in. "Please hold for Mary Jo White." I was ecstatic. It was widely known that Mary Jo, who'd been running the Office for eight years, called applicants only with offers, not rejections. I was going to be an assistant U.S. attorney for the Southern District of New York.

Like all new prosecutors, I started in General Crimes and then graduated to the Narcotics Unit. I'd never aspired to work on narcotics cases, but I knew all prosecutors spent a year in Narcotics after completing General Crimes, and I figured I wouldn't spend one day over the required minimum.

That changed after I started working for Richard Sullivan, the Narcotics Unit's chief. He was actually an odd match for me. A tall, intense, deeply religious man who had never touched a drop of alcohol in his life, Rich worked tirelessly: he was always already at work when I arrived, and he often stayed after I'd left. There were a lot of brilliant lawyers at the Office, and Rich was definitely one of them. But what struck me about him was how deeply committed he was to the work. Working for Rich was a revelation, and I started following him around like a puppy.

In 2002, Rich formed the International Narcotics Trafficking Unit, known as INT, to go after the most sophisticated transnational narcotics organizations. He saw evil in the drug world and believed that he could make a difference. Joining INT meant buying into that mission completely and learning how to be a prosecutor under Rich's exacting standards wasn't easy. But it proved invaluable. Rich firmly believed that the greatest sins a prosecutor could commit were being outworked or underprepared. You would have a short and miserable time in his unit if you ever went into court without having done your homework.

Once he assigned me to a case that was set to go to trial in just three weeks. The defendant was the first to be extradited from Colombia solely on money-laundering charges, and Rich let me know the gravity of the case when he assigned it to me.

"Losing is not an option," he told me. "If you lose this case, extradition from Colombia will end as we know it." He repeated that warning to me every day through the end of the trial. I didn't sleep much, and I probably lost about ten pounds, but the anxiety and hard work paid off: the jury was out for less than an hour before convicting the defendant on all counts.

Years later, when I had a staff of my own at SIGTARP, the question "What would Sullivan do?" was an important guidepost in navigating the treacherous waters of Washington. I tired to make his ethos of "always the right thing, rarely the easy thing" my own.

Little did I know how relevant the experiences I would gain through investigating, prosecuting, and fighting over those cases would be when I later tried to gain my bearings in Washington as the special inspector general for TARP.

In early 2004, Rich had asked me to jump onto an investigation into what would prove to be the world's largest narco-terrorist cartel, the Revolutionary Armed Forces of Colombia, or FARC. FARC was one of South America's oldest insurgencies, an old-school Marxist-Leninist guerrilla organization that had fallen on hard times after one of its sources of funding, the former Soviet Union, collapsed. To fund its terrorist activities, FARC forcibly moved into the nuts and bolts of cocaine production. It wasn't your typical cartel of powerful traffickers, it was a 20,000-member army that operated out of the Andean jungle and controlled a large portion of the Colombian countryside. As we later learned from our investigation, they ruled with an iron fist, ripping children from local peasant families and forcing them to "enlist," routinely raping their female recruits, and often engaging in the gruesome torture and murder of those who dared to steal from their narcotics enterprise (including dismembering a suspected thief alive with a chainsaw in front of his friends and family). The FARC would even murder the child "recruits" who later tried to escape, often ordering other children to carry out the executions.[3] When I asked Rich how I was supposed to proceed, he told me simply to go down to Bogotá and figure it out.

In doing so, we were going to be stepping on the toes of the Justice Department, a preview of the hostility I would later have to deal with at Treasury. The Office had an occasionally contentious relationship with Main Justice, or DOJ, the Washington division of the Department of Justice. All U.S. Attorney's Offices report to the deputy attorney general of the United States, who in turn reports to the attorney general. Also reporting to the deputy attorney general is an assistant attorney general who oversees a bevy of Washington-based prosecutorial sections that are divided into subject matter areas such as fraud, organized crime, money laundering, narcotics, civil rights, and terrorism. Those sections have overlapping jurisdiction with the U.S. Attorney's offices, which occasionally leads to turf battles over which office gets to prosecute high-profile cases.

The Office, though, had become an island of independence from Main Justice, with prosecutors generally able to avoid the usual politics. We were allowed to just be prosecutors, while the U.S. attorney fought the necessary battles to keep DOJ at bay.

In the FARC case, however, Rich was asking us to be the ones to invade someone else's turf. He gave us marching orders to essentially pick a fight with three different offices in Washington that had been investigating the FARC—unsuccessfully—for years: DOJ's Narcotics and Dangerous Drugs Section, the Counter Terrorism Section, and the U.S. Attorney's Office for the District of Columbia. Together with the leadership at the Drug Enforcement Administration (DEA) and the FBI, they had developed an official FARC narrative: though certain rogue groups within FARC, called "fronts," might have been engaged in narcotics trafficking, the organization as a whole was not.[4] That narrative was fully supported by the State Department, which likely wanted to keep its options open in case an opportunity arose to broker peace between FARC and the Colombian government. It also justified DOJ's tepid results after years of investigation: only a handful of charges against FARC guerrillas. I was to learn while at SIGTARP that "adopting a narrative" was a tried-and-true tactic in Washington: define the status quo as a success, and then ignore all evidence that suggests otherwise.

Rich was stepping in on the FARC case because the Office had received a request from a DEA group working in Colombia. By working with nontraditional sources, including military intelligence agencies from both Colombia and the United States, our agents had gathered evidence that proved that FARC's leaders had transformed their "revolution" into a sophisticated and fully integrated drug-trafficking organization. But when the agents had taken their preliminary findings to the DOJ attorneys handling the FARC case, they were rebuffed. They then brought the evidence to us.

Once I jumped on board, my partner on the case, Eric Snyder, and I soon established a near-constant presence in Bogotá, supported by two DEA groups, one in Bogotá and another in New York. Before long, we were awash in evidence that the FARC was the world's largest narcotics cartel, responsible for producing more than half of the world's cocaine. Within months we'd developed enough proof to support an indictment that would charge the top fifty FARC leaders in a sprawling conspiracy to import cocaine into the United States—a remarkable accomplishment by some of the most committed and hardworking law enforcement agents whom I have had the pleasure to know.

If, like me, you'd never worked in Washington, you'd think that DOJ and the higher-ups at DEA would've been thrilled. After all, in a few short months we had advanced a moribund case to the precipice of becoming one of the largest narcotics prosecutions in U.S. history. The political reality was far different. DOJ apparently viewed our success as proof of its own failure, and following the logic that is unique to Washington, it worked to kill our case. By July 2004, the three different groups of prosecutors were working with each other with an energy that they had never applied to actually investigating FARC. On July 15, 2004, I was summoned out of Colombia to Washington to "brief" the DOJ leadership team. It was, as Rich later described, an "ambush." I spoke for less than five minutes before a preordained "consensus" was reached by everyone in the room—except, of course, our investigative team—that the New York–led FARC investigation would take a backseat to the Washington-based prosecutors.

We ignored the edict and continued to move forward, but we started receiving pressure from all sides. The DEA leadership in Washington became hostile, and our agents began getting messages that pushing too hard on the case could be detrimental to their careers. When the head of our Bogotá group was hauled up to DEA headquarters, I went too and had to watch him get dressed down by DEA's chief of operations for simply doing his job.

The State Department also started getting into the act, and several times I was called in from the field to the embassy in Bogotá to be yelled at by the deputy chief of mission (the number two person in the embassy), who threatened to toss me out of the country for imaginary offenses, such as violating country clearance protocols and supposedly "duplicating" the efforts of the DOJ prosecutors—all apparently planted by DOJ sources in Washington. That summer we easily spent as much time fighting DOJ as we did investigating FARC.

Apparently the State Department had played this role in drug cases before. On one of my train rides between Washington and New York, I was working on my laptop when a man sat down next to me and started looking over my shoulder. I twisted the computer screen around so he couldn't see what I was working on, but he arched his head and moved so close that I could smell the coffee on his breath. Annoyed, I turned to him to tell him to back off when I recognized that he was then Senator Joseph Biden. We chatted at length about narcotics law enforcement, and he told me that he worked extensively on international narcotics legislation. Right as we were approaching his stop in Wilmington, he turned to me, handed me his card, and told me to stop by his offices next time I was in Washington. Then he offered a parting thought.

"Neil, you know what the biggest single hurdle is to enforcing the narcotics laws internationally?" he asked.

"What, Senator?" I dutifully responded.

"Not the traffickers. Not the corruption. The State Department. The United States State Department." He turned and headed off the train.

By August 2004, notwithstanding the interference from Washington, we had made tremendous progress. I was in Bogotá preparing the agents to go to the grand jury in New York to seek the indictment of dozens of the top FARC leaders when Rich forwarded to me a memorandum from the Washington-based prosecutors to the deputy attorney general, or DAG. The memo essentially requested that the DAG order us to shut down our case and fall in line behind the Washington prosecutors.

I was dumbfounded. I knew turf battles were normal when you were going after big traffickers, but this was different. We were in the midst of a fully developed investigation, and I couldn't believe that all of our hard work might end up being for nothing, buried in a filing cabinet.

The DAG's office made the Solomonic decision to split the baby in half. Though we would continue to "lead" the case, we were going to have to charge and try the case out of the prosecutors' offices in Washington.

It was maddening. The DOJ attorneys had done little work on the case except disrupt our investigation, and instead of being punished for their obstructionism, they were now being rewarded with a prize. Because the case would be brought out of their offices, they would be able to claim a landmark conviction without having done any of the work.

After I hung up the phone and relayed the news to the agent I was having a drink with in Bogotá, I declared, "I'll tell you what I learned from this whole thing. I will never, ever take a job in Washington. The people down there don't care about justice or protecting the United States. It's all about bullshit, ego, politics, turf, and credit."

I had no idea at the time how wrong I was about myself and how right I was about Washington.

ULTIMATELY, IT WAS the FARC case, in a roundabout way, that put me on the path to SIGTARP. One of the breakthroughs in the case was the Colombian army's willingness to share the names of former FARC guerrillas who had defected and sought asylum. One of the best was "Jane," who gave us detailed, corroborated evidence of FARC's dominance of the Colombian cocaine trade. During my third meeting with Jane in Bogotá, I told her that she was going to be one of a handful of witnesses whom we'd be bringing back to the United States and putting into the Witness Protection Program. Pregnant, she seemed excited by the news. As we wrapped up the meeting, Jane told me, "Mr. Neil, there's something I must tell you."

"Okay," I said.

She looked around the room at the DEA and Colombian agents, and said, "If it's okay, I'll tell you in New York, okay?"

"Sure," I responded. By that point I'd spoken to scores of former FARC guerrillas and knew all too well about the sadistic violence and abuse that FARC leaders inflicted on their female members. I thought that she was too embarrassed to talk about it in front of her Colombian handler.

A couple of months later, back in New York, she told me her news. The FARC, she said, had learned of our case and sent fake defectors to infiltrate the investigation. The most successful of them was Jane herself, who had gone back into the jungle to debrief the FARC after our first two meetings. Before our last meeting, the FARC had directed her to kill me, but she had refused. Instead, they had sent her back to Bogotá with a militia group that would kidnap me, if possible, and murder me if not. Jane was supposed to call in the location of our last meeting to the waiting terrorists during one of our breaks.

She told me that she had been fully prepared to carry out the plan, but had changed her mind after I offered to put her into U.S. witness protection, which she considered a better deal. Her decision was not without consequences, though. Jane was shot at before we took her out of Colombia, and she lost the baby. She told us that FARC had also killed her last remaining family member, a brother, in retaliation for her betrayal.

I was lucky. We had offered to bring only a few witnesses to the United States, and it was pure happenstance that I chose that particular meeting to tell Jane that she was one of them. To remind me of that luck, I still keep an inscribed bayonet knife on my desk that I was told was taken off a dead FARC soldier and given to me by the Colombian National Police.

Though we were eventually able to charge the top fifty leaders of the FARC and extradite a handful of defendants (including one of the leaders responsible for plotting my kidnapping), I decided after the near miss that my days of chasing drug lords in Colombia were over, and I soon transferred to the Office's Securities Fraud unit.

MY NEXT BIG CASE came a year after my transfer and was against the executives of the commodities giant Refco, which had collapsed in 2005 under the weight of a multibillion-dollar accounting fraud. It was the latest in a string of massive accounting frauds that had brought down firms such as Enron, WorldCom, and Adelphia.

I threw myself into the case, which would later prove instrumental in my understanding of some of the causes of the financial crisis. I also received an amazing education in securities fraud and Wall Street. My professors included forensic accountants, investment bankers, experienced securities lawyers, private equity executives, and, for the lessons in fraud, a cooperating witness, Santo "Sandy" Maggio. He had spent almost his entire career on Wall Street committing fraud, and at Refco he had acted as the hatchet man for Refco's chief executive officer, Phillip Bennett. Maggio had executed his boss's orders to create false book entries, engineer fraudulent transactions, and lie to investors, lenders, and counterparties with a zeal and efficiency that was breathtaking. But Maggio was also smart enough to turn on his boss as soon as things started to fall apart at Refco. By working closely with him for the better part of two years, I learned the ins and outs of how a financial services company operates, particularly one built on a foundation of fraud.

A significant part of Refco's funding came from what was known as sale and repurchase agreements, or repos, from which it obtained what in essence were overnight secured loans from a variety of creditors. Refco leaned on the repo market because the company was highly leveraged (meaning that its operations relied heavily on borrowed money) and it needed those borrowed funds to make up for a billion-dollar hole in its books that Bennett and Maggio were constantly trying to cover up through fraud. Because of its reliance on overnight funding, Maggio had to take care to hide Refco's losses lest Refco's lenders in the repo market began to suspect something was amiss and refuse to renew the nightly loans. Maggio explained that if that were to happen, Refco wouldn't have enough cash on hand to meet its daily obligations and would collapse.

Maggio also explained how easy it was to trick the credit-rating agencies into giving Refco inflated investment-grade ratings by presenting them with false information and fraudulently massaging numbers to make the company look as though it were in far better shape, and taking far fewer risks, than it actually was. Once it got a decent rating from the credit-rating agencies, it was then a cinch to get creditors to buy Refco's bonds and lend it even more money that Bennett and Maggio could then use to plug the various holes in the company.

In my first taste of the risks inherent in investing in mortgage securities, bold new breeds of which would be at the heart of the financial crisis, Maggio showed me how one set of losses that Refco covered up came from a bet Refco had made with its own money on mortgage-backed securities. They were highly rated and therefore supposedly safe investments, but in the 1990s a bubble had broken in subprime mortgage securities, causing Refco significant losses.

Maggio also showed me how easy it had been for him and Bennett to fool the big banks and investors when Refco raised about $2 billion in 2004 and 2005 by selling bonds and shares of its stock to the public. The most important lesson I learned, however, was that virtually no one doing business on Wall Street—rating agencies, accountants, investment banks, or others—cared to look very hard at a fraud that was occurring right under their nose as long as they were getting paid their astronomical fees.

Bennett was charged in 2005, about a year before I came onto the case. In January 2007, we added a second defendant, indicting Refco's former president Tone Grant. While Bennett, Maggio, and Refco's chief financial officer, Robert Trosten, all pled guilty, Grant went to trial in March 2008. We convicted him after a grueling trial, and I became engaged to my girlfriend, Karen, without whose support I never would have survived the trial, within days of the verdict. In addition to being the kindest and most amazing person I've ever met, her ability to keep me steady without once complaining about the insane hours I worked during the trial helped confirm the obvious—she was the one with whom I wanted to spend the rest of my life.

I almost immediately moved on to preparing for the trial of the next Refco defendant, Joseph Collins, Refco's outside counsel. No outside counsel had been charged in any of the big accounting fraud cases, and I wanted to convict Collins in order to send a strong message to the bar that lawyers who actively assisted an accounting fraud could and would be brought to justice.

Then one day in June 2008, Mike called me into his office and said, "We're getting killed on mortgage fraud, killed." He filled me in that the FBI had made it a major priority and that the Office needed to ramp up its efforts.

"This is an epidemic, and we need to get on top of it," he said.

He had decided to set up a group in which seven or eight prosecutors would act as a SWAT team for mortgage fraud cases, and he asked me to run it.

The job gave me an inside look at the burgeoning housing crisis and its causes, and the more I dug into the cases, the more I saw that the creation of the housing bubble and the explosion of mortgage fraud were caused by the same thing: the Wall Street–inspired ravaging of mortgage-underwriting standards in order to generate more mortgages, which in turn provided the Wall Street financial institutions with higher fees. As the real estate bubble was being inflated, some of the most basic aspects of good underwriting—verifying a borrower's employment and income, making sure that the borrower had enough income to cover his or her debts, making sure that the mortgaged property was worth more than the loan—were thrown out the window, clearing the way for rings of fraudsters who would execute complex schemes that netted billions of dollars in illicit proceeds.

NOT SURPRISINGLY, this decline in underwriting standards opened the doors wide to fraud. In our mortgage fraud group, I focused our efforts not on individual borrowers but on criminal rings typically made up of corrupt lawyers, mortgage brokers, notaries, loan officers, appraisers, and insiders at the mortgage lenders. One category of cases involved "predatory lending." In these, mortgage brokers and originators, seeking to increase their fee income, lied to potential borrowers (such as about the amount of the required payments or the interest reset provisions) in order to trick them into taking a loan they couldn't afford.

Some of the activity we found in those investigations was immoral but impossible to prosecute because it had been endorsed by the banks and the regulators. For example, the banks and other lenders formally agreed to pay brokers an extra multithousand-dollar bonus euphemistically called a "yield spread premium" if they were able to convince a borrower who qualified for a prime loan to take a more expensive higher-interest-rate subprime loan. In other words, the lenders were paying brokers to steer unsuspecting borrowers into more expensive loans that they had less of a chance of being able to repay. From the lenders' perspective the economics were simple: because of higher interest rates and fees on subprime loans, they could resell them for a higher profit than they would earn on prime loans, and so were willing to pay brokers to generate more. The worse the mortgage was for the borrower, the more profitable it was in the short term for everyone else. As for the regulators, particularly the Federal Reserve, they had more or less abandoned any semblance of consumer protection during this time period and looked the other way at reported instances of predatory lending.[5]

More easily proven were the wrongdoings of fraudsters who exploited the banks and other lenders' indifference to underwriting standards. There were many variations of those frauds, but they generally involved "flipping" houses. In a typical case, the fraudsters would buy and then sell the same house: first they would buy the house at one price, and then, in a second, controlled transaction, they would "resell" the house to a straw (fake) buyer recruited into the scheme. This second transaction would typically involve a grossly inflated purchase price that was far higher than the first purchase price and would be financed entirely by the lender that was tricked into making the loan for the second transaction, which of course would never be repaid. The fraudsters' profit was the difference in the purchase price between the two sales along with any fees that they could squeeze out of the process.

In order to be able to engage in back-to-back transactions at such different prices, the schemes required a number of corrupt professionals, all working together. For example, there would often need to be a corrupt appraiser who could paper the file with a false appraisal that justified the higher price for the second transaction, a corrupt lawyer willing to do the two transactions at radically different prices and sign off on paperwork that typically hid that information, someone to generate a fake title report at closing that would disguise the first half of the transaction, and insiders at the lenders who would look the other way while generating fees and taking a cut of the action. The profit from any single transaction could easily clear $100,000.

Although the banks and other lenders were typically the "victims" in these cases, I didn't feel much sympathy for them, given their own complicity in the ever-declining underwriting standards. Though the number of professionals who had to participate in these frauds makes them sound complex, they were actually simple to perpetrate because of the lack of underwriting and the complete absence of effective antifraud measures.

Two other types of fraud we investigated involved targeting struggling home owners and came into prominence after the housing bubble began to burst. The first, called "advance-fee" schemes, were straightforward. The bad guys would troll property filings to find borrowers who were in default and would offer them "legal services" or "foreclosure relief" for an up-front fee of thousands of dollars. After they received the fee, the fraudsters would tell the victims that they were making progress in renegotiating their mortgages when in fact they were doing nothing. The borrower often wouldn't realize that he had been scammed until after the bank evicted him following a foreclosure sale. This scam later became endemic in a TARP-related mortgage modification plan after Treasury refused to heed my warning about how easily those preexisting frauds could be adapted to exploit its program.

The second set of schemes was "foreclosure rescue" scams of the type that I was working on when Mike called me up to his office to talk about the job at SIGTARP. In that particular case, we ended up charging thirteen defendants in a $10 million scheme that included a number of different types of fraud. The scam was run out of a mortgage brokerage in Long Island, and we eventually charged attorneys, loan officers, mortgage brokers, a loan processor, and others.

In that case, the defendants used an alternative method of finding houses to flip: they stole them by targeting properties facing foreclosure and convincing the borrowers that they could "save" their homes by temporarily signing over their deeds to their houses for a period of time, during which the fraudsters would supposedly clear the backlog of missed payments. In reality, the signed-over houses were "sold" to straw borrowers who submitted fraudulent mortgage applications for values far greater than the size of the existing mortgages already on the houses. The defendants walked away with the profits, while the victims were left in foreclosure with any remaining equity left in their homes stripped away.

BETWEEN MY EXPERIENCE investigating mortgage fraud and the work I had done as a securities fraud prosecutor, I felt I had the right qualifications for the job at SIGTARP. As I had followed the unfolding financial crisis, I saw many of the same vulnerabilities in the financial system that had been present at Refco. For example, one of the main causes of Bear Stearns' collapse was its overwhelming reliance on short-term overnight lending in the repo market. As Bear's lenders became frightened about the possible losses the investment bank might suffer because of its exposure to subprime mortgages, they began to refuse to renew their overnight loans to Bear. It was the equivalent of Maggio's worst nightmare for Refco, news about the company's losses hitting the street and ending its access to repo funding. Eventually, after enough lenders pulled back, the government had to step in with a bailout that drove the firm into the arms of JPMorgan Chase as part of a taxpayer-funded sweetheart deal.

Similarly, Lehman Brothers collapsed in part because of market worries about its exposure to mortgage-related investments that seemed to be safe—until they were not. And it had become breathtakingly clear that the credit-rating agencies that Refco had so easily fooled had repeated their mistakes on a far grander scale in their generous awarding of the highest level of rating, AAA, to a variety of mortgage-related bonds.

Though I thought it was the right thing to do to put myself up for the job, I was conflicted about what it would entail, and I told Mike that I had to consult my then fiancée, Karen. She had weathered all of the craziness of my work on the trial of Grant just six months earlier, and although I knew she was resigned to endure my similar absence with the upcoming trial of Refco lawyer Joseph Collins, that was a known burden. Building an agency from scratch would require a commitment of time that would make the Refco cases look like summertime frolics. My interest was also tempered by the scars I still bore from my political battles with DOJ over the FARC case, and I had little interest in diving into Washington politics.

I discussed all of it with Karen when she got home that night, telling her the little that I knew about the job and how unlikely it was that I'd actually get it.

"Look, I really don't think this is going to happen. People like me just don't get jobs like this," I said.

"But why not go ahead and do it, go through the process, meet a bunch of people? No real harm in trying," Karen observed.

We had so many issues to consider. For one thing, we'd have to live apart for a period of time because I'd have to work seven days a week in Washington and Karen couldn't just pick up and move. She is a therapist, and she couldn't just abandon her patients. She offered to commute to Washington on the weekends and said she'd get licensed in Washington and try to transition her practice; she thought that eventually she could limit herself to just one night a week in New York. We would also have to postpone the honeymoon to South Africa we'd planned, although I promised her that our January wedding in Costa Rica wouldn't be touched.

I knew our decision was made when finally Karen looked at me, with tears in her eyes, and said, "You're going to do this. You *have* to do it."

If she'd expressed even the slightest resistance, I'd have told Mike that

I couldn't do it, that it was too much to ask of Karen and me as we started our life together.

Looking back at it now, I had no idea that night what I was in for and what I'd learn. I hadn't yet understood the degree to which the entire crisis was unleashed by the greed of a small handful of executives who exploited a financial system that guaranteed that no matter what risks they took, they'd be able to keep the profits and lavish pay those risks generated with the assurance that if their outsized bets went wrong, the U.S. taxpayer would cover their losses. I had no idea that the U.S. government had been captured by the banks and that those running the bailout program I'd be charged with overseeing would come from the very same institutions that had both helped cause the crisis and then become the beneficiaries of the generous terms of their bailout. And despite my experience with DOJ, I couldn't have imagined the ugliness of the Washington that I'd experience as someone who went against the grain by challenging powerful government officials and the Wall Street powerhouses.

2

Hank Wants to Make It Work

O N OCTOBER 23, 2008, eight days after Mike called me into his office to tell me about the TARP job, I was in Miami Beach to attend my nephew's Bar Mitzvah. Karen and I were having a late breakfast with my parents when my BlackBerry started to buzz.

"Neil, it's Lou Reyes. How are you?" Reyes was the lawyer from the White House Office of Personnel who had been handling the logistics of my interviews.

"Good, Lou. Just down in Miami with my family. How are you?" I answered. My heart was thumping. I don't think I really knew how much I'd come to want the job until that moment. I was confident that my interviews earlier that week had gone well, but I still knew I was a long shot.

"I've got some news for you," Lou continued. "This morning Joie Gregor [the head of White House Personnel] will recommend to the president that you be nominated as the special inspector general for the Troubled Asset Relief Program."

I was speechless.

Lou explained that the next step was that the president had to sign off on the nomination, and then they would do a background check. I'd have to fill out a number of forms, and then I'd still have to be confirmed by the Senate. He said the White House was putting a rush on the process, so hopefully I'd be cleared in a few weeks.

He finished by saying "One thing. You can't tell anyone. This can't get out."

Though I told him not to worry, I immediately thought of my mother, nicknamed by our family "Radio Free Gail," because she instantly broadcast all family news far and wide.

When I sat back down to breakfast, I announced, "Well, at some point today the name 'Barofsky' will be uttered to the president of the United States of America."

The week before had been a whirlwind.

The same morning that Mike had sent my name down to Washington for the job, I'd heard from a secretary at the White House that I would have my first interview by telephone, the following day, with Reyes. During that call, Reyes had told me to come down to Washington for interviews at the White House and Treasury the following Tuesday.

Mike, who had been through the nomination process twice before, for U.S. attorney and for the head of Immigration and Customs Enforcement, advised me on how to handle the interviews. He said that most of the people I'd be talking to didn't know the first thing about complex fraud cases and they'd be fascinated by the investigations I'd done. He stressed that coming from the Southern District of New York would drape me with credibility; the Office had a tradition of sending strong job applicants to Washington. He then walked me through a series of do's and don'ts for the interview as I furiously took notes:

Do talk about trials.

Don't be afraid to talk in platitudes; it's Washington, the home of platitudes.

Don't get into the weeds of TARP.

Do talk as much as possible about mortgage fraud and Refco.

He also warned that, above all, I needed to make clear that if I got the job, I would bring a cooperative attitude. "They're looking for someone who can help protect their program, not someone who is going to be playing a game of 'gotcha.'"

I immediately began boning up on TARP. There had been a good deal of controversy about the program, and I wanted to be sure I was up to speed.

* * *

CROSSING 15TH STREET onto Pennsylvania Avenue on the way to my interviews at Treasury the following Tuesday, I was struck by the amazing sight of the White House, the Eisenhower Executive building, and Treasury all lined up next to one another. The Treasury Building, instantly recognizable from its image on the back of the ten-dollar bill, is an impressive block-long granite behemoth full of history. The marble floors of the hallways are patterned in black and white diamonds, and you can make out the shapes of a stray nautilus and other fossils imprinted into the floors here and there, lending a prehistoric touch to the building's august past.

After a rigorous security check, I was escorted to my interviews, which went more or less exactly as Mike had predicted. The Treasury officials I met with were in awe of the Southern District, and even with Mike's heads-up, I was still a little surprised by how much the pedigree mattered. Mike was also right that they didn't know the first thing about mortgage or accounting frauds, and, as far as I could tell, they had not spent one second contemplating the many ways TARP could be victimized by criminals looking to steal taxpayer money. I was also to find that they weren't exactly thrilled about the creation of SIGTARP.

One of the first people I met with was Neel Kashkari, the so-called TARP czar, whose official title was actually interim assistant secretary of the Treasury for financial stability. The thirty-five-year-old former Goldman Sachs vice president had been brought to Treasury by Paulson, who, before taking the Treasury secretary post in 2006, had been the CEO of Goldman. Kashkari initially worked on one of Treasury's early housing programs before being promoted to assistant secretary for international economics and development.[1] Kashkari had served as a close adviser to Paulson as the financial crisis had unfolded, and Paulson had put him in charge of TARP soon after the legislation was signed into law.

Kashkari seemed exhausted and a little confused at first about what I was doing in his office. The interview was awkward, just tracking my résumé, which he explained he hadn't read yet. "So, SDNY, how's that been?" "So tell me about Refco?" "How about that FARC?" I found it odd that Kashkari had a role in selecting his eventual overseer, but I got the sense that he wasn't the one who would be making the call on whether I would be hired. That seemed to be Jim Wilkinson, Paulson's chief of staff.

Wilkinson exuded raw politics. I had learned from a Google search that he was a longtime Republican operative, who prior to joining Paulson at Treasury had served under Karl Rove at the White House and before that worked on the Bush-Cheney campaign. Among his reported accomplishments was helping to peg Al Gore as having claimed to have "invented the Internet."[2] He'd also run the media center in Doha, Qatar, during the second Iraq War,[3] and was part of the "protester" group in Florida during the Bush/Gore recount.[4] He started off the interview by helpfully telling me his view on Congress's inclusion of a special inspector general in the TARP legislation.

"We didn't want it. The White House didn't want it. We fought it. We already have an inspector general who is just fine and thought that this was a waste of money. But Baucus [Senator Max Baucus, the chairman of the Senate Finance Committee] insisted on it, and it was a small price to pay for the bill."

Okay, I thought, *he's going with the warm and welcoming approach.*

"But we're stuck with it," he continued, "and we've got to make the best of it, and Hank has made it clear that he wants it to work, so we'll make it work."

Toward the end of the interview he called Bob Hoyt, Treasury's general counsel, who had not been on my original interview schedule, and arranged for me to speak with him before heading off for my interviews at the White House. I figured if Wilkinson was adding the general counsel to the list, things had to be going well.

Before I left Wilkinson said, "One more thing, Neil. I want to give you some advice. When Hank asked me to take this job, I made sure that there were certain conditions he agreed to, certain requirements that had to be met. And I made sure that I got those commitments in writing. I highly advise you do the same before accepting this position. Do you understand what I'm saying?"

I had no idea what he was talking about, nor did anyone else to whom I later repeated his warning, but I told him I understood and thanked him for the advice. It was my first taste of the paranoid weirdness of Washington.

The White House interviews followed the same script as at Treasury, with even more love expressed for the Office. The penultimate and most important interview was with the White House counsel, Fred Fielding. He is a Washington legend and served as Ronald Reagan's White House counsel for the first five years of his presidency. He was brought back to the White House by George W. Bush to right the ship after the troubled tenures of Alberto Gonzales and Harriet Miers. As I was escorted into his office, I was cheered to see that William Burck, a recent Office alum who was now deputy White House counsel, was sitting in on the interview.

On Mike's advice, I had spoken with Burck before coming down for my interviews. He was junior to me in the Office, and he'd left years before to go to Washington to work at the White House and at DOJ. I didn't know him well—mostly from two Office bachelor parties we had both attended—but he seemed like a great guy. Though I'd been hesitant to call him, he was very supportive, and years later I found out that he had been instrumental in the decision to nominate me. For a moment, seeing him there, I felt a teeny bit like an insider. The interview was a succession of softballs that included Fielding thanking *me* for even considering the job.

As with my interviews at Treasury, there seemed to have been little focus at the White House on the fraud dangers presented by TARP. I found this lack of attention particularly troubling because the previous week Paulson had announced the first major outflow of taxpayer money: a controversial new TARP program, the $250 billion Capital Purchase Program, or CPP, which would provide direct equity injections into the banks and which I thought could be highly vulnerable to fraud.

CPP had provoked some howls of outrage because it took the spending of TARP money in a very different direction from how TARP had originally been pitched to Congress. The initial TARP proposal, made by Paulson, was for the money to be used to buy large quantities of the "troubled" or "toxic" mortgages and mortgage-related bonds that were clogging so many banks' balance sheets; hence the name Troubled Asset Relief Program. The sharp decline in the value of those assets, starting in 2007, was what had precipitated the crisis, and the argument was that the banks could not be stabilized until large quantities of them were taken off their books.

Congress had approved of TARP in large part because buying those assets from the banks would not only—hopefully—prevent the banks from failing but because Treasury would then be in control of so many of the troubled mortgage loans that had gone into the toxic assets. That would allow Treasury to modify the terms of the loans in order to give foreclosure relief to struggling home owners across the country—a major priority for many Democrats in Congress—which would in turn help to stabilize the cratering housing market. With the announcement of CPP, though, Paulson used the wide latitude given to him by Congress in the TARP bill to abandon the plan to purchase those mortgage-related assets.

When, on September 20, 2008, Paulson submitted what appeared to be a hastily crafted three-page original TARP plan, he had requested $700 billion strictly for the purchase of mortgage-related assets.[5] Congress quickly rejected it because, among other things, it included no oversight provisions, had virtually no reporting provisions, and protected Treasury from any type of administrative or legal review of any decision it made.[6] It replaced it with a several-hundred-page bill that included broad over-sight provisions and a virtually unlimited expansion of the definition of "troubled assets" that Treasury could purchase.

Paulson took full advantage of that discretion when he decided to switch to CPP and use TARP funds to inject capital directly into the banks by buying preferred shares of stock from them. He began thinking about doing so even as the bill was still making its way through Congress,[7] as the team at Treasury soon realized that the original asset purchase plan would take too much time to implement. The market was crashing *now,* and Paulson feared a massive meltdown of the entire financial system.[8] Paulson later told me that he believed that Morgan Stanley was just days away from collapse, and Ben Bernanke, the chairman of the Federal Reserve, similarly confided that he believed that Goldman Sachs would have been the next to go. After that, all bets on the country's financial system would have been off.

After initially being voted down, TARP was amended and finally passed by Congress and signed into law by President Bush on October 3, 2008, authorizing the spending of an immediate $350 billion and per-mitting the administration to petition Congress for an additional $350 billion at a later date. Eleven days later, Paulson, Bernanke and Timothy Geithner, then the president of the Federal Reserve Bank of New York, put CPP into motion.

In its simplest form, CPP was a straight bailout. On terms that Citigroup CEO Vikram Pandit and JPMorgan Chase CEO Jamie Dimon described at the time as "cheap"[9] and that the Congressional Oversight Panel later determined were too generous by 22 percent,[10] on October 12, 2008, Treasury put $125 billion of taxpayer money into nine of the largest banks and on the same day committed to making another $125 billion available to other banks that wanted to apply for TARP funds. Under the CPP, none of the toxic assets would be taken off of the banks' books and no mortgages would be purchased or modified.

This left open two big questions: how the festering pools of bad assets could be dealt with and how mortgage modifications could be achieved on a large scale.

Members of Congress soon began voicing strong objections to Treasury's broad interpretation of its authority to use TARP funds for CPP, furious with the shift away from purchasing troubled assets. A key complaint was about how the banks were using their newly received TARP funds. Paulson had justified the change to CPP in three separate press releases, in which, rather than acknowledging that the original infusion of $125 billion into the first nine recipients had been made to try to keep several of them from collapsing, he announced that CPP was intended to stimulate lending. It had been designed, he said, to enhance the ability of the recipient banks to "perform their vital function of lending"[11] and was intended to "get credit flowing."[12] The banks were expected to "deploy" and not "hoard" taxpayer funds in order to "provide credit to our economy," "make more loans to businesses and consumers across the nation,"[13] and improve "credit to households and businesses."[14] In addition, the newly injected capital was intended "to help struggling home owners who can afford their homes avoid foreclosure."[15]

As part of the announcement of CPP, Paulson, along with the Federal Reserve and the FDIC, endorsed the "health" of the nine original banks that had received funds (Bank of America, Citigroup, Wells Fargo, JPMorgan Chase, State Street, Morgan Stanley, Merrill Lynch, and Goldman Sachs) and also declared that additional CPP funds would be available only to similarly healthy and viable banks. Of course, as Paulson and Bernanke told me many months later, they actually knew that some were on the brink of collapse. For his part, Geithner, who had helped design and implement CPP, later confirmed that he had made no judgment as to whether the first nine banks were actually healthy or viable.[16]

The truth was that there was no real focus in CPP on either increasing lending or helping home owners avoid foreclosure. So when Treasury lawyers drafted the contracts that would govern the injection of cash to the banks, they imposed only a few token restrictions on how the money could be used, and were almost entirely silent on the primary justification provided for the program: increasing lending. Instead of requirements or even incentives to make more loans, all that appeared in the nearly one-hundred-page boilerplate agreements was some aspirational language on the front page that said that the banks would strive to "expand the flow of credit to U.S. consumers and businesses."[17]

It soon became apparent that the banks were going to do nothing of the sort, and some members of Congress were incensed. Kashkari bore the brunt of Congress's anger, and he was routinely hauled up to the Hill so that members could vent their frustrations on him. In a hearing in late November, for example, Republican Congressman Darrell Issa told Kashkari, "You are here today because Congress is feeling that you played a bait-and-switch game, and you are not convincing anyone that you haven't."[18] At the same hearing, Democrat Elijah Cummings suggested that Kashkari was a "chump" for the banks.[19] And at a hearing in December, a number of prominent Republicans further criticized Kashkari for not putting conditions related to lending in the CPP contracts or having the banks account for how they were using TARP funds.[20] Representative David Scott, a Democrat, probably best summed up the anger in Congress over CPP:

We have been lied to; the American people have been lied to. We have been bamboozled; they came to us to ask for money for one thing, then used it for another. They said we would have oversight, and no oversight is in place. We have given these banks $290 billion for the sole purpose of so-called buying these toxics. They change it, and all of a sudden now they are not lending it but using it for acquisitions, using it for salaries. These are lies. We have been bamboozled.[21]

During my interview at Treasury with Jim Wilkinson, he mentioned that Paulson was still considering a toxic asset purchase program in addition to CPP, in which Treasury would purchase both mortgage-related securities and whole mortgages. I warned him about some of the potential dangers involved, including that banks might seek to dump onto the taxpayer the bonds most riddled with the types of fraud I had been investigating at the Office. I also warned about what I thought might be an even bigger danger with the CPP plan: I expected that some banks would try to cook their books through accounting fraud to make their balance sheets look "healthy and viable" in order to get their hands on TARP funds. Though Wilkinson was clearly interested in what I was saying, I found it troubling that apparently neither he nor anyone else at Treasury had seriously considered those dangers before. If I did get the job, I knew that putting in fraud protections would be a first order of business.

AFTER I GOT word from the White House that it intended to nominate me for the job, I settled into a several-week purgatory as the FBI conducted its background check on me. Fortunately, during that time I had some people working behind the scenes on my behalf, including Burck and another Office alum, Preet Bharara, whom Mike had also suggested I reach out to.

Preet had been about a year senior to me in the Office, and other than having gone for a few drinks with him now and again, I didn't know him well and hadn't really spoken to him since he had left for Washington to become Senator Chuck Schumer's chief counsel. At the time he left, Preet's nontraditional choice raised more than a few eyebrows in the Office, but he thrived in Washington, leading the congressional investigation into the firing of several U.S. attorneys for political reasons by then Attorney General Alberto Gonzales. Preet was widely credited with having forced Gonzales's resignation, and soon-to-be-proven-correct rumors were flying that if Obama won the election, Preet might succeed Mike as U.S. attorney for the Southern District of New York.

Before I called Preet I checked with Burck to make sure that I wouldn't be violating the "don't tell anyone" rule. He told me there was no problem; he'd already discussed my possible nomination with Preet. Burck warned that Preet had said there might be some pushback on the nomination because of my age. The staffers on the Hill were already concerned that the Neel running TARP—Kashkari—was only thirty-five years old, and a similarly named thirty-eight-year-old inspector general might look like a "kiddie show."

Preet was friendly when I called and invited me to come down to Washington to have drinks with him and some of the Democrat staffers on the Joint Economic Committee, which Schumer chaired. As Preet said, the idea was that they would see that I was "normal" (which I think meant a fellow Democrat) and had the right experience for the job. I thanked Preet and told him that I'd check my schedule but was not sure if I'd go.

Mike looked at me as if I were some sort of space alien when I told him I didn't want to schlep all the way down to Washington just to have drinks with Preet.

"You've got to go," he said. "None of this happens if Schumer is not on board, and Preet can help. You need to go down there and show him and the other staffers what a good Democrat you are."

Burck was equally adamant and offered to join us.

When I met up with Preet, I asked if Burck was definitely coming, and a staffer who had met Burck before referred to him as "the good Republican."

It was fascinating. Here were two guys, Preet and Burck, who, despite being on completely opposite poles of the political spectrum, were good friends (Preet was later in Burck's wedding party) brought together by their shared experience in the Office, where they had only barely overlapped. Now, largely because of my own membership in that club, they were welcoming me to Washington with open arms and conspiring with each other to get me through the confirmation process.

A couple of weeks later I got a call from Treasury telling me that it wanted me down in Washington on November 12 for three days of preparation for my confirmation hearing, which might be scheduled for the following week. I was told to prepare for a "murder board," in which Treasury officials would play the role of senators in a mock hearing. Despite its scary name, it sounded like an extreme version of the practice moots we had done in the Office before an argument before the Court of Appeals.

It was anything but "murderous." Each day, for about an hour or two, the Treasury legislative affairs people and some lawyers chatted with me about the process and gave some generic advice on how to answer the senators' questions at the hearing, some of which actually proved to be very helpful. Tidbits such as:

"When they give you a multipart question, just pick the part that you like the best and answer it, and ignore the other parts."

"Most of the time they don't really care what your answer is, they just care about getting their question on the news."

"Don't feel like you actually have to answer their questions. You can just say what you want to say."

"Try not to be distracted about what they're doing when they're not talking to you. They will be talking, laughing with one another while you or another senator is speaking. They might even ask a question and leave during your answer."

"When you get any substantive questions and they insist on an answer, just tell them that you didn't have access to anything other than what is already in the public domain, so you can't really answer."

"Tell them that, if confirmed you'll keep an open mind, and that whatever their concern happens to be, you'll make it a top priority."

THINGS SEEMED TO be going very smoothly, but then, on the morning of my second day of prep, Thursday, November 13, *The Washington Post* broke the news of my impending nomination in a front-page article. I felt a surge of anxiety reading the piece, not only because my name had been divulged but because the current Treasury inspector general, Eric Thorson, was also quoted in the piece as saying about TARP, "It's a mess. I don't think anyone understands right now how we're going to do proper oversight of this thing."[22]

I was still too inexperienced in the ways of Washington to recognize that my name had actually been given up by the White House. Burck told me not to worry about it and said this kind of thing was all part of the game. The White House didn't have the time to lobby all one hundred senators, so they used the *Post* to assure the Democrats who controlled the Senate that although I was a Bush appointee, I was still one of theirs, making sure that the article emphasized my contribution to the Obama campaign. (Later I found out that both Burck and Preet had had a hand in placing the article.) I calmed down, but I also decided that I wanted to meet with Thorson as soon as possible to find out what was so out of control with TARP. So I called Peter Dugas, the legislative staffer from Treasury who was handling my nomination (and one of the nicest guys I met at Treasury), to see if he could set up a meeting with Thorson later that day. He set up a "meet and greet" but warned me not to ask substantive questions about what oversight Thorson had been doing. Paradoxically, apparently for the hearing, the less I knew the better.

Thorson's office was breathtaking. Located on the fourth floor of Treasury, it seemed like it was the size of two or three of any of the executive offices I had previously seen. The walls were adorned with giant framed photos of his time as a pilot in the air force.[23]

Thorson was in a full-on tizzy about the *Washington Post* article, and he told me to beware the press, complaining that the article had quoted him out of context. At one point he took a telephone call and voiced apologies to whoever the caller was, even offering to write a letter to the editor of the *Post* saying that the article had misconstrued his thoughts about TARP (which he did go on to write).[24] I didn't understand why he was so upset. The article noted that in the almost six weeks that had passed since TARP had been signed into law, Congress had not yet appointed the members of the Congressional Oversight Panel, the other pillar of oversight for TARP, and the administration had obviously still not formally nominated a TARP inspector general. The article seemed to capture Thorson's understandable frustration with the failure of Congress and the administration to act and that although he was doing his best to fulfill his role of providing interim oversight, more help was urgently needed.

I wanted to hear more but decided to follow my directions and avoided asking him about the program, instead making the mistake of commenting about his magnificent office and asking where the rest of his staff sat. After a ten-minute lecture on the office's history (my mind started to stray when he mentioned that the floor had been raised to put in updated electrical wiring), Thorson explained that his staff was in a different building. When I asked whether that made it harder for him to manage his office and whether he would prefer being in the same building as them, Thorson looked around the room as if Allen Funt from *Candid Camera* were about to come through the door. My question was insane. This was Washington, where nothing matters more than the size and location of the ultimate status symbol, your office. He mumbled something about having to be in the building to consult with the secretary (with whom, though, I later found out, he met relatively infrequently), and we wrapped up the meeting. My many questions about TARP oversight would have to wait until after I was confirmed.

The next morning, Burck e-mailed me the White House's official announcement that I was indeed the nominee to be the special inspector general, and my phone started buzzing almost immediately. So began my wild ride on the media merry-go-round. I had always been shielded from the press at the Office, and I wasn't prepared for the onslaught. *The New York Times, The Wall Street Journal, The Washington Post,* the *New York Post,* and the New York *Daily News* all wanted to interview me. CNBC wanted a picture, and so did the White House, to give to the press. I even heard from DEA agents down in Colombia who'd heard the news.

I also got a voice mail that morning from my mom asking me what to do about the flood of calls my parents were getting from the press. I called back and left a message telling them to just say that they had no comment. My dad is not known for his tact (something I inherited) and was no fan of President Bush. I could easily imagine him saying something with which the press could have a field day.

I couldn't believe the attention. Who ever cared so much about an inspector general?

After my final murder board at Treasury later that day, I walked over to the White House to visit Burck, and while I was waiting outside the West Wing security gate my BlackBerry rang.

It was my dad, and I right away asked him, "You got my message, right, about not talking to the press?"

"Well, I did," he said, pausing, "but not until after I had a very nice conversation with someone from the *Daily News.*"

"Oh, God," I said. "What did you do, Dad, what did you do?"

"Nothing, we hardly talked at all, it was nothing," he assured me.

"Dad? Really, what did you say, Dad? What?" I pressed, sure he'd dropped some bombshell.

"Mostly we talked about Italy, nothing much more than that," he said, referring to his online tour business.

"No more, Dad, please, no more. You can't talk to the press, never again. Okay?" I chided.

"Okay, Neil, but it really wasn't a big deal," my dad responded.

"Promise?" I asked.

"Promise," he sighed. It wasn't always easy being my father.

The next day, when the articles hit, it was surreal seeing friends quoted about me in *The New York Times* and *The Washington Post*. But the best, of course, were the quotes my dad gave the *Daily News,* which made me cringe at the time but which I now treasure. The "proud dad" said that "you should congratulate the country," but "I don't envy him. It's not going to be an easy thing. It took a lot of hard work to get us into this mess." Best of all was my dad's evaluation of why I could handle the job: "He has two older sisters and they were pretty tough."

It was strange seeing personal details of my life in print. On Friday, there was almost nothing about me on the Internet. By Saturday major news publications reported that I was a Yankees season ticket holder and an adoring uncle; that I was getting married in January and planned to cancel my honeymoon if I got the job; that I had given $200 to the Obama campaign; and even that I was the plaintiff in an ongoing medical malpractice lawsuit over a botched surgery. Why would anyone want to know those things?

But if the media christening was odd, my first encounter with the culture of Congress was even stranger. I was scheduled for a hearing in front of the Senate Finance Committee for Monday afternoon, November 17, but first I had to be "vetted" by the senators' staffers that morning. Some of the questions were perfunctory, but others were pretty tough, probing about my plans and how I intended to staff and launch the office. Still other questions were downright hostile. The most memorable came from a staffer to one of the Republican senators, who had apparently read *The Washington Post* and couldn't believe that Bush would appoint an Obama-contributing Democrat to such a high-profile job.

"Just tell me the truth," he said. "Did you, Paulson, and Bush come to a secret agreement that you wouldn't look into certain areas in return for this nomination?" I laughed at the suggestion and explained, among other things, that I had never even talked to either Paulson or Bush.

The initiation continued when, after lunch, Karen and I, accompanied by Dugas, arrived at the room in the Senate office building in which my hearing was going to be held. A long line of homeless-looking people stretched down the hall from the door.

"Peter, is this us?" I asked.

"Yep," Dugas said.

"Umm, these people waiting in line, they don't exactly look like the type of people who would normally attend a TARP-related confirmation hearing," I commented.

Dugas laughed. "Lobbyists pay them a few bucks each to stand in line for them to reserve a seat for the hearing. It's a good sign, means you're in the big leagues," he explained chipperly.

Even stranger to me was the reaction when I approached the long table that was set up in front of the U-shaped elevated dais behind which the senators would soon take their seats. A pool of photographers sprang up from the well in front of the table and converged on me like a swarm of locusts. I tried not to burst out laughing and turned to Karen to have a fake conversation as the photographers pressed their cameras inches from my face, whispering to her, "Well, I guess they'll have a photo of me now."

Most IGs escape with one confirmation hearing, which is usually barely attended and in which hardly any tough questions are asked. I was lucky enough to have two, because with TARP being a new program, the Senate Banking, Housing, and Urban Affairs and Finance Committees were wrangling about which of them would have jurisdiction over TARP and SIGTARP. In a preemptive move, Finance had gone ahead and scheduled this first hearing, but the ploy hadn't worked. As I settled into my seat, I learned that the Senate parliamentarian had just ruled in favor of Banking but that the Finance hearing was going to proceed anyway. I was going to become perhaps the first nominee to have a nonconfirmation confirmation hearing.

Senator Baucus, the chair of the committee, kicked off the proceedings by asking me to introduce any members of my family in attendance. I felt a pang of guilt for telling my parents not to come up and then looked at

Karen. *Oh shit,* I thought, *I can't lie to Congress.* We were scheduled to be married in front of friends and family in Costa Rica in January, but we had actually already had a small legal ceremony in New York about which we hadn't told anyone except our parents. For us, the real wedding would be in January. Now our secret was about to get out.

"My wife, Karen, is here today," I said.

"Wife? Did he say wife?" my sister Vickie asked my mom down in Miami Beach, watching C-SPAN. My friends at the Office were also watching, and some worried that I had just committed a crime by lying to Congress. Maybe, someone suggested, I had lied to hide from some of the conservative Republican senators that I had been living in sin with Karen. I would have some explaining to do later.

During the hearing, the senators kept returning to several overriding concerns they had with TARP and on which they wanted me to focus should I be confirmed. They expressed almost a sense of helplessness that so much TARP money had already gone out the door without having a special inspector general in place. Senator Baucus set the tone at the very beginning in his opening statement:

> You are also going to confront the harsh reality that almost half of the $700 billion is already out the door. . . . For a while, you are going to be playing catch-up. You will be looking back at Treasury's use of about $290 billion in about 43 days.[25]

The other main concern was the lack of transparency with which the money was being distributed, and a number of senators emphasized that I should investigate how the banks were spending the money they received from TARP.[26] Senator Ron Wyden summed up the concerns colorfully: "Given the fact that Treasury still declines to say exactly how it spent the taxpayer money, nor has it said who the beneficiaries are or what conditions have been placed on them, I would characterize the operation of this program now in terms of oversight as like Dodge City before the marshals showed up. I think it is critically important that you get on top of this."[27]

Baucus closed the hearing by telling me what I should do in the job with words I would later lean on heavily:

[T]his is not just a garden-variety Inspector General within a Department. . . . You are independent. You are special. . . . [Y]ou are not an oversight board, you are not these other oversight institutions that are mentioned and created in the statute. You are targeted with laser-like focus and all your resources on this program. You are independent. You are fully independent.[28]

I felt the hearing had gone extremely well, with most of the senators supportive of my nomination. At my second hearing, two days later in front of the Banking, Housing, and Urban Affairs Committee, things were a little rougher. Senator Jim Bunning, a conservative Republican from Kentucky and a former Hall of Fame pitcher for the Philadelphia Phillies, told me in his opening comments that he had opposed the bailout plan and saw SIGTARP as a potential waste of taxpayer resources.[29] He said I would "serve the public far better in the Southern District of New York" prosecuting mortgage fraud than in Washington as the special inspector general.[30] Later, while barking at me about my lack of qualifications for the job, he held his hand out in a strange clawlike way, as if he was about to throw me a three-finger changeup, and I couldn't help thinking of the professional wrestler Baron von Raschke, whom I'd used to watch as a kid with my dad, goose-stepping around the ring getting ready to apply his famous "brain claw" move.

The rest of the hearing went well, though, and Dugas called me the next evening while I was back up in New York to tell me to turn on C-SPAN and watch myself get confirmed. As I sat in my office waiting to go out for "confirmation drinks" that my friends had already started without me, I watched the session close without my name being mentioned. I soon got a call from Dugas.

"It's a hold," he told me. "A Republican, one of ours, put a hold on your nomination."

"Who? Why? What does it mean?" I asked, ignoring Dugas's use of the word "ours."

"The vote has to be unanimous. Under Senate rules, if any one senator puts a hold on your nomination, you can't get unanimous consent, and without that, you aren't confirmed."

I asked if it was Bunning, and Dugas explained that the hold was anonymous (although I later found out that it was indeed Bunning who had placed the hold).

Now my life was completely in limbo.

Congress had finished its session for the year and might not be back until after the inauguration. In that event, my nomination would expire. Although I had been told that there had been an "understanding" with the Obama team on my nomination, I had never spoken to anyone about what would happen if I weren't confirmed.

I thought that my nomination was dead, but in the next couple of days some rays of hope emerged. Senators Dodd, Baucus, and Schumer all issued public statements condemning the anonymous hold, and bloggers on both the left and the right took up my cause.

Then, about two weeks later, on December 4, while the Senate was still in recess, the Banking, Housing, and Urban Affairs Committee held an emergency hearing with the CEOs of Ford, General Motors, and Chrysler, who were asking for a $34 billion bailout.[31] The combination of their poor business practices, high levels of debt, and the severe drop-off in car sales due to the recession had put them on the brink of bankruptcy. Their first trip down to Washington looking for a handout, on November 18, 2008, had been a disaster, with all three acknowledging that they had traveled there by corporate jet. Now they were back, begging for their companies' lives and a taxpayer handout, and rumors were flying that the House and Senate leaders might call back all members the following week for an up-or-down vote on a Detroit bailout. And if the Senate came back, my nomination could go through, if the White House could only get Bunning to release his hold.

That is exactly what happened, and on the following Monday, December 8, 2008, I watched on C-SPAN as I was finally confirmed.

The next day I called Eric Thorson. I didn't have to hold off on my questions any longer, and with an initial report due from me to Congress on February 6, 2009, I needed to get up to speed on the work his office had been doing on TARP as quickly as I could.

I made the mistake of starting off the conversation by asking him if he had any tips.

"Make sure you get an account at the Treasury Dining Room. It's very good and it's very affordable. As a presidential appointee you get to use it," he told me.

That wasn't exactly the type of tip I was looking for. "Also, the guys here at Treasury are great, but you don't have to tell them everything that you're doing. It's important to maintain your independence. So, for example, I won't tell the chief of staff that I have a meeting up on the Hill in advance; instead I will wait until I am already there and then send him an e-mail," Thorson bragged incongruously.

I started to feel the first bite of panic. Why would I tell Treasury where I was going and who I was meeting with? I was supposed to be fully independent. Senator Baucus had gone out of his way to say so, and he had repeated the point in his press release about my nomination. There was no way I was going to be reporting my every move to Jim Wilkinson or anyone else.

After I pressed Thorson on what he and his staff had been doing to oversee TARP, he told me that they had sent document requests to Treasury and sat in on some briefings with the Government Accountability Office (GAO), the auditing arm of Congress, which also had TARP oversight responsibilities. He then told me that he was launching an audit of City National Bank, a Beverly Hills–based bank that had received TARP funds. "We're going to do a cradle-to-grave audit of the process that Treasury used to approve the bank for CPP," he told me.

Huh? I had just been confirmed, and *now* he was launching an audit? I suggested that my office could take over the audit once we were staffed up, but Thorson batted the suggestion down.

I couldn't nail Thorson down on any other specifics during the call and figured that it would be easier to do in person after I started. I hung up with a bad feeling that Thorson might not be all that helpful. I might be completely on my own.

3

The Lapdog, the Watchdog,
and the Junkyard Dog

M Y ALARM WENT off on Monday morning at 5:30 a.m. It was December 15, my first day on the job and two months to the day from when Mike had first called me into his office. Although that would soon become my default wake-up time, that first morning it was a shock to my New York system. Other than when I was on trial, I usually hadn't sauntered into the Office until a little after 9:30. Bolting out of bed in the dark, I could just make out the cheap, unfamiliar artwork on the walls of the furnished apartment Karen and I had hastily rented. She was going to stay in our apartment in New York during the week, see her patients, and come down to Washington on weekends. She was booked on an early train up to New York for our first week apart. We got ready quietly. Both my heart and my brain were racing as I put on my lucky suit and tie (the outfit I had worn on my first date with Karen).

We fumbled with the apartment's alarm system and walked out onto R Street, me carrying an old briefcase I'd dug up—the first and last time I'd use one while at SIGTARP. I prefer a backpack, but I figured that I shouldn't walk into the office of the secretary of the Treasury hauling a JanSport.

On the drive to the train station, we said hardly a word to each other, dreading the week's separation. We listened to Howard Stern discuss the arrest of Bernie Madoff for running a massive Ponzi scheme. As we said good-bye in front of the station, our eyes welled up.

"See you Thursday night, I guess," I said, dreading that I would have to get through this first week without her.

She told me I needed to call her all the time.

"Jesus." I laughed at myself. "I'm going to Treasury, not Iraq." I told her I loved her and, as I would say many times in the coming months, "Couldn't do this without you."

So began our gloomy Monday ritual. My next stop was to meet Kevin Puvalowski, my friend from the Office, who'd agreed to be my deputy.

IN THE THREE days between my confirmation and moving to Washington, other than trying to clean up, organize, and send to archives my files from eight years of prosecutions, I had one key mission: I wanted to take someone from the Office with me to help set up SIGTARP. My group of friends from General Crimes had colorful and stupid nicknames for one another, which included The King of Mean, The General, Sandman, J-Rod, Bird, The Super Freak, and The Large Beautiful Man, a small way to lighten up our very serious jobs. (Others at the Office rightfully ignored our attempts to get them to join the merriment. Nicknames such as "Teabag" and "Coco" were quickly swatted down by their recipients.) Kevin had been dubbed "Dog" (as in Pavlov's).

A year junior to me, he and I had become fast friends after he joined the Office. He didn't fit the traditional mold of a Southern District prosecutor. Most have an Ivy League degree, and it's not uncommon for them to be second- or third-generation lawyers. Kevin was a graduate of Fordham Law School and came from a working-class family outside of Detroit where, as he will tell you on any given day, he was the starting shortstop for his state championship high school baseball team. Clearing six feet and bearing the physique of a high school athlete who, well, was no longer as active as he had once been, Kevin could be an intimidating figure. His father had worked for thirty-five years as an electrician for Pontiac and his brother worked in sales at Ford. His grandparents, Polish immigrants, had been farmers and bakers. I was the first person in my family to go to graduate school, a relative rarity in the Office, but Kevin was the first person in his family to go to college. He also had an incredibly diverse set of interests, which included a sprawling garden at his house in New Jersey, bird-watching, woodblock printing, guitar, astronomy, Detroit sports, and God only knows what else. (I almost got him to raise chickens in his backyard so I could have an unending supply of fresh eggs, but his wife put her foot down.)

Most important for our work at SIGTARP, Kevin was a remarkably talented lawyer. He is the best writer I've ever met, is fantastic in court, has impeccable judgment, and has a work ethic that I could only compare to our common mentor, Rich Sullivan. The only problem was that he'd announced that month that he was leaving the Office to take a lucrative partnership at one of the premier litigation boutiques in New York.

I figured there was no way he'd walk away from that to join me at SIG-TARP, but I had to at least try.

To my shock, he expressed interest. I told him, "Kev, it'll be my name on the door, but this'll be a partnership. You name the title you want; you design the job description. You can target whatever part of TARP you want to focus on, it'll all be up to you." I was begging.

I then gave him my own adaptation of Mike's "God and country" speech and finally tried to explain how this was such a unique opportunity.

"Think about it," I said. "If someone came up to us last year while we were down in Curaçao chasing Colombian traffickers and said, 'Okay, guys, here's the deal. In a year or so, the world is going to implode, and Congress is going to create from scratch a brand-new law enforcement agency. And the agency will conduct only the most complex and highest profile white-collar investigations imaginable. And you two assholes are going to build and run it, because President George W. Bush is going to appoint one of you to be in charge of it.' We'd say that person was out of his fucking mind. Well, guess what? That just happened."

He agreed to talk it over with his wife, and the next day, he came into my office and exclaimed "I'm in!" It was the single most important moment in SIGTARP history. I personally wouldn't have survived Washington without Karen, but without Kevin, SIGTARP wouldn't have had a chance.

My last day at the Office was Thursday, December 11. I was both elated and nervous as I left that night for the last time as an assistant U.S. attorney. Every day for more than eight years I had walked into that dilapidated building at 1 St. Andrews Plaza and looked up at the giant seal over the entrance. And every day I had felt a surge of pride: pride at being part of that amazing team and of the work we did. It was hard to believe I was walking out of the building for the last time as a prosecutor.

That night, my friends from the Office went for drinks after the holiday party, and when my colleague Marc Litt arrived late, I gave him shit about it. But he had a good reason.

"I'm sorry, I just got a new case today," he said. "It's unbelievable, the FBI just walked in some guy who's confessing to a $50 billion fraud."

"Billion? With a B?" I asked.

"Yes. Billion. His name is Madoff."

The Office was clearly, somehow, going to survive without me.

KEVIN AND I had agreed to meet at a Starbucks near the Treasury Building at 7:15 the following Monday morning so we'd have plenty of time to strategize about what we might say to Secretary Paulson at our scheduled meeting with him that morning. I really didn't know what to expect; I had simply been directed by Paulson's assistant to report to his office at eight to take the oath of office. She didn't tell me whether we would be shuttled out of the office after a quick ceremony or if we'd have time to talk afterward. In case I did get the chance to meet with Paulson, I wanted to be prepared, and I had some points I wanted to make.

The former CEO of Goldman Sachs, Paulson had joined the Bush administration as secretary of the Treasury in 2006. On the one hand, I felt that he bore some responsibility for the crisis. Some of Wall Street's great abuses had occurred under his watch while he was running Goldman Sachs, and he had then become a key part of the regulatory apparatus that had so devastatingly failed to prevent the crisis. His initial actions in response to the crisis had also been disjointed and had surely contributed to the uncertainty that had helped fuel the panic. On the other hand, I thought he had proven to be a forceful leader who was able to move a Republican president along with a Democrat-controlled Congress to pass a piece of historic legislation that helped tamp down the very worst of the panic. Paulson may have acted with too little transparency and too much deference to the Wall Street banks, but I thought him primarily responsible for the bold steps that helped prevent the crisis from escalating totally out of control and causing a second Great Depression.

More than anything else that morning, I wanted the opportunity to follow up on Jim Wilkinson's statement to me during my interview that "Hank wants to make this work." If I got the chance, my plan was to encourage Paulson to set the tone within Treasury that we would be a welcome partner in protecting TARP from fraud.

My plan to brainstorm with Kevin fell through. He was beginning his own difficult Monday-morning ritual that day, commuting from his home in New Jersey, and he had to leave at the far more depressing time of four in the morning. He showed up about a half hour late, so, with no real time to talk, I handed him a now-cold coffee and we darted down the block to Treasury.

As we walked past the gate facing Pennsylvania Avenue, I noticed Kevin glance over at the White House and then at the statute of Thomas Jefferson's Treasury secretary, Albert Gallatin.

"This is pretty crazy, right?" I said.

"Insane," he replied.

We climbed the ornate staircase to the third floor, and after taking a few wrong turns, we finally arrived at the door to the large anteroom to Paulson's office. Neel Kashkari met us at the door, looking even more haggard than when he had interviewed me nearly two months earlier. With good reason too: the financial crisis continued to rage, and in the time since I had last seen him Kashkari had overseen additional TARP bailouts of AIG and Citigroup and the announcement of a new $20 billion TARP program intended to spur consumer lending, and, as we would soon find out, he was currently hard at work on TARP-funded bailouts of General Motors, Chrysler, their auto-financing companies, and Bank of America.

Wilkinson was also there, along with Treasury's general counsel, Robert Hoyt. They greeted us warmly as I introduced them to Kevin, making the perfunctory round of handshakes. Wilkinson's earlier comments to me, that he and others at Treasury thought the entire concept of a special inspector general was a waste of resources, echoed in my ears. He and the rest of this group now giving us an enthusiastic welcome had lobbied against the creation of SIGTARP, and my swearing in was the direct result of a political defeat for them.

After about a minute, Paulson's office door opened and he came lumbering into the anteroom, greeting us warmly. A former offensive lineman at Dartmouth, he is a large man and can be imposing, but his body language was welcoming that morning, even though he looked worn down and was almost twitching with nervous energy. As I shook his right hand, I couldn't help but notice the pinky of his left hand jutting out at a ninety-degree angle, the result of an old football injury.[1] He nodded at Kevin and led me to the corner of his office to administer the oath. Paulson is famously a devout Christian Scientist, and as I put my Jewish hand on the Paulson family Bible, I fleetingly pictured it bursting into flames. As I took the oath, I kept telling myself that I belonged there, and gradually my nerves settled. When I then started to leave the room, he half smiled and stopped me, gesturing toward the couch. Everyone else took a seat, and our half-hour conversation was a revelation.

Paulson first noted, with visible relief, that the "futures" weren't down that morning, referring to the indices of pre-market trading, which generally predicts how the Dow Jones, NASDAQ, and S&P will move once they open. I shot Kevin a look, amazed. Could it be, nearly four months into this crisis, that the secretary of the Treasury was still keeping daily score of his efforts by charting the day-to-day movements of a futures index? Was that how tenuous our situation still was?

Paulson emphasized that he thought SIGTARP had an important role to play and that he was fully committed in his short time left as secretary to make sure that we'd have whatever support we needed.

"It's important for the American people to know that someone is looking out for fraud in this program," he said, and he wanted us to be Treasury's partner in making the program better. He sounded as if he meant what he was saying, and I think he did. What Kevin and I didn't realize at the time, however, was that this meeting would mark the high point of our relationship with Treasury.

I told Paulson that one concern I had from what I'd so far learned about TARP was that, as I had said to Wilkinson, the Capital Purchase Program might be vulnerable to fraud by struggling banks. When Paulson had announced CPP, he had stressed that the money would only go to banks that could demonstrate that they were "healthy and viable." It seemed to me that with the continuing stresses of the financial crisis—collapsing real estate prices, a growing recession, defaulting borrowers, and an overall credit crunch—it was inevitable that some banks on the edge of insolvency would turn to accounting fraud to make themselves appear to be healthier so they'd qualify for CPP money. As for banks that were already covering up weaknesses on their balance sheets, it would take no additional effort to defraud Treasury now; all they needed to do was bring their already cooked books to the TARP window and take home a big pile of taxpayer cash.

In the parlance of security fraud cons, a gullible mark with a lot of money was sometimes called a whale. In my view, with the way TARP money had been flying out the door so far, Treasury looked like the mother of all whales.

I assured Paulson that we would strive to make sure that anyone who stole from TARP would be locked up, but I stressed that it was going to be far more important for us to keep fraud out of the program in the first place. Paulson agreed, and I then explained that an important first step with respect to any recipients already approved to get funds was to require them to acknowledge in their agreements that SIGTARP would have full access to their books, records, and personnel. This, I explained, would let them know that we were on the job, which would, hopefully, deter bad behavior. Again, Paulson was receptive to my concerns.

He then changed the subject to the automobile industry. A few days earlier, Congress's $14 billion rescue package for the automakers had died in the Senate, and the past Friday the White House had announced that it was considering using TARP funds instead.[2] The Republicans largely opposed the bailout, with future Speaker of the House John Boehner describing the congressional proposal as asking "taxpayers to further subsidize a business model that is failing to meet the needs of American workers and consumers."[3] Similarly, Senator Shelby explained his view that "[u]nless Chrysler, Ford and General Motors become lean and innovative and competitive in the marketplace, this is only delaying their funeral."[4]

Paulson told us that GM and Chrysler would almost certainly have to declare bankruptcy by the end of the year without assistance, and he confirmed that he planned to use TARP to rescue them.

Even though the CEOs had publicly begged for a bailout just days earlier, it was still jarring to hear the Treasury secretary say that those two icons of American industry really were teetering on the edge of bankruptcy.

"So what do you think?" Paulson asked me.

What do I think? I think that the only thing I know about the domestic automobile industry is that sweet '95 Chevy Camaro I parked outside, I thought to myself. To Paulson, I reemphasized that I thought it was important to put provisions into the contracts that explicitly acknowledged SIGTARP's oversight authority. I also mumbled something about Kevin being our auto expert (based on his being from Detroit and his dad's career at GM). Paulson agreed that there should be such provisions, and Hoyt, who as Treasury's general counsel was responsible for drafting the agreements, nodded. *Our first win!* I thought. *Okay, these guys really are on board.*

With that the meeting was over, and we all stood up and shook hands again. We were then escorted by someone from Human Resources down to our new quarters, which were a revelation.

Now, to this point I had been in five different Treasury offices, each more impressive than the last. Kashkari had a sprawling office, replete with signed photographs of him with Paulson, as well as a signed presidential commission and a number of large pictures of President Bush. Wilkinson's office was equally impressive, and Bob Hoyt had an office that looked more like a museum than a working space (it is a roped-off part of the weekend tour of the Treasury Building). Thorson's enormous office was nicer than all of theirs, and Paulson's office, of course, was spectacular. Though I don't generally care much about things like how big or how well decorated my office is, I had come to assume that as Treasury's most recent presidentially appointed and Senate-confirmed official, I was in for a huge upgrade from the 1970s chic of the U.S. Attorney's Office.

Reality began to hit as Kevin and I were escorted down two flights of stairs to a drab hallway on the first floor. We were struck by the smell of bacon and eggs as we arrived at an office numbered 1064. "Great location," our guide told us, "right next to the Vault, our cafeteria, very convenient!"

As the door to the office was unlocked, it became glaringly apparent that our red-carpet welcome did not extend past the threshold of Paulson's anteroom. The office literally stank, and although it was technically on the first floor, due to the downward slope of 15th Street, our side of the building was mostly underground. Our office "suite" consisted of an anteroom with two offices on either side and a set of *Laverne & Shirley*–like barred windows onto the street. Instead of looking out onto the grandeur of the White House, like some of the offices I had visited, our view was of the ankles and shoes of passersby. If either Kevin or I forgot to pull down the blinds, particularly at night or on weekends, tourists would gather by the windows to look down on us. That first night, Kevin called me into his office, laughing, and pointed up to a family staring down at him through the bars. (He jokingly suggested that Treasury might be conducting a sociology experiment on us.)

My office had been recently, and only partially, vacated, with the desk drawers and cabinets still filled with pamphlets and materials from my predecessor. The walls were bare, and the room featured only a desk, chair, phone, and computer; no table, no guest chairs, and not even a garbage can. Then there was the smell, a musky socklike odor, which we later learned emanated from a broken sewage pipe directly under the office suite. The office, which would be our home for several months, screamed, "Welcome to Washington, asshole. Fuck you. Really, I mean it. Fuck. You."

As we waited for a parade of administrators to come by and do all of the typical first-day-on-the-job processing, Kevin turned to me and said, "Well, congrats."

"Thanks, that was pretty intense," I replied.

"Not on being sworn in," Kevin said with a laugh. "For giving Treasury your blessing, less than ten minutes into the job, to use TARP funds to bail out GM and Chrysler."

He was right. My first official act of oversight had been essentially to approve of Treasury spending tens of billions of TARP dollars to rescue two decidedly nonfinancial institutions. Not exactly what Congress had envisioned when it had passed TARP. Given the anger already generated by CPP and the opposition to the congressional bailout of Detroit, there was clearly going to be some backlash for expanding TARP to cover GM and Chrysler, and I told Kevin to make a note that we shouldn't leave that night until we made sure that I hadn't made a colossal blunder.

A big part of that first day was getting an education on all of the things that we couldn't get done. We couldn't get access to our personal e-mails, we couldn't get a fax machine, and we couldn't even get trash cans. Worst of all, we couldn't hire people without posting position descriptions of their jobs online for thirty days. When I heard this, my heart began to sink. How could I stand up an agency when I couldn't bring anyone on board? (We were eventually able to get that barrier temporarily lifted.)

The one thing we could do was spend money. When Congress passed TARP, it made sure that SIGTARP was well funded, with $50 million allocated right off the bat. But figuring out *how* to spend it was another matter entirely.

Bizarrely, I began receiving calls from various government agencies pitching services to us, at a steep cost. I had never heard that there were whole subdivisions of government agencies that served as intragovernmental profit centers. Money in Washington is always sure to attract those who are seeking to get some, and although I had expected to be inundated by those in the private sector seeking to part us from our funds, I had no idea of the flurry of pitches I'd get from other governmental agencies. Before I knew it, we were signing contracts with Treasury's Bureau of Public Debt, which, in addition to overseeing how the government raises funds to meet its obligations, operates a massive one-stop outsourcing business from which we purchased, at exorbitant rates, back-office operations, accounting, human resources, and other services. Even more rapacious were the costs we were to be charged by Treasury's IT department for computers, printers, and BlackBerrys ($2,194 per BlackBerry with prepaid service).

We were also pitched that day by the Treasury inspector general for tax administration and his deputy, who oversaw the IRS. They gave us a laundry list of "services" they could provide us, everything from lending us personnel to start building our administrative core to building our website to handling our human resource functions. After that meeting, I turned to Kevin, impressed by the generous level of support that our brother IG was offering.

"Wow. Those guys are going to be really helpful. No one else has stepped up and has been willing to help out like that," I said.

Kevin smirked at my naiveté. "Did you hear what they said at the end? About a memorandum of understanding and a meeting on specific services?"

"Yes," I replied.

"They're going to charge us for everything. And my guess is through the nose."

He was right. But we really had no other choice, as getting through the morass of government procurement procedures would have taken months that we did not have. And although we would have to pay above-market prices, at least the money was all going to other governmental agencies. I was confident that if we ever had to defend the expenses, we could explain that because they were intragovernmental transfers, they were at limited expense to the taxpayer.

Rochelle Granat, the head of Treasury's Human Resources Department, was also helpful in finding us a secretary who had been bouncing around the building from job to job, including most recently with TARP. She also gave us some advice on navigating through some of the no's we had been encountering, including how to hire people faster.

As night settled in, we learned that no food delivery was allowed to the building, so we emptied the vending machine outside our office and settled in to figure out what was next.

As we gazed over the expanding landscape of the vending machine detritus on the office floor some hours later, Kevin reminded me of my earlier approval of Paulson's proposed use of TARP to bail out GM and Chrysler. I had reviewed the TARP statute before my confirmation hearings to make sure that CPP was legal, and I knew that the language was pretty broad, but I had not yet considered specifically whether it would authorize the bailouts of GM and Chrysler. I pulled out the prep materials Treasury had given me for my hearings and went over the statute.

The bill explicitly gave Treasury the authority to purchase "troubled assets" from "financial institutions," so the breadth of Treasury's authority depended on the definition of the two terms. If defined narrowly, Treasury would've been restricted to only buying a small range of assets and making those purchases only from banks. But as I reread the full text that evening, I saw that the definition of "troubled assets" included not only bank-related assets but also "any other financial instrument that the Sec-retary" deemed necessary to buy in order to "promote financial market stability."[5] In other words, a "troubled asset" could be just about anything, as long as Paulson (and later Geithner, who had already been named by the incoming president as his choice for Treasury secretary) declared to Congress that its purchase was "necessary." Remarkably, the definition of a "financial institution" was even broader, including "any institution" that is "established and regulated under the laws of the United States or any State."[6] Given the broad regulatory scope in this country, that included just about every company in the nation. Under TARP, Paulson could make any loan or investment in any company that struck his fancy.[7]

After I finished reading, I walked over to Kevin.

"Well, the good news is that we didn't approve an illegal transaction as our first official act," I told him.

"And the bad news?" Kevin asked.

"There really is no such thing as an illegal transaction. These guys can do whatever they want, whenever they want."

"Well," he shot back, "there is a one good thing about that."

"What's that?" I asked.

"It'll be your ass, not mine, who gets to tell the members of Congress who didn't bother to read the legislation before voting for it that they gave Hank Paulson and Tim Geithner a blank check."

As we called it a night and locked up the door to our new home, I made a mental note to try to get a SIGTARP sign for it, and Kevin and I searched for an exit that was still open (no one had told us, but through trial and error we learned that only the rear of the Treasury Building was open after hours). Kevin turned to me as we headed to our separate cars and said, "Good day for SIGTARP," which became the last thing we said to each other just about every night for the next nineteen months.

With the frenetic pace of the day ending, the reality of having to build an agency from scratch, with little help or support, smacked me in the face as I got in my car. I was in a low-level panic. There was just so much that needed to get done. I was also worried about Paulson's comments about GM and Chrysler that morning. Part of me had thought that by starting right before the holidays, I would have a couple of weeks to get my bearings and devise an overall strategy. I now realized how foolish I had been to think that I would have any break. Vast sums were pouring out of Treasury every day, and I just didn't have the luxury of meticulously building the perfect agency. I just had to get rolling. Now.

THE NEXT MORNING, I got to Treasury before sunrise and started preparing outlines for the full day of meetings that Kevin and I had scheduled. Our plan was to do a minitour of some of the sixty-plus different inspectors general offices around Washington to gather the best advice about how we should set up our office and how we should operate. Every major Executive Branch department and many large agencies had IGs, which were ostensibly independent offices that shared a common mission to root out waste, fraud, and abuse within the agency they oversaw. They varied greatly in size, from just a handful of people to more than 1,500 on staff,[8] as well as in reputation. Some IGs were viewed as effective watchdogs that served as strong, independent voices, while others were never really heard from at all. We were hoping that by canvassing widely, we'd learn how to avoid pitfalls and become one of the offices that was widely respected.

We met with anyone who agreed to meet with us, and with few exceptions, the meetings followed the same script, merging into one disquieting composite meeting.

Although the idea behind IGs was that they would be fiercely independent watchdogs, I soon learned that they were mostly just like any other government agency. As such, their priorities were, in order of importance: maintaining and hopefully increasing their budget; giving the appearance of activity; and not making too many waves. The common refrain went like this:

"Neil. There are three different types of IGs. You can be a lapdog, a watchdog, or a junkyard dog. A lapdog is too timid, perceived as being in the pocket of the agency. If you're seen as a lapdog, Congress will have your head and make life really miserable for you. So, for example, you don't want to have a weekly golf game with the guys you're supposed to be overseeing or go to their house for a Christmas party."

Check, I thought. I've never played golf in my life and could not imagine that Paulson could get much of a grip on a golf club with that mangled pinky anyway. But I also couldn't help but notice that the reason that they gave me for not curling up on Paulson's lap was that it might annoy someone in Congress, not that it would be a complete dereliction of my duty to be independent.

"You also don't want to be a junkyard dog. You don't want to be perceived as someone who is out there promoting himself or playing games of 'gotcha' with management. If you get that reputation, you're going to alienate the people with whom you're trying to forge relationships, and you'll end up getting buried with requests from Congress to conduct all sorts of audits and investigations, which you really want to avoid."

Check.

"What you want to be is a watchdog. The agency should perceive you as a constructive but independent partner, helping to make things better for the agency, so everyone is better off. You want Congress to know you're doing something, but you don't want it to think that it owns you."

The first few times I heard that, I thought the advice made sense. Be aggressive, but not too aggressive, so as to lose credibility. Be visible, but not too much so, and try not to piss everyone off. That way you can live to fight another day. But as the day progressed, I began to realize that there was a troubling subtext. First, those guys viewed Congress as a potential enemy, one that could come down hard on you. Over and over again we were warned about the two dangerous beasts of Congress who had it out for IGs: Chuck Grassley, the ranking Republican on the Senate Finance Committee, who, I was told, made terrorizing IGs he thought weren't doing their jobs his favorite pastime; and Darrell Issa, the Republican ranking member of the House Oversight and Government Reform Committee, whose name was usually spat out venomously. I also couldn't help remembering that Senator Baucus had told me at my hearing that I should aspire to option three by being "as mean as a junkyard dog."

The IGs also seemed way too concerned about how they would be perceived, whether by Congress, the senior management team at the agencies they were supposed to be overseeing, or other IGs. They seemed obsessed with finding a perfect Goldilocks balance—being perceived as "just right," not too hot and not too cold.

As far as the content of their work was concerned, many of the IGs seemed disdainful of the investigation part of their jobs, emphasizing that their offices revolved around the other core function that Mike had originally described to me: audits. The audit process was lengthy and cumbersome, I heard time and time again, and it was vital that all audits be up to "yellow book" standards (which I later learned referred to a book with an appropriately yellow cover put out by GAO on how to conduct an audit). These were not like the financial audits done by the big accounting firms, with which I had become familiar as a prosecutor. The "performance audits" I'd be conducting were supposed to evaluate the "process" that the agencies used to execute their policy decisions. The IGs explained to me that "process" was a fairly ambiguous term—it could refer to anything that went into how the agency chose to implement a particular policy or program, what internal controls the agency adopted to make sure that it didn't violate its own policies, and its performance in executing its policies.

I was told repeatedly, however, that the *policies themselves* were outside of my jurisdiction; it was not for me to second-guess the decisions Treasury made on how and where to spend TARP funds. Instead, it was my job to assess how it was implementing those policies and running its programs and make recommendations so that it could fix any breakdowns or mistakes.

Finally, I learned that one of the most important things for IGs was performance statistics, the metrics on which IGs were judged by Congress and the White House. Specifically, IGs were judged by how many audits were completed, how many individuals were arrested, and what percentage of recommendations was adopted by the agency they oversaw. The higher those numbers, the higher the agencies' funding would be, I was told, so it was important that I start churning out audits and making recommendations that could be adopted as soon as possible.

Beneath it all was an undercurrent of fear. Nearly all of my fellow IGs, like myself, were Bush appointees, and we could all be fired at will by the incoming president. In many ways, their advice was as much about surviving the transition as conducting robust independent oversight. I would get a good look of that survival instinct in the coming months, after President Obama fired several IGs, including Gerald Walpin, the AmeriCorps IG. Walpin did not go quietly, charging that his dismissal had been in retaliation for his investigation of a close political ally of the president. It quickly got ugly, with the administration hinting that Walpin was senile and claiming that he had acted "confused" during meetings.[9]

In the midst of the swirling controversy, I went to a meeting of the Council of Inspectors General on Integrity and Efficiency, a group of IGs that met monthly. Walpin had asked the council to conduct an investigation into his firing or at least for a statement of support, and when the request was raised in the meeting, the IGs were like rats scurrying to the closest corner. Statements by the supposedly fiercely independent watchdogs included "We've got to keep our heads down on this" and "Jerry got himself into this mess, and we can't let him drag us down with him." I asked what procedural mechanisms there were to comply with his request and was told that there was none. By that time, I had become an outspoken critic of Treasury, and as I was walking out of the meeting, another IG commented on my most recent public fracas and said, "I wish I could do the same thing, but I've got kids in college. I need this job."

As I was conducting my initial round of IG meetings, though, I was just beginning to understand their motives and fears, and what I learned was that to succeed as an IG: (1) investigations should be a secondary concern; (2) I should instead focus on audits; (3) in carrying out those audits, I should stay away from the policy decisions made by Treasury and instead just focus on process; (4) I should try not to be too aggressive and seek to meet management halfway; and (5) it was vital to avoid Congress like the plague and to churn out as many mostly agreeable audits as fast as possible so that I'd have enviable stats. In other words, every instinct that I had about the job was dead wrong.

My confidence was shaken. My plan had been to focus on investigations, not audits. I had assumed that Treasury generally knew what it was doing in implementing TARP and my job would be to keep criminals from putting their hands in the cookie jar. My only relevant experience was in investigating fraud, not conducting audits, and I was now being told that SIGTARP would be judged almost exclusively on something with which I had almost no familiarity.

Maybe hiring someone like me, who had no audit experience, had been a mistake. Or, more troubling still, maybe Treasury had picked me for that reason? Because it didn't want someone with extensive audit experience poking around?

* * *

My introduction to the IG community, and to the world of oversight in Washington, took another dispiriting turn Wednesday evening in an e-mail exchange with the Treasury IG Eric Thorson. He had been part of a whirlwind of introductory meetings on Monday, but we had not yet had a chance to have a substantive conversation since our phone call the week before. The TARP statute required us to submit an initial report to Congress within sixty days of my confirmation, and the February 6 due date was now just seven weeks away. Kevin and I needed to get a handle on what Thorson's group had been doing so we could use that work as a jumping-off point. I was concerned that my initial request that he send over the TARP documents that he had already acquired had gone unanswered, and I was still bothered that Thorson had initiated the City National Bank audit only after I had been confirmed. I needed to know what exactly he had been doing in the ten weeks between TARP's passage and my arrival in Washington.

The e-mail exchange stoked my concerns. Shortly after five, I received a message from Thorson's chief counsel, Richard Delmar. He clearly considered the message important, as in addition to me he had sent it to a number of Treasury's top brass: Hoyt, Wilkinson, and Treasury's press secretary, Michele Davis. He'd also copied Thorson, Thorson's deputy, and Kevin. The e-mail said that even though it had not yet publicly announced the City National audit, the *Los Angeles Times* had sent Delmar an e-mail asking if the Treasury inspector general's office was examining TARP payments to any banks in California. Delmar included in the e-mail his proposed response: "We are reviewing the process by which one bank in southern California, City National of Beverly Hills, was found to be eligible for participation in the Capital Purchase Program."

I was thoroughly confused. I still had no understanding of the art of planting a question from a journalist, which is what I later suspected Thorson had done. Even more confusing was why the top brass at Treasury was being copied on what seemed to me to be an internal IG matter. I remembered that Thorson had told me that he notified Treasury about his visits to the Hill—a practice which, thankfully, was thoroughly rejected by the other IGs with whom I had been meeting—and wondered:

did this e-mail mean that he also ran his press by the department? Was Treasury going to expect that I would also be so closely tethered to it?

But the most important thing to me was that I didn't want Thorson sending out a press release on a TARP matter, at least until I'd had some time to think it through. After all, any release at this point would likely be attributed to me and could set a precedent I was not sure I wanted. At a minimum, I first needed to speak with Thorson about his oversight efforts to date and the mechanics of our transition.

I hit "Reply to All," typed a draft response, and called Kevin over to take a look at it. "Before any reply goes out," I wrote, "let's discuss this at our meeting tomorrow. Since I have not yet been briefed on this matter, I cannot evaluate the proposed response or whether a response is warranted." With Kevin's assent, I hit "Send."

About a half hour later, Thorson responded that he had briefed the Congressional Oversight Panel on the audit, and "it is clear" that the reporter must have learned about the audit from someone on the panel. He added that Delmar was only "advising" us of his response, which Thorson planned to send. He then explained that he "must" respond, because he had "a responsibility here to have accomplished some work" and that this was "the one job that we would demonstrate our required involvement" in TARP oversight.

Whoa. The *one* job? He'd said nothing to me about the audit being essentially for show, though the timing of it certainly raised my suspicions. Now he was blithely admitting that he'd wanted to get some press for doing this "one job," apparently so that he wouldn't be accused of having done absolutely nothing while hundreds of billions of dollars were surging out of Treasury's coffers. After all, he had told *The Washington Post* that he was actively engaged in TARP oversight and written a letter to Congress that said he was "gearing up to provide the Congress with the first 60-day report that the SIG TARP is required to file per the Act."[10] But here he was apparently admitting, in a forthright e-mail to me and to top officials at Treasury, that he had initiated no significant projects until after my confirmation and that he now wanted to cover his ass by citing this audit.

I fired off an irritated message in which I asked him to hold off until the next day, reiterating that we had not yet settled on a press policy regarding notification of ongoing audits (we would later decide to announce everything proactively). Any steps he took now could be construed as precedent, I wrote, and his statement could be attributed to us. I closed by saying that we could find other ways "to demonstrate your oversight to date," which we could discuss in our meeting. When I didn't hear back from him that night, I assumed that the matter had been resolved, but I told Kevin that we needed to assume that we might not be getting a lot of help from Thorson for the initial report.

My e-mail exchange with Thorson was actually the highlight of the evening. I had started interviewing people for key positions. My leading candidate to run the investigations division told me flat out that she was not interested, and some leading candidates for other key jobs either had terrible interviews or their references weren't checking out. By the time I headed home I was in a state of high anxiety. I called Karen.

"How'd it go today?" she asked.

"It's a nightmare," I replied.

I unloaded, telling her how little I had understood about what it meant to be an IG and how I was going to be judged primarily on being an auditor, which I had no idea how to do.

"Even worse," I said, "it is not as if nothing is happening. TARP money is literally streaming out the door. A hundred billion dollars could go out over the next two weeks alone, on top of the hundreds of billions that have already been committed. I'm supposed to be watching it like a hawk, and I can't even figure out how to get in and out of the parking lot."

"What about Treasury, are they being helpful?" Karen asked.

"All I hear is how things can't get done. For three days I have been trying to get garbage cans, and I can't get anyone to listen. How am I going to build an agency if I cannot even get a place to put the trash?"

Karen, God bless her, laughed. "Where do you put trash?"

"We pile it up and take it to the cafeteria. Which is conveniently next to our office," I said, laughing back.

Ever the psychologist, she asked how Kevin was dealing with things. "What does he say when you tell him about how you're feeling?"

That was part of the problem, I explained. I couldn't tell Kevin how worried I was. I knew he must be asking himself every other hour why he had given up his great gig at a prestigious New York City law firm to come down here for this, and I couldn't let him or anyone else see how panicked I was.

Karen reminded me that I had dealt with greater stresses; after all, unlike FARC, no one in Washington was going to try to kill me over an audit.

"Don't think of all the things you have to do, just the one thing right in front of you," she wisely advised.

THE NEXT MORNING started on a great note: garbage cans arrived! Confident that a new day was dawning, the first thing I did was to try to smooth things over with Thorson by writing him a cooperative e-mail. I'd met the day before with Jon Rymer, the FDIC IG, and he suggested that we conduct a joint audit of all the banking regulators—which included the FDIC, the Federal Reserve and the two Treasury regulators, the Office of the Comptroller of the Currency, and the Office of Thrift Supervision—with Thorson and the Federal Reserve IG. I wrote Thorson an e-mail about the idea, thinking that consulting him would be a nice conciliatory gesture that would get us on a better path. *Quite the diplomat,* I thought.

I had not heard back from Thorson by the time Kevin and I made the trek up to his fourth-floor palace a little before two for our meeting. Tension filled the air as we walked in. Thorson was sitting at the head of his large conference table, looking pissed, with a handful of his staffers lined up on one side of the table, across from where Kevin and I were to sit—a setup not exactly suggestive of the cooperative spirit I was shooting for.

As we sat down, Thorson said nothing, so I started the meeting. Kevin and I had agreed earlier that in meetings with agencies that had overlapping jurisdiction with SIGTARP, we should try to take control. The statute that had created SIGTARP said we were responsible for "coordinating audits and investigations" related to TARP, and we hoped that if we asserted our authority firmly enough, we'd encounter few objections. At this particular meeting, however, that approach might not have been the wisest strategy.

"Okay. Let's go through what you guys have actually done, so we can figure out the handoff," I said.

For the next few minutes I questioned Thorson's staff, but I didn't get far. When I asked what they had done to oversee the hundreds of billions of dollars that had already gone out the door, they simply repeated what Thorson had told me, that they'd sent staff to briefings that Treasury had set up with GAO. Okay, I thought, but what oversight had *they* done? I asked about the documents that Thorson had told me he'd been compiling and was told that the staff had sent an e-mail request to Treasury back in November.

That's it? I wondered, the sinking feeling in my stomach returning once again. When I next asked to see the e-mail requests to Treasury and any responses, Thorson exploded.

"How dare you? How dare you question how I handle the press? I've been dealing with the press for years, and you come in and question me?"

So he was clearly still annoyed about our exchange the night before.

I tried to respond, but he cut me off; he was just getting started.

"And how dare you send an e-mail like that to the chief of staff, the general counsel of Treasury?" Thorson asked, spitting out the two titles. "Why would you ever do such a thing? Why?"

In a measured tone, I responded, "Eric. I have to admit I thought it was quite odd that Delmar had copied them on his initial e-mail to me, but since he did, I assumed that you thought it was appropriate that they be kept in the loop in the ensuing conversation. I was just following your lead."

"But to send an e-mail like that to them, saying you didn't want me to send the response after we'd obviously already responded to the *L.A. Times*. What were you trying to do?" he snarled.

Sometimes as a prosecutor I'd had to talk to victims who were so upset that they would just irrationally start screaming at me, even though I was the one trying to help them. I now adopted the same tone I'd used with them.

"Well, Eric," I said slowly, "I didn't know you'd already sent a response. In Richard [Delmar]'s e-mail, it said that you *planned* to send a response, so I thought that you hadn't done so yet. I'm sorry if I didn't read it correctly. I was only trying to slow down the process and wanted to talk about these issues with you before there was a response."

Thinking that would settle the matter, I changed the topic.

"Now let's talk about the joint audit proposed by Rymer," I suggested.

"Not interested!" Thorson snarled. "We won't be doing another single thing on TARP other than City National. Nothing."

"You won't do *anything*? Really? We do all have an obligation here," I said, my voice rising.

"Nothing," Thorson replied.

Now I was really mad. I couldn't believe this was happening. This audit was potentially important for us; it would give us the chance to coordinate a comprehensive report on an important topic with minimal resources. Was this guy really going to torpedo the project because of an *e-mail*?

My voice sharpened. "Well, you'll need to keep us in the loop on City National. And we'll likely go forward with Rymer on the joint audit and do your parts ourselves."

"Fine. We'll keep you up to speed on City National," Thorson replied (which would turn out to be untrue), "but we'll not be doing anything else with you. We don't have the resources."

Then, remarkably, he once again returned to the issue of the previous evening's e-mail exchange.

"Obviously it was *suggested* in the e-mail that our response had already gone out. How dare you second-guess me?" he ranted. I could see his staff inching away from him.

Losing my patience, I snapped back at him that I was sorry about the misunderstanding but that he needed to get over it so we could move on to actually doing our jobs of overseeing $700 billion in taxpayer money.

I then turned to his head of audits and resumed asking about the documents requested from Treasury, but Thorson declared the meeting over and got up from his seat.

"Really? Eric," I said, "Because I hurt your feelings. In an e-mail?"

Really. As we walked out of his office, his deputy grabbed us and said he would get us what we needed.

Although I tried to mend fences with Thorson over the years, he avoided talking to me from that day forward, refusing to personally show up to a council that I created of nine inspectors general who had overlapping oversight on TARP-related matters, and ignoring my requests to coordinate overlapping projects with us, even after we received joint letters from Senator Grassley a few months later to do a coordinated audit of the $168 million in bonus payments made by AIG to its executives.

The meeting was unnerving. The worst revelation was that there had apparently been no meaningful IG oversight of the hundreds of billions of TARP dollars that Treasury had already spent.

As I started talking to congressional staffers and interviewing applicants from other IG offices, I came to understand some of the reasons for Thorson's hostility, which should have been obvious to me. I was told that Thorson and the rest of the IG community were as adamantly opposed to the creation of SIGTARP as Treasury was. They viewed us both as a congressional incursion on their jurisdiction and as a rejection of the IG community's ability to police its own agencies. Indeed, for no one was the creation of SIGTARP more of a rebuke than Eric Thorson, who would have otherwise had primary jurisdiction over the program.

I got even more insight into Thorson several months later. When I walked into my office one day, I found a printout from Kashkari's online calendar from November 13, 2008, sitting on my desk. That was the day the article appeared in *The Washington Post* that quoted Thorson as saying that TARP was "a mess." The calendar entry included an e-mail sent by Thorson to Kashkari that morning in which he said he wanted to meet with him to apologize for the quote and said he had meant to refer to his own handling of TARP as being a mess. The groveling apology also obsequiously heaped praise on Kashkari and the rest of the leadership team at Treasury, noting how offended Thorson would be if anyone ever thought that he had anything but the highest respect for them.

I realized that this message, more than anything else I'd encountered in Washington, explained so many of the problems I was having with Treasury by that time. This type of capture, this type of utter subservience by the IG, had become the expectation within Treasury about how an IG was *supposed* to act.

Though my meeting with Thorson was seriously troubling, an encounter later that night with Bill Burck clarified for me how I would move forward.

Around seven that evening, Kevin and I called it an early day and walked over to Fogo de Chao, a Brazilian steak house where the Office's Washington alumni network was having a dinner in honor of us and of those departing Washington with the change of administrations. As I was waiting for a cab in front of the restaurant, I got a chance to talk to Burck, who was winding down his time at the White House. I filled him in about my problems with Thorson and how concerned I was about getting SIG-TARP off the ground.

"Don't worry about Thorson," he said. "He's a total clown, and no one will care about what he does or says. He's a joke."

"But what am I going to do about building this office? What do I know about audits?" I asked.

Bill gave me a puzzled look. "We didn't nominate you because of your auditing skills. We couldn't care less. You were hired because you prosecuted Refco. Because you put mortgage bad guys in jail. Because you went down to Colombia and fucked with the FARC. If we wanted another bullshit IG office, trust me, there were plenty of bullshit IG types that we could've picked. We picked you because we want you to be the exact opposite of these assholes that you are talking to."

"But what about stats? How important is it to have high numbers?" I asked.

"You have at least a year to worry about that, and there's a good chance that no one will even care about TARP a year from now. Congress isn't going to care about your numbers, they're going to care about results. And they're going to love you," Burck said.

He paused, letting it sink in, before continuing to buck me up.

"Look, I've told you this before. You've got to understand, you have a real bully pulpit here. You'll be able to say things and people will listen. They'll have to listen, and Treasury won't have any idea of what to make of you. So just don't worry about the other IGs or Thorson or Treasury. You just need to do the exact same things that you did to those guys in Refco that are rotting in jail. To the leaders of the FARC. Just do what seems right to you."

A cab pulled up almost on cue. I thanked Burck, and we made plans to get together after the holidays. By the time I got back to my apartment, I was buzzing.

Karen was down for the weekend, and I realized just how much I'd missed her when I saw her in her pajamas waiting for me. "How was it?" she asked.

"I just had the most amazing conversation with Burck," I told her. "I've been doing this all wrong. I've been thinking that I should build an IG office that looks like every other IG office. But why? Why do I want to be like them?"

The next morning, I woke up and couldn't wait to see Kevin. As soon as he came in, I told him, "I talked to Burck last night. Change in plans . . ."

4

I Won't Lie for You

K EVIN AND I felt liberated by the Burck-inspired revelation that we should run SIGTARP our own way. We *were* "special," damn it, and didn't have to adhere to some bullshit IG code that made no sense for us. Breaking free of the cage of traditional IG expectations, however, didn't reduce the challenge facing us. With the GM and Chrysler bailouts still on deck, Treasury had been showering Wall Street with hundreds of billions of dollars for two months now, with $250 billion committed to the Capital Purchase Program, $40 billion to AIG, and $20 billion to a new Treasury/Fed program that was unfortunately named the Term Asset-Backed Securities Loan Facility (TALF). Further, although the transaction was still being finalized, in November Treasury had committed to giving the still-struggling Citigroup another $20 billion in addition to the $25 billion in CPP funds it had already received and along with the Federal Reserve and the FDIC, agreed to provide the bank with a guarantee relating to $300 billion of its toxic assets. All of these transactions and commitments had been executed with no oversight by or input from Thorson's office, and Kashkari and his team had become accustomed to calling their own shots without having to listen to an IG's concerns about potential waste, fraud, and abuse.

One thing I quickly realized was that we needed a good press person. I'd had no experience whatsoever with handling the press. For prosecutors, the Office made it very simple: you did not talk to the press. Ever.

Under any circumstance. Only one person spoke to the press, and that was the U.S. attorney himself.

During the nomination process for SIGTARP, I had gotten away with simply refusing all interview requests, but I knew that strategy of sticking my head in the sand wouldn't work much longer. I'd already gotten enough of a glimpse of how the game was played in Washington to know that we needed a professional.

Most of the IGs I spoke to expressed hostility toward the press and seethed against the "media whore IGs" who cultivated press relationships. The person most associated with this label was Stuart Bowen, the special inspector general for Iraq reconstruction (SIGIR). Stuart was, in many ways, the anti-IG. Although many within the IG community viewed him as something of a self-promoter, to Congress SIGIR was considered a success story for its hard-hitting and widely distributed reports. Stuart had brought much-needed transparency to the pervasive fraud in the Iraqi reconstruction effort and was specifically cited during my confirmation hearings as an example that I should emulate. Whereas most others IGs, including Thorson, had their counsel handle press inquiries, Stuart had people on staff whose sole job was to deal with the media. Previewing what I would later be told by a senior congressman, Stuart explained to me that in order to have an impact as an IG it was vital to have a good relationship with the press. The only way to make things happen in Washington, he explained, was to ensure that Congress and the public were aware of the problems you saw, so that they could then pressure the agency to resolve them. One of the best ways to do that, Stuart explained, was through the press.

Fortunately, my old partner in the FARC battles, Eric Snyder, sent me the résumé of a friend of his, Kris Belisle, who was working as Stuart's communications director. Kris is from Minnesota, and speaks with a singsong accent straight out of the movie *Fargo*, but the accent only adds to her earnestness. During her interview, Kris opened our conversation dramatically, saying, "I should tell you right off the bat, if you're looking for the traditional type of press officer, you shouldn't hire me."

"What does that even mean?" I asked.

She responded that in most governmental agencies, it is often expected that the press officer will spin, shade, or even hide any facts that might put the agency in a negative light.

"The number one goal of most agencies is, frankly, to try and make the principal [Washington-speak for the head of the agency] look good, no matter what the actual facts are, even if it means lying to or misleading the press," she explained. "I won't do that. I won't lie for you. I won't compromise my integrity, and I won't comprise this office's integrity." She had my full attention.

"So what would your strategy be?" I asked.

"We'll be completely transparent with the press," Kris responded, correctly presuming that she already had the job. "We'll admit and even highlight our mistakes."

"Okay. I understand not lying, but my guess is that as a start-up, we're going to have more than our fair share of screwups. Why would we want to bring them to the press's attention?" I asked, intrigued.

"Because if we do, we'll earn the press's trust. They'll know we're not spinning like everyone else. SIGTARP will quickly become the only credible source for information in Washington about TARP. We might be embarrassed at times and disclose things that we could—and others would—easily hide, but we'll shock the press with our honesty. No one else does this, and before long we'll have a built-in defense when we're attacked. No matter what they hear, the press will come to us first and believe us, because we'll prove to them that we tell the truth."

"Why do you think we'll be attacked?" I asked. I didn't yet see the giant target that I was slowly beginning to paint on my back.

"I've watched your hearings, I've read up on you, I can see how you describe what you plan to do here, and I've talked to Eric about you. If you're really going to find the truth and tell it without any political consideration, you're going to be opening up a real can of worms and have real enemies before long, here at Treasury and on Wall Street."

I was taken aback and thought of the haunting line from former Clinton staffer Vince Foster's suicide note in which he described Washington as a town where "ruining people is sport."

I asked her what kinds of things they'd do.

"You'll start seeing unattributed quotes from Treasury or Wall Street officials saying all sorts of things about you and SIGTARP."

"Like what?" I asked.

"You'll read in the newspaper that a 'senior Treasury official' or a 'high-ranking bank executive' made negative comments about what you're doing, which could run from criticisms about specific audits or reports to outright lies," Kris calmly told me. "Or you may see a quote attributed to 'a source familiar with so-and-so's thinking,' which almost *always* means that it's so-and-so providing the quote."

"So how do we respond?" I asked. "Would we do the same?"

"I won't let you. Our strategy will be to never play their game, always be above it. That's how we'll maintain credibility. If you're not comfortable putting your name behind a statement, then I can say it, or we can have someone else in the organization say it. But if you're not comfortable with *anyone* from SIGTARP saying it on the record, then you'll just have to keep your little mouth shut," Kris declared, her Minnesota accent coming through.

"But wouldn't that put us at a disadvantage? We wouldn't be able to fight fire with fire," I asked.

"In Washington, everyone is obsessed with the news cycle, twenty-four to forty-eight hours. That won't be us. We may lose occasionally in the short term, but we're going to win in the long term. Credibility will make us different," Kris answered.

I would interview a lot of people for a lot of different jobs over the next couple of years, and no one was as impressive as Kris. Over the course of a sixty-minute interview, I found more than just a communications director; I found an expression of the philosophy I wanted to adopt for the entire agency.

I felt a little guilty hiring Kris because I'd also found our head of audits, Barry Holman, at SIGIR; Stuart Bowen was a good friend to us, and he had good people. I didn't know the first thing about conducting a "Yellow Book" audit, and Barry had decades of experience running audits while working for GAO and then SIGIR. Stuart also came to our rescue by lending us one of his legislative affairs experts, Paul Cooksey, while we looked for our own permanent legislative director.

Our legislative strategy was simple. Members of Congress, for all of their pettiness, bipartisan bickering, and self-destructive idiocy, were our gods. We were their progeny, created over the objections of Treasury, the White House, and even the inspector general community. And sure enough, as we soon started to feel the tension from our brother, sister, and parent agencies in the Executive Branch, it became apparent that if we were going to have any friends at all in Washington, they were going to come from that confounding branch of government known as the legislature. One of our first legislative efforts was to approach Senator Claire McCaskill, a known "friend" of inspectors general who had introduced a bill that would expand SIGTARP's already extensive jurisdiction even before my confirmation. Paul and I immediately went to work on McCaskill's staff to fulfill our legislative wish list and to make sure that her bill had the strong support of other known supporters, including Senator Grassley, the senior Republican on the Senate Finance Committee who had fought alongside Senator Baucus for SIGTARP's creation. Ironically, Senator Jim Bunning, in an apparent change of heart, also became a cosponsor of the bill.

While searching for legislative directors, one for the House and one for the Senate, I had a difficult time finding someone who had the necessary experience and who could also be bipartisan, which was a necessary but difficult prerequisite to find. My search spoke volumes about the way Washington works. I had a large selection of remarkably experienced Republican applicants; after all, December 2008 was a bad time to be a Republican in Washington. Applicants included high-ranking Bush administration legislative affairs officials as well as staffers for recently ousted Republicans in Congress, all about to be out of work. I was tempted by the prospect of bringing someone on board who already had extensive experience in legislative affairs, but Kevin pointed out that we couldn't have our representative on the Hill be someone who reminded the Democrat staffers who were now in control of both houses of the political rancor of the past eight years. Any face associated with President Bush could not be the face of SIGTARP.

Finding Democrats with relevant experience, however, was no easy task. The same factors that brought us a flood of Republican applicants resulted in a drought of qualified Democrats. We spoke to several, but most senior staffers were looking to get jobs in the incoming Obama administration, staying on the Hill to work on what promised to be game-changing legislation, or cashing out for high-paying lobbying jobs. What they were *not* looking to do was join an anonymous former prosecutor in an unknown agency.

That may have been just as well; an overly partisan Democrat would have been as problematic for us as a die-hard Republican. Traditionally, IGs are the favorite of the party that does not have power in the White House and thrive during split government. As John Angell, a Democrat who served as a senior staffer to the Senate Finance Committee, jokingly told Kevin and me during those first few weeks, "Look, we love you today, but once January twentieth comes around and we have a new president, we'll be coming after you." I laughed at the time, and John warmly replied, "I'm not joking." Despite his warning, John and his boss, Senator Baucus, never wavered in their strong support of SIGTARP. But until the day I stepped down, whenever I ran into John he joked, "You know, Neil, it's just a matter of time . . ."

As I interviewed candidates for the position, the battle scars left by the partisan battles of recent years became apparent. I realized that the model I was looking to establish, which necessarily provided for equal love for both Democrats and Republicans, was a hard sell, to say the least, to those who had been fighting in the political trenches against the other side for years. Some applicants, who had not done their homework, assumed that as a Bush appointee I must be a Republican, and they would bash Democrats during their interviews. Others, knowing that I was a Democrat, would delight in the recent sweep of the elections and gloat about how unimportant the Republicans had become. I was beginning to lose hope and told Kevin that we'd have a better chance finding Bigfoot than someone who met our bipartisan criteria.

In early January, however, I interviewed Lori Hayman, and I knew right away we had to hire her. She was a Democrat staffer from the House Oversight and Government Reform Committee but had no rancor whatsoever toward her Republican colleagues and actually seemed to like some of them. A lawyer, Lori was smart and personable and thoroughly understood the inner workings of the House of Representatives. Though I had planned to hire one person to cover the House and another to cover the Senate, Lori was so proficient in working with both houses and on both sides of the aisle that I made her director of legislative affairs and let her hire an assistant to help her do both jobs. Lori's uncanny ability to maintain SIGTARP's apolitical, nonpartisan reputation on the Hill, even when we later came under brutal attacks by the sitting administration, made her, along with Kevin and Kris, one of the most valuable members of my team.

The other key job we had to fill was a head of investigations. I spoke with a number of agents from the FBI and other big law enforcement agencies that made compelling pitches based on the types of criminal investigations they envisioned. But Kevin and I knew as much about putting together complex white-collar investigations as anyone, so we opted instead for someone who knew how to run an IG law enforcement agency. Kevin and I knew well from our days working drug cases together that when you put together guns, badges, and testosterone, you need someone who knows how to keep things under control. We got our wish in the form of Chris Sharpley, the head of investigations for the inspector general for the Energy Department. What he might have lacked in experience in investigating the types of financial institution accounting frauds that I planned to be the focus of our investigations, he more than made up for in terms of his knowledge and understanding of how to build a law enforcement agency from scratch. He was a great hire.

As we were bringing Chris on board, he pointed out an issue in the bill that had created SIGTARP that Kevin and I had missed. Although it had been apparent during my confirmation hearings that Congress had intended for me to build a law enforcement agency to hunt down those who would try to profit criminally off of TARP, Chris pointed out that it seemed to have forgotten to give us full law enforcement authority. That meant no guns, no search warrants, and no arrests. It also meant that it would be very hard to recruit experienced agents; no law enforcement officer wants to give up his or her gun.

Kevin found some ambiguity in the IG statute itself. It conferred full law enforcement authority on "The Inspector General offices of . . ." and, in a lengthy list of agencies, included "Treasury."[1] We decided that for the short term we would assert full law enforcement authority under the provision (after all, we were an "inspector general" and we were part of "Treasury") until we could get a legislative fix. In the meantime, knowing that our interpretation might not legally hold up if anything went wrong during an arrest, we agreed that we would hold off on issuing firearms and make sure that any arrests were executed by one of our law enforcement partners. We got Senator McCaskill's staff to tack on some "clarifying" language to the SIGTARP bill that they were working on, and until the bill was signed by the president in April, I was able to roll over anyone who questioned our law enforcement authority with Kevin's interpretation of the statute.

With Chris on board, our core team was complete, and we could let them start filling the ranks. Having such a strong team saved us, because Kevin and I had our hands full just trying to deal with Treasury. Right away, we began sitting in on a string of TARP briefings. At first Treasury didn't seem to understand our role, initially refusing even to give us copies of its contracts, insisting instead that we could only "inspect" them. It was only after I pointed out the provision in the TARP statute that *required* me to report to Congress whenever Treasury was being less than fully cooperative that our requests started to be fulfilled.

We were dismayed by the complete absence of oversight and compliance conditions in the CPP contracts that we received. Kevin and I decided that our first priority should be to get Treasury to incorporate as many oversight mechanisms into its new TARP contracts as possible, particularly with Treasury finalizing more than $45 billion in TARP deals with Citigroup, the auto companies and their finance arms in the coming two weeks.

We started with the first suggestion that I had made in Paulson's office, to get the new TARP recipients to explicitly acknowledge in their contracts that SIGTARP would have unfettered access to their documents and personnel. We'd never have the resources necessary to police every deal, but if we could put into those executives' minds that SIGTARP agents and auditors would be swarming over their every move, it might at least keep them in line as stewards of billions of dollars of taxpayer money. Unfortunately, even though Paulson had indicated support for this idea, Hoyt and Kashkari's initial reaction was not receptive. "Why do you need this if you think you already have statutory jurisdiction over them?" asked Hoyt.

I explained that even with full jurisdiction, we couldn't compel employees at the TARP recipients to talk to us, and that even though we could subpoena documents, they could always force us to go court to compel production. We could get stuck in court wasting resources and needlessly delaying our efforts.

They countered by arguing that there was no way that GM, Chrysler, or Citigroup would refuse to cooperate with us; any type of stonewalling would trigger a nuclear reaction from Congress.

"Of course they'll cooperate now," I conceded, "but what about a year down the road, or three, when they'll hopefully be back on their feet and public attention has moved on?"

"We are pretty far down the line in these negotiations, and we don't want to start inserting new terms; we don't know what their reaction will be," Hoyt answered.

After I noted that it was unlikely that those companies would risk bankruptcy over an oversight provision, Hoyt and Kevin were able to finally hammer out what I thought was mutually acceptable language for the Citi, GM, and Chrysler agreements. It felt as if we were gaining some traction with Treasury, but when we started recommending that similar provisions be included in the contracts for the hundreds of banks still getting TARP funds from the Capital Purchase Program, we hit a brick wall.

Hoyt and Kashkari refused to consider any changes to the CPP contracts. In an argument that would be repeated both by them and by their successors in connection with a number of different recommendations, they said that they feared that any alteration of the terms would frighten banks away from participating. I countered by asking if they really wanted banks in TARP if they were the type that would be scared away simply by having to acknowledge SIGTARP's oversight. Apparently, that was exactly the type of bank that they wanted in the program; the answer remained an emphatic no.

I was also becoming increasingly concerned about what was happening to the hundreds of billions of dollars in taxpayer funds that Treasury was pouring into the banks' gaping capital holes. Banks were beginning to talk to the press, and they were saying that they were using their taxpayer-supplied funds for just about everything other than the increased lending that had been Treasury's justification for CPP. Buying securities, great; buying other banks, no problem; saving it for a rainy day, sure; but lending?[2] It wasn't happening. And without increased lending, the economy would not be able to crawl out of the recession and into a robust recovery.

As *New York Times* columnist Thomas Friedman explained in January 2009, notwithstanding CPP the banks had "gone from lending money to anyone who could fog up a knife to now treating all potential borrowers, no matter how healthy, as bankrupt until proven innocent. And, therefore, you're either not lending to them or lending under such onerous terms that the economy can't get any liftoff."[3]

In addition to failing to include terms that would provide incentives to increase lending, Treasury didn't require the banks to report on how they were using TARP funds. Congress had noted this failure of transparency, and senators from both parties repeatedly told me of their discomfort with this policy during my confirmation hearing.[4] Senator Shelby summed up the thoughts of his colleagues when he told me that it was "important to know what the recipients are doing with the funds and the details of where this money is going."[5]

We began to push Treasury to require the banks to report on how they used TARP funds. At first glance, it seemed obvious: taxpayers could get transparency on how their money was being used by the banks; Treasury could monitor whether the banks were acting as they had hoped (increasing lending); and banks could thus be held more accountable. If it turned out that the banks were using the taxpayer money responsibly, Treasury's strategy would be validated, which would be great for the program. If not, Treasury could make fixes so that its policy goal of increased lending could be achieved.

Before making a formal recommendation, though, I wanted to firm up my facts. My one year of undergraduate accounting that I took at Wharton was nearly twenty years in my rearview mirror, so I went to some of my accountant friends and asked them if it was possible for the banks to account for how they used their taxpayer-supplied cash. I'd already heard Treasury defend its position by arguing that it was impossible for the banks to do so because money was fungible, meaning that since all money looked the same, once TARP dollars got mixed in with the other dollars held by the bank, it was impossible to tell whether any given expenditure came from TARP or some other funds. After speaking to my friends, reviewing stacks of materials that they gave me, and speaking with an economist, I became convinced that there were in fact ways to tie a bank's activities to its uses of TARP funds.

It wouldn't necessarily be easy, they warned, and any reporting requirement could potentially be gamed, but a rough accounting could be done of what they did with the money by asking the right questions. What changed on their balance sheet after they received the funds? How did different balances compare before and after the funds came in? Did lending increase or decrease? How about cash on hand, securities investments, acquisitions? By looking at the typical things that banks do with cash and taking before-and-after snapshots, Treasury could limit how much the banks could game their answers. Also, my friends suggested, Treasury could ask the banks for their internal estimates of what they intended to do with TARP funds, which could help guide Treasury's review. More practically, most senior executives are likely going to have a pretty good idea what the company is going to do with a huge capital infusion. It was clear to me that although no survey would be perfect or impossible to game, it was still a potentially powerful tool for transparency.

We informally floated the idea to Kashkari and Hoyt by asking them if they would consider requiring Citigroup to track how it would use the additional $20 billion in TARP funds that it was scheduled to receive by the end of the year. Though they didn't exactly say no, they said that they thought it unlikely that Citigroup would go along with it.

By December 23, 2008, our eighth day at Treasury, we had received a number of similarly ambiguous answers to our recommendations, and I realized that my approach of trying to be an informal adviser to Treasury and hoping that I could persuade it to improve the agreements wasn't going to work. We were giving it too much wiggle room. I told Kevin that we had to put on our big-boy pants and make formal recommendations, in writing.

"We do that, we're locked in," he said. "Written recommendations mean that they go in the book." That was his term for our initial report, due to Congress on February 6. "And if they go in the book, you'll be defending them at a hearing."

That was exactly what I wanted. It was time to step up.

We sat down that evening to put together our first set of written recommendations. First, we wanted to address compliance—Treasury's obligation to make sure that TARP recipients were living up to the terms of their agreements. Though there had not been many conditions in the

TARP agreements, there were some restrictions related to executive compensation, dividend payments, and stock buybacks.[6] We knew from our initial briefings that Treasury had neither the manpower nor much inclination to monitor the TARP recipients' compliance with the conditions in the agreements. So we thought it a prudent first step to push some of the burden onto the recipients themselves. We therefore recommended that Treasury require new TARP recipients to establish internal procedures to monitor their compliance with TARP conditions and regularly report to Treasury on how they were implementing them. Since lying to the government was a crime, we also recommended that Treasury require the recipients to provide signed certificates of compliance from their senior officers, thus putting them on notice that they could be subject to criminal prosecution if they lied on the forms.

Next, we included the recommendation that would dominate SIG-TARP's early months, that Treasury should require upcoming TARP recipients to use their "best efforts to account for their use of TARP funds, to set up internal controls to comply with such accounting, and to report to TARP on the results, with appropriate certification."

We also included what we thought was the ultimate ground ball, recommending that Treasury post all of its TARP-related agreements on its website.

We put all of this in an e-mail and sent it to Hoyt the night of December 23.

With the Christmas holiday, Treasury cleared out the next day. Hoyt sent a message confirming receipt, but we received no other response that day. Kevin also left, heading on a prescheduled, prepaid, weeklong cruise of the Caribbean with his family, leaving me alone in Washington.

It had been a rough couple of weeks, and I promised myself that on Sunday, December 28, at 4 p.m., I was going to go to a sports bar to watch the final game of the 2008 regular NFL season for the Miami Dolphins. I'm a rabid Dolphins fan, and the team had been just terrible in recent years, posting an abysmal 1–15 record in 2007. But they'd had a renaissance in 2008, and that Sunday they were playing their hated rival, the New York Jets, for the AFC East Divisional Championship. Karen found a bar near our apartment that was showing the game, and all week I was looking forward to three straight hours of focusing only on football, not bailouts.

Then, at 3:04 p.m., fifty-six minutes before kickoff, Hoyt responded to my December 23 e-mail. I cringed when I saw the subject line on my BlackBerry, "Provisions in citi and auto deals," and the very long e-mail that followed.

The news initially appeared to be mostly good. He noted that agreements were close to being finalized and that he had included provisions consistent with our recommendations concerning internal controls. He also said that he had forwarded our request regarding use of funds to Citigroup's lawyers but noted that they were pushing back, using the fungibility argument to complain that it would be difficult for them to distinguish TARP funds from non-TARP funds. But when I read the "final" language that Treasury intended to include in the agreements regarding SIGTARP oversight, my heart sunk. It wasn't the language we'd agreed upon. Over the next couple of hours, while watching one of the most satisfying Dolphins victories in recent memory (it was and remains the only year that the Dolphins made the play-offs since the 2001 season), I negotiated the terms via BlackBerry.

As I was sitting at a table in the back of the bar pecking away at my BlackBerry, I suddenly realized that this was the first time in two weeks that I had gotten out of that putrid office and into a normal, real-world setting. The magnitude of what I had been doing, negotiating oversight terms for contracts under which more than $45 billion of taxpayer money would be committed, also dawned on me for the first time.[7] I couldn't believe how much my life had changed over just a couple of weeks.

When the agreements were finalized, we had achieved a mixed bag of success with respect to our initial recommendations. Although we'd succeeded with the oversight language and internal control requirements and, for Citigroup, a use-of-funds requirement, Treasury balked at posting all of its agreements on the Internet (it agreed to post some) and said that it "would look into" another request that we had made regarding adopting similar conditions with respect to its already executed agreement with AIG.

I had hoped that Treasury's concessions in this set of agreements would set a precedent, but when we next recommended that *all* new CPP recipients be required to agree to the same terms, Kashkari and Hoyt responded that they wouldn't do it. "The banks won't participate," they repeated.

Kashkari and Hoyt's goal was to get as much TARP money out as quickly as possible to qualified banks, and they seemed completely unconcerned with what the banks then did with the money. As we pressed our points, their responses became more and more extreme, to the point where Kashkari suggested that requiring banks to report on their use of funds could actually destroy CPP and thus TARP and perhaps, as a result, the entire banking system. He accused us of being either politically motivated or just plain stupid. His favorite argument, always dripping with condescension, was that "all money was green." Because money was fungible, he argued, any reporting requirement would be useless; the banks could simply assign all of their lending to TARP funds and anything else to non-TARP funds. When I pointed out that he had signed the agreement with Citigroup that contained a similar provision, thereby putting his name on a document that contained a "stupid, useless, and political" provision, as he had described it, he just shrugged off my argument.

Kashkari steadfastly refused to acknowledge the set of methods for reporting on the use of the funds that the experts I'd consulted had recommended, including having them compare before-and-after snapshots of the different ways banks spend or invest capital (such as lending, investing, securities on hand, acquisitions, etc.) to see what had changed. We argued the point over and over because I truly believed—and later proved correct—that meaningful information on the banks' use of taxpayer funds was possible. I wouldn't let that point go. After one meeting, in which Kashkari exploded in front of a group of SIGTARP and GAO auditors, Kevin chided me for pressing Kashkari's buttons. "I know it's fun, but you really were an asshole."

I may have been, but I was remarkably frustrated; I just couldn't figure out why they wouldn't budge. At the time, I didn't know what our audit into the CPP decisions would later uncover, that Treasury didn't really view the initial CPP recipients as "healthy and viable" and that the stated core policy goal of increasing lending was apparently more of a public relations move than an executable policy. If I had known the truth, I would have better understood Treasury's stonewalling of our requests.

But I was still operating under the naive assumption that the program was being implemented as intended, to encourage lending by healthy and viable banks, and that Treasury would welcome close oversight of those deals because it would help validate the legitimacy of the TARP in the eyes of both Congress and the American people. I didn't yet realize that the type of transparency that we were pitching risked exposing CPP as the pure bailout that it was, given to teetering "too-big-to-fail" banks, some of which were on the brink of extinction. Of course they were fighting back.

We pinned hope of any improvement on the change of administrations. I was avidly counting down the days until Obama's inauguration on January 20, 2009. An Obama Treasury Department had to be better than this. It just had to be.

5

Drinking the Wall Street Kool-Aid

GETTING INTO THE building was brutal. Security everywhere in Washington was tight, but with our newly issued Treasury law enforcement credentials, Kevin and I were able to move pretty freely around town. Not here, though. Standing in front of a metal detector in an unmarked office fortress about ten blocks from Treasury, the security seemed tighter than at the White House for my job interview. It was the morning of January 7, 2009, and we were at the offices of the Presidential Transition Team.

It had been thirty days since I'd been confirmed and two and a half months since I'd been told that I was going to be the nominee, but I'd not yet had a single conversation with anyone from the incoming president's transition team. All of the banging of our heads against the wall at Treasury had been with a group of short-timers. They'd be vacating their opulent offices within a couple of weeks. This meeting was our first chance to get a sense of where the Obama administration planned to take TARP from here.

I was a little nervous. Although when asked by job applicants I always played it down, I didn't exactly feel I had job security. I had been told by the Bush people that there was an "understanding" that I would be kept around, but I had never gotten any assurances beyond that. And as I'd gained my own understanding of the dreadful way Washington works, I realized that I had done one of the stupidest things possible: I had trusted someone. I was already making some waves at Treasury with my clashes with Kashkari and Hoyt, and with all of the pomp of the inauguration, I could easily be shipped back to New York without anyone noticing. As the last Bush nominee to be confirmed by the Senate, I would soon be serving at the pleasure of a president who hadn't appointed me and whose advisers might not want me around.

Our meeting was with Lee Sachs, who was rumored to be in line to take either Kashkari's job as the head of TARP or the slot above that as undersecretary for domestic finance.

This was going to be Sachs's second spin through the revolving door between Wall Street and Treasury. He had left Bear Stearns in the 1990s to work under Treasury Secretary Robert Rubin toward the end of the Clinton administration and then returned to Wall Street as the vice chairman of Mariner Investment Group, where, among other things, he had overseen the management of the firm's involvement in certain mortgage-related assets.[1]

After brief introductions, I walked Sachs through a letter we had sent to Congress that morning, setting forth our modest accomplishments thus far. When I shared our view on requiring banks to report on how they used TARP funds, Sachs was dismissive, waving us off with the same fungibility argument so favored by Kashkari and the banks. Overall, I got the impression that he was only vaguely aware of who we were and what we were doing there.

His interest picked up a little, though, when we started discussing a new TARP program that had been announced in November and was about to be launched: the Term Asset-Backed Securities Loan Facility, or TALF. Through that program, the Federal Reserve Bank of New York would provide up to $200 billion in cheap loans to hedge funds, financial institutions, and other qualified investors.[2] With that money, borrowers would be required to buy bonds that had been generated from pools of car loans, student loans, credit card debt, or small-business loans.[3] The idea behind the program was that the market for those types of bonds had frozen due to the crisis, and the Fed hoped TALF would bring it back to life. The TALF-targeted bonds had previously funded a good chunk of consumer lending in the country as part of the so-called shadow banking system, and with the banks still not lending, kick-starting this market would hopefully get some money to consumers.

But I saw a big red flag. The TALF bonds were being created through the financial innovation known as "securitization," the same method used by Wall Street to create the toxic mortgage-related bonds that were still clogging the big banks' balance sheets. Fortunately, as chief of the mortgage fraud group at the Office, I had received a crash course in how the creation of those toxic bonds had spun wildly out of control before the financial crisis struck. With that background, I was better able to understand how the implosion of those bonds had nearly wiped out our entire financial system, and I could recognize the potential flaws in the government's proposed approach to reviving some of the markets left devastated by them.

DECADES AGO, banks funded mortgage loans with cash received from their depositors. Their profits came from collecting the difference between the low interest they paid to depositors and the higher interest they charged home owners for their loans. The banks had a strong incentive to make sure their mortgage loans were sound, because if they screwed up and made too many bad loans they could suffer substantial losses from foreclosures and might even face insolvency.

The government also had an interest in ensuring that the banks made prudent lending decisions because of its guarantee, through the Federal Deposit Insurance Corporation (FDIC), of a large portion of the banks' deposits. As a result, if a bank failed because of imprudent lending decisions and didn't have enough to pay back its depositors, the FDIC would be on the hook to cover its insured depositors. That gave bank regulators a strong incentive to pay careful attention to what the banks were doing.

Over time, however, this reliable system had become radically altered, and mortgages gradually became more like a commodity, to be bought and sold like a stock or a bond. Instead of holding on to the loans they originated, banks and other lenders started to sell them off to third parties, earning instant profits from the buyer's up-front cash payments that they could use to originate more loans.

In the beginning, this practice presented little risk to the financial system because, for the most part, the purchasers of the loans were the two massive government-sponsored entities (or "GSEs"), Fannie Mae and Freddie Mac. The system began to change, however, when the GSEs began to "securitize" the mortgages, which essentially meant selling off the rights to receive mortgage payments to investors. The GSEs would gather together thousands of loans to form bonds, called mortgage-backed securities, and then collect the payments made by the borrowers on those loans into a single pool of cash. Bonds would then be created, which would give the purchasers of the bonds the right to receive a steady stream of payments from the pool of cash, including interest, over the life of the bonds. Because the GSEs guaranteed the payments promised by the bonds, they, not the investors, bore the risk if some borrowers failed to make their mortgage payments and the pool fell short of cash. Though the GSEs would later participate in the mortgage mania of the 2000s, including purchasing all sorts of loans as investments to hold in their own portfolios, prior to that they were largely restrained by Congress and their regulator in the types of mortgages they could purchase and, recognizing the risk that they were taking on by issuing the guarantees, they adhered to certain minimum underwriting criteria and legally defined loan size limits.

For many years, the system worked relatively well and allowed for a healthy expansion of the mortgage market because the bonds were backed by mostly high-quality mortgage loans that had low rates of default. As a result, there was generally plenty of cash coming in from the mortgage borrowers to make the regular bond payments.

Enter Wall Street. The banks realized that they could create the same kind of mortgage-backed securities as the GSEs, only without having to guarantee the payments, by focusing on the types of loans that fell short of the GSEs' requirements. Those were called "subprime" loans because banks made them to borrowers with lower credit ratings, who lacked certain documentation or who had less money for a down payment. Wall Street banks began purchasing the subprime mortgages and putting them into pools that backed what were called "subprime bonds," separate and apart from the GSEs. Because the risk of default was higher for subprime loans, the banks charged a higher interest rate to the borrowers and then offered a higher rate of return to those purchasing the bonds. However, because those new subprime bonds—unlike those offered by Fannie and Freddie—were not guaranteed, the banks had to devise a way to convince investors to purchase them.

First, the banks would pay the investors higher interest rates depending on the level of risk an investor was willing to bear. They did so by issuing a number of different bonds, called tranches, off of a single pool of mortgages with each offering a different interest rate corresponding to the riskiness of the bond: the higher the risk of default, the higher the interest payment offered to the investor. The cash gathered in the pool would then be paid to the safer highest-ranked tranches first and to the riskiest lowest-ranked tranche last.

This way of apportioning the cash has been likened to a bartender pouring a pitcher of beer into a number of mugs lined up on a bar. The beer in the pitcher is the cash generated from the mortgage payments the bank receives each month from the borrowers whose loans were placed in the pool, and the mugs represent the different tranches of bonds (we'll use five here, but in reality the mortgage-backed securities had far more tranches). The bartender fills the highest-ranked mug first, then the second highest, and so on down the line until either all five mugs are full or the pitcher runs out of beer, which would happen only if a number of borrowers in the pool stopped making their monthly mortgage payments. If there are enough defaults, the fifth, fourth, third, or even second mug might go dry, and if a housing catastrophe strikes, even the first mug might not get filled.

The second way in which they enticed investors to purchase the bonds was by convincing them that higher-ranked tranches of bonds posed almost no risk. First, they built the bonds in accordance with complex mathematical models that indicated that there was a very small chance that large chunks of the loans going into any single pool would default at the same time. Their mathematicians, hired from top universities, ran analyses that assured them that if they mixed in mortgages from different parts of the country with different characteristics, there would almost certainly always be enough cash to pay out the higher-ranking bonds. No housing crisis since the Great Depression had been national in scope, so as long as they came up with the right mix of loans, the bond payments would be safe.

The second and perhaps most important step in marketing the bonds as safe investments was convincing the credit-rating agencies to bestow high ratings on the bonds. With five thousand subprime mortgages potentially stuffed into a single bond and no loan-level detail offered to investors, it was impossible for investors to research and analyze all of the underlying loans to make sure that their investments were safe. Credit-rating agencies helped solve that problem.

In theory, the agencies were supposed to do their own analysis of the underlying loans and give an unbiased rating, which was essentially the agencies' opinion on the likelihood that a bond would pay off. But the agencies were working under an enormous conflict of interest that highly incentivized them to provide the Wall Street banks with their stamp of approval on the subprime bonds, and that conflict would eventually help fuel the financial crisis.

Originally the rating agencies earned money primarily from subscription fees paid by investors, such as big investment funds, to get access to their credit ratings for bonds and other investments. More accurate ratings theoretically led to better outcomes for investors, which therefore led to more paying subscribers, which meant more profits. But by the 1970s, that began to change,[4] and instead of investors paying for the ratings, the Wall Street banks underwriting and issuing the bonds began hiring the rating agencies and paying them fees in exchange for rating the products they were selling.

The rating agencies charged more for complex bonds, such as subprime mortgage-backed securities. As a result, because they stood to make a good deal of money from issuing the ratings, and because the small handful of agencies bitterly competed with one another for the business, they had a strong incentive to please the banks. If they were too tough, the banks would just walk away and shop for a more compliant agency. That ultimately resulted in lax analyses of the bonds and inflated ratings.

The highest rating offered for a mortgage-backed bond was AAA, and the Wall Street banks and their complex models were able to convince the ready, willing, and able credit-rating agencies to assign that top rating to up to 80 percent of the bonds issued off a particular pool of subprime mortgages, or the first four out of the five mugs on the bar.

The mortgage-backed securities were a huge boon for the banks. At every stage of their creation and sale, the Wall Street institutions offering them raked in large fees, and every firm that participated in the transactions (from loan origination through the final sale of the bonds) enjoyed huge profits. With high credit ratings in hand, the AAA subprime bonds became wildly attractive to investors and other financial institutions because they paid a higher interest rate than other AAA-rated bonds, such as those issued by the U.S. government, and because regulators began giving such highly rated bonds favorable treatment.[5]

Before long, the demand for the bonds became so great that banks were having a hard time scrounging enough mortgages together to buy to make more of them. So mortgage lenders got inventive. They started offering mortgages that required remarkably low payments at first, but which would later reset to a much higher rate that the borrower might no longer be able to afford. They then lowered lending standards even further. In what were widely described as "liar loans," a borrower no longer had to prove that he was making a certain salary or even that he had a job; now he could get a mortgage by just writing in his income on the forms. As I saw far too often when I was investigating mortgage fraud cases, even when a borrower truthfully wrote down an income that was too low to qualify for a mortgage, it wasn't necessarily a problem. The mortgage broker or loan originator, who earned fees based on the number of loans he could generate, would often just tell the borrower to write in a higher number, or the broker himself would make the false entry, sometimes without even telling the borrower.

For their part, the banks buying the mortgages weren't terribly concerned about the obvious problems with the mortgages being thrown into those pools. The profits from the securitization mill were too high, and the losses would not be borne by them but by the investors buying the bonds. Later investigations would demonstrate that several of the largest banks had been on full notice that the mortgages they were packaging were littered with fraud but continued to sell and package them.[6]

This further decline in underwriting standards led to what were, in essence, sub-subprime bonds, but those too were given AAA ratings by the conflicted rating agencies based on their mathematical models and similar lack of concern about the quality of the loans that were being pooled.

So voracious had the market for highly rated mortgage-backed securities become that even as Wall Street and the mortgage lenders radically expanded the supply of mortgages by destroying lending standards and ignoring fraud, there still weren't enough loans to supply the unquenchable demand. The banks were also looking to move some of the lower-rated, non-AAA-rated tranches of the bonds (the fifth mug on the bar), which they sometimes found themselves stuck holding, particularly as investor appetites began to wane for the lower-rated tranches.

Wall Street managed to kill both birds with a single stone: the banks created brand-new bonds by purchasing the lower-ranked tranches, to which they gave the arcane name Collateralized Debt Obligations, or CDOs. They were created by the same basic mechanism used to create the first generation of mortgage-backed securities. Instead of directly filling the pitcher of beer with payments from mortgage borrowers, however, the CDOs took whatever beer happened to make it into a whole bunch of the fifth mugs of beer—the lower-rated tranches of bonds that were at a higher risk of suffering losses—from a number of different mortgage-backed security pitchers and poured that recycled beer into a new pitcher. Thus was created the CDO, with the pitcher filled with the regular cash payments made by dozens of lower-rated bonds from the already issued mortgage-backed securities.

The pitcher was then poured into a new set of five mugs lined up on the bar, which formed the new tranches of the CDO. The banks then once again sold the rights to each of the tranches, making a new money machine out of what was essentially recycled fifth-mug beer. And incredibly, the banks and their mathematicians were once again able to convince the rating agencies to bless a large portion of these new tranches with the coveted AAA rating. Voilà. Through "financial innovation," the banks were able to meet the fervent demand for AAA-rated bonds while also ridding their balance sheets of some unwanted assets.

Those elaborate machinations allowed the mortgage-related securities business to explode into a multitrillion-dollar industry. And because many of those loans were largely made by nonbank lenders and affiliates that funded themselves through borrowed money, not deposits, the process often didn't put the FDIC's deposit insurance program on the hook.

As a result, the government looked the other way, leaving this "shadow banking" business almost entirely unregulated.

The new wave of subprime and sub-subprime borrowers, coupled with low interest rates, created a huge demand for houses, which in turn caused huge increases in prices. How big were the increases? Between 1998 and 2006, housing prices across the country reportedly increased by 67 percent.[7] Even more tellingly, the total amount of mortgage debt in the United States almost doubled in just six years, from \$5.3 trillion in 2001 to \$10.5 trillion in 2007.[8]

Starting in 2007, when the out-of-control housing bubble began to burst nationwide, the magic of the banks and rating agencies' mathematical models proved a myth. With large numbers of borrowers defaulting on their mortgages across the country, many of the supposedly "safe" mortgage pools began to come up short of cash, and the values of the AAA mortgage-related bonds began to collapse.

The housing crisis created the ensuing near meltdown of the whole financial system in part because many of the banks had started to eat their own cooking, both holding and purchasing vast quantities of the bonds, which they funded almost entirely with borrowed money rather than with their own capital.

Through TALF, Treasury and the Federal Reserve were proposing to put a huge new stake of taxpayer money into the purchase of bonds created by the very same securitization process, albeit backed not by mortgage loans but by a range of types of consumer loans. That was an obvious cause for concern, but even more troubling were the rumors we started to hear that Treasury and the Fed were already considering expanding TALF to include the purchase of the now-toxic fraud-laced mortgage-backed bonds still clogging the banks' balance sheets. That was a recipe for potential disaster.

THE PLAN FOR TALF was to use taxpayer funds to lure investors back into the consumer loan–backed bond market by increasing their potential profits and limiting their losses. Profits would come from the New York Fed lending money to investors at cheap interest rates that were well below what the bonds themselves promised to pay out. For example, under the terms of one TALF-eligible bond issued by Ford's finance company, an investor could take out a TALF loan for $100 million that required him to pay the New York Fed 3.0445 percent interest (about $3 million) for a bond that paid out 6.07 percent (about $6 million),[9] allowing the investor to pocket the difference of 3 percent (about $3 million) each year. That's the investor's equivalent of shooting fish in a barrel.

Although a borrower would have to put up some of his or her own money to buy the bonds, the government planned to allow loans of up to 95 percent of the purchase price. And in order to protect investors from significant losses, the loans to the purchasers would be "nonrecourse." That meant that if the bond crashed in value, the purchaser could simply stop making payments on his TALF loan without any additional liability as long as he surrendered the bond. Though borrowers' losses would be capped at whatever portion of a bond's purchase price they had to put up (which was as little as 5 percent), the taxpayer would be on the hook for the entire unpaid portion of the loan. Treasury had agreed that TARP would cover the first $20 billion in losses from the program, and it was my job to protect that $20 billion.

At our meeting, I told Sachs of my concern that Treasury and the Fed had put so much emphasis on making TALF loans attractive that they had all but ignored taxpayer-protecting antifraud provisions. I had, of course, already raised similar concerns with Kashkari, Hoyt, and others with respect to TALF, CPP, and the other nascent TARP programs. Their response was always the same: I just didn't understand that the biggest players in these programs—the big banks and the investment firms—would never risk their reputations by trying to rip off the government. The reputational damage they'd suffer would be far greater than any potential profit, they argued, so it just wouldn't happen. I always responded by noting that the events of the past two years had proven that the banks seemed willing to put profit over just about everything, particularly their reputations.

I was to hear this argument about "reputational risk" so many times that finally, in the spring of 2009, I blurted out to one of the TARP officers, "Please, don't waste any more of our time with that argument. I understand that you guys think that it's relevant, but for me, it means absolutely nothing. I hear the words 'reputational risk,' and my brain turns off."

A particular concern I had about TALF was that it created the possibility of an extremely difficult-to-detect fraud: collusion between the bond's buyer and seller. To use a very simplified example, if the seller had a bond that was worth only $50, he could sell it for $100 to a colluding buyer who had taken out a $95 TALF loan. The corrupt seller would instantly recognize a $50 profit. Normally, the buyer would be on the hook for the $50 difference in value. But with the TALF loan, he stood to lose only the $5 he'd had to put up as his "skin in the game." He could just walk away from the loan and more than make up his $5 loss by collecting from the seller a kickback of, say, half the seller's profits. In that scenario, everyone would win—except for TARP, which would be left holding a bond truly worth $50 but effectively bought for $95.

Unfortunately, Sachs also showed no particular interest in my concern about fraud in TALF, so I moved on to our second worry, the rumor that the Fed might expand TALF to include toxic mortgage-related securities. When I brought that up, Sachs finally became fully engaged.

"We see TALF being expanded to absorb both new and legacy RMBS," he said, using the Washington/Wall Street jargon for residential mortgage-backed securities. "Legacy" meant that they were bonds issued before the housing bubble had burst; they were the subprime and sub-subprime bonds stuffed with fraud-riddled loans that had been given to anyone, in Tom Friedman's words, whose breath "could fog a knife."

This is bad, I thought as I shot Kevin a look. TALF was supposed to stimulate consumer lending so people could go buy cars and attend college, not be yet another bailout of the banks. The financial crisis had been triggered in large part by investors and financial institutions making ruinous bets on these same RMBS *with their own money.* Now Sachs thought it was a good idea to make a new set of bets on the exact same toxic bonds, only now with hundreds of billions of taxpayer dollars. In other words, he was betting that investors' decision making would somehow *improve* when it was the taxpayer, instead of the investor itself, who funded the bulk of the transactions and potentially bore up to 95 percent of the losses. It made no sense.

"Why do this through TALF?" I asked.

Sachs explained that he thought it was the best way to bring the real estate–related bond markets back to life, which, of course, would finally allow the banks to get the bonds off their books. "We plan to go big with TALF on RMBS," Sachs said.

He wasn't kidding. I later found out that "big" meant up to one trillion dollars.

There was no question that getting the toxic assets off the banks' books—TARP's original mandate—was pressing. The market didn't know what evil might still be lurking on the banks' balance sheets, and that uncertainty was a major factor leading to the government's guarantee of a portion of $300 billion of Citigroup's toxic assets as part of its most recent bailout, as well as a similar promise that Treasury would announce the following week regarding $100 billion in Bank of America's assets. With a lack of transparency, the market was concerned that other large banks holding toxic assets might still fail, and I completely understood Sachs's drive to find a solution.

But the risks of expanding TALF were considerable. By one measure, the prices for the bonds had already fallen more than 40 percent in the previous year.[10] "We're going to have so much exposure," I said. "The values of these bonds have already dropped like rocks, and given that so much of the money that will be used by investors to purchase these bonds will be borrowed from the government, if the prices drop even a small amount more, we're going to end up with massive taxpayer losses."

"This type of leverage is typical," Sachs responded, "as is the nonrecourse nature of the loans; we see it all the time in this market. There's no difference in how this will work and how it worked in the private market," he observed.

That, of course, was why I was so worried.

Sachs ended the meeting by saying "Well, nothing has been decided, and we do look forward to working with you."

As we walked out, I turned to Kevin and saw that he was as worried as I was. We had pinned so much hope on the changing of the guard with Obama's inauguration. We'd expected that the new team we'd work with would care about holding the banks accountable for the billions of dollars they were receiving and would prioritize fraud prevention. But we'd just gotten a glimpse of the new TARP team, and it looked and sounded an awful lot like the old one.

Sachs, however, ultimately didn't get either of the Senate-confirmed Treasury positions that had been the subject of rumors. The speculation in the press was that his recent history on Wall Street, where he had reportedly "sat atop [his] firm's C.D.O. management committee,"[11] may have made him unconfirmable. Prior to joining the transition team, Sachs had apparently made millions by trafficking in mortgage-related CDOs.[12] In addition to his other responsibilities, *The New York Times* later reported that Sachs had overseen a subsidiary, Tricadia, which had assembled and sold CDOs to investors in the run-up to the crisis. The *Times* reported that several of those CDOs had experienced heavy losses as the real estate market turned. But though Tricadia's clients had suffered significant losses, according to the *Times*,[13] the firm had profited handsomely by making bets against the housing market in one of its hedge funds.[14] It was even reported that one of Tricadia's CDOs, which had lost 75 percent of its value, had been purchased by the New York Fed in November 2008 as part of the AIG bailout.[15] In other words, Sachs had worked at a firm that had successfully exploited the financial crisis and that could potentially profit off of TALF (it later reportedly obtained more than $200 million in TALF loans).[16]

Tricadia was not alone in reportedly betting against the real estate market at the same time that it was convincing potential investors to bet in the opposite direction. As investigations by Congress and the Securities and Exchange Commission (SEC) later detailed, when signs that the real estate bubble might pop began emerging, several banks took this two-sided approach, including Goldman Sachs and Deutsche Bank.[17] The SEC also accused Citigroup of making a $500 million bet against a bond that it had created, marketed, and sold,[18] while others such as Goldman Sachs[19] and JPMorgan Chase[20] settled cases in which the SEC accused them of failing to disclose that bonds they had marketed had essentially been built to fail by investors who were betting against them.

Ultimately, Sachs settled in as one of Geithner's "senior advisers" and was later credited with being one of the architects of Geithner's financial crisis response policies.[21]

*   *   *

THE DAY AFTER our meeting with Sachs, Kevin and I had a conference call with officials from the New York Fed. We wanted to hear from them what protections they were setting up to prevent fraud in TALF. During a perfunctory round of introductions the Fed official leading the call identified himself as William Dudley. At the time, we had no idea who Dudley was; he was just yet another disembodied "voice of the Fed" on the other end of the line giving us yet another briefing. I later learned that he was the acting president of the New York Fed and yet another alum of Goldman Sachs, where he had been chief economist. Dudley was officially made president of the New York Fed once the Senate confirmed Timothy Geithner as Treasury secretary.

We asked "Bill" what measures were in place to protect taxpayers against potential TALF fraud.

He explained that first, as we already knew, the borrower would have to put up a "haircut," say 5 percent of the purchase price, so he would have "skin in the game." Dudley explained that investors would therefore have a powerful incentive to do due diligence on the bonds before purchasing them. That diligence, Dudley believed, would help ensure that the loans standing behind the bonds were properly underwritten. I told Dudley that I didn't think that would provide much protection, given how woefully inadequate investor due diligence had proven leading up to the crisis, and that had been without the government being on the hook for up to 95 percent of the purchase price.

Dudley brushed off my concerns, saying that the Fed had confidence in the economic models it had run on TALF, which projected minimal losses.

That set off another alarm. The economic models used by the banks and the rating agencies to evaluate loan-backed bonds had failed miserably in the lead-up to the crisis because they had failed to incorporate certain scenarios that had come to pass, such as house prices declining across the country simultaneously. Betting taxpayer money on similar models seemed unacceptably risky.

I asked Dudley if the models accounted for the likely impact of the government's involvement in TALF, such as the nonrecourse loans that would limit how much an investor could lose. I was also concerned that investors might perceive that a bond deemed "eligible" by the Fed bore a government stamp of approval and would therefore view it as a safe investment. Both of those factors, I thought, could reduce the investors' incentive to conduct the vigorous due diligence upon which Dudley was apparently relying.

"No. They don't," Dudley responded dismissively.

I felt a pit form in my stomach.

I then asked Dudley if the models contemplated any type of expansion of TALF, as Sachs had suggested, to include "legacy" mortgage-backed securities. I was somewhat relieved when Dudley responded by saying that the program was neither modeled for nor intended to include such assets. I then raised the question of compliance—the important procedures that Treasury and the Fed needed to establish to make sure that the investors and issuers followed the program's rules. The most basic front against fraud in any program was a robust compliance regime that let the participants know that the government would be closely monitoring their every move.

"We're not planning on doing anything with compliance other than have them submit certificates. If we had to oversee compliance, we wouldn't participate in TALF," Dudley said.

"I'm sorry, what does that mean?" I asked.

"We'd walk away from the program. We don't have the resources to conduct compliance," Dudley responded.

The pit in my stomach sank lower.

I then asked him what other protections were in place, other than the investors' "skin in the game."

Dudley told me that the only other protection was that the Fed was going to require that all eligible bonds earn a AAA rating by not one but *two* credit-rating agencies. That would, he confidently asserted, further assure that the loans backing the bonds were properly underwritten.

I gulped. "What else?"

"Just those two things," Dudley replied.

After he said that, I asked for a moment and pushed "Mute." I really thought that I might have not heard him correctly and had had an aural hallucination. I looked at Kevin and asked, "Did he really just say that they were going to bet $200 billion of taxpayer money on the credit-rating agencies?"

"He did," Kevin replied.

"That's fucking crazy, right?" I asked.

"You are correct. That is fucking crazy."

I unmuted the phone. "Bill," I said, "Let me get this straight. We're going to put $200 billion of taxpayer money on the line to buy asset-backed securities that are similar to those that got us into this whole mess in the first place, and we're going to rely only on the credit-rating agencies and investor due diligence, nothing else?" I asked.

Dudley replied, "Right."

In what wasn't my most professional moment, I exploded. "Really? *Really?*" My voice rose. "Isn't that *exactly* the same formula that caused this financial crisis? *Exactly?* What makes you possibly think that now, after all of this, the rating agencies are suddenly going to get it right?"

Dudley paused, understandably annoyed at my tone. "Well, the ratings agencies performed pretty well in these asset classes," he continued, "and we're confident they won't risk being embarrassed again."

It was my turn to pause. "You don't think that the credit-rating agencies will *embarrass themselves again*?" I challenged.

"Correct," Dudley confirmed.

I was flabbergasted. These guys were going to risk hundreds of billions of dollars of taxpayer money on the integrity of the exact same rating agencies that had sold their souls for a few basis points of profit. The same rating agencies that would downgrade 90 percent of the AAA ratings given to subprime residential mortgage-backed securities in 2006 and 2007 to junk status.[22]

Treasury and the Fed weren't just trying to restart a securitization market that had ground to a halt, they were proposing to replicate the very same flaws that had just crippled the global financial system: lax regulatory oversight, overreliance on conflicted credit-rating agencies, incomplete risk models, and an inherent trust in investors' good decision making. But to that flammable mix they were going to add the accelerant of a government-guaranteed floor on potential losses. In other words, Treasury and the Federal Reserve looked at those factors and didn't see them as flaws that should be eradicated from the system but as a great way to sell some bonds.

In retrospect, I shouldn't have expected otherwise. Almost all of the people we were dealing with, after all, came from the same Wall Street banks. Paulson, Dudley, and Kashkari were Goldman Sachs alumni, as was the man who would later become TARP's chief investment officer, David Miller. The current chief investment officer, James Lambright, came from Credit Suisse First Boston (via the U.S. Export-Import Bank). Even in the face of the mounting devastation of the crisis, they were apparently unable—or unwilling—to question the inherent goodness of their former employers and the other Wall Street institutions. They were sure they would never "risk their reputations" or "embarrass themselves" again.

After we hung up, I turned to Kevin and said, "These guys haven't just drank the Wall Street Kool Aid, they ripped open the packets, added the water, stirred it up, and are now serving it to us on a $700 billion taxpayer-funded service platter."

"I'll get started on some recommendations," Kevin replied.

THE NEXT MONDAY, dropping Karen off at Union Station for her 7 a.m. train to New York wasn't nearly as painful as it usually was; I was going to see her late the following night at Newark airport before flying to Costa Rica for our wedding. We had set the date for January 17, 2009, and I had agreed on the night that Mike first told me about the SIGTARP job that it was nonnegotiable. But as it turned out, the timing couldn't have been worse.

The deadline for our initial report to Congress was looming over us, and we'd actually lost a day after a staffer for the Senate Banking Committee had "requested" that we move the release up so that it could be the topic of a Senate hearing on February 5, 2009. The hearing was to star me; the acting head of the Government Accountability Office, Gene Dodaro; and Elizabeth Warren, the soon-to-be-famous chair of the Congressional Oversight Panel. Warren had already achieved some notoriety in the bailout world by criticizing Treasury's failure to directly answer several of the panel's questions that had been posed in her first report, citing its "shifting justifications" for the bailout.[23]

The report was occupying every free minute of our time. Although congressional staffers and other IGs told me repeatedly that congressional expectations were low, I viewed it as our coming-out party. The pressure had intensified when, a week earlier, Senate Majority Leader Harry Reid had declared that he wouldn't even consider a request from either Bush or Obama to release the second half of the $700 billion in TARP funds until he had a chance to review "that inspector general report."[24] (He eventually relented).

I told our team that we were going to heed the warning of the old Head & Shoulders shampoo commercial that "you never get a second chance to make a first impression" by putting out a strong report that was both comprehensive and comprehensible, written in plain English so that the average taxpayer could understand what was happening with his or her money. The book was going to be our vehicle to broadcast to Congress where we thought Treasury was falling short and our recommendations on how its mistakes could be fixed. I wanted to make a powerful statement.

I had spent hours working with Kevin on how to cover our recommendation to Treasury that it require the banks to report on how they were using TARP funds and Treasury's refusal to adopt it, and now, as Karen's head rested on my lap as she slept on the flight to Costa Rica, I couldn't stop thinking about it. Finally, it occurred to me that I wasn't powerless. If Kashkari and Sachs were going to insist that banks couldn't report on how they spent TARP funds, I would prove them wrong. Instead of whining about Treasury's recalcitrance, I'd just do it myself. We would audit the banks, I decided, every one of them, by sending out subpoenas demanding that they report on how they were using the TARP money. While trying not to disturb Karen, I excitedly tapped out an outline of how the audit would work on my BlackBerry and sent it to Kevin as soon as we landed.

Poor Karen. When she woke up, I regaled her about my epiphany, and though, as always, she was encouraging, I could sense an undercurrent of despair as she realized I was going to spend the entire trip fixating on the exciting topic of banks' abilities to report on their use of TARP-supplied capital.

In my rush of enthusiasm and showing my characteristic lack of patience, I told Kevin to start getting the subpoenas out the next day. He wisely counseled that we should wait until I was back in Washington. The audit would make Treasury apoplectic, and members of Congress would inevitably have questions.

Kevin cautioned, "What happens after this goes out and we start getting calls from Congress asking why we're doing these audits and demanding to speak to you, and I have to say, 'Sorry, he can't talk to you. Sure he's only been on the job for a month, but he's on vacation right now in Costa Rica?' Do you want to be taking that call by the pool?"

He told me to put the audits out of my head for the rest of the long weekend and enjoy myself because, as he put it, "it's going to be a 24-hour a day shit-show when you return."

I of course obsessed anyway about the audit a good part of the weekend, worried that the Treasury team might try to thwart us. Even when Karen tried to walk me through the drill for the ceremony, I couldn't stop.

As she explained, "So we'll come down this elevator and then walk down these stairs to this area, where we'll have the ceremony," I responded, annoyingly, "Treasury is going to fight this. Kevin's right, they're going to flip. It's going to shine a light in an area they want to keep dark."

"And this is where the band will set up," Karen said, ignoring me and pointing out where the party would occur.

"Treasury could just go out and tell the banks to respond with the 'all money is green' argument, and the banks will just say that they can't respond to the request. We're going to have to get real specific in the subpoena," I blurted out, more to myself than her.

"This is where the buffet will be; we can taste some of the food tonight at dinner if you'd like," Karen placidly continued.

She very smartly refused to engage with my obsession, and she finally got some degree of peace after I walked into the pool with my BlackBerry still clipped to my bathing suit, frying it. I still haunted the hotel's computer room but was generally untethered for the rest of the trip.

In retrospect, the timing of the wedding was probably a blessing. The weekend was amazing, and it was exactly what I needed before launching into high gear with the change of administrations.

6

The Worst Thing That Happens,
We Go Back Home

T HE ENERGY ON the packed train was palpable. Even though it was past midnight and freezing outside, people were streaming into the city to camp out for the inauguration ceremony. I was also excited. Even after my meeting with Sachs and a recent announcement that Kashkari would be staying on for a couple of a months, I was confident that an Obama-led Treasury Department would be more receptive to our ideas and more reluctant to toe the Wall Street line.

The Treasury Building was closed for the parade on inauguration day, so I worked on the letter to go out to the banks from my apartment with the television on, watching Chief Justice John Roberts administer the oath of office to President Barack Obama. Kevin convinced me that it would be far more efficient to send letters instead of subpoenas to the banks and use our friends in Congress rather than court proceedings to compel wayward banks to respond. Our arguments for auditing the banks' use of TARP funds had been reinforced that preceding Sunday. A front-page *New York Times* article reported statements made by executives at a handful of banks about what they were doing with TARP money in which several scoffed at the idea that they would use it to increase lending. John Hope III, the chairman of Whitney National Bank in New Orleans, which had received $300 million in TARP funds, was quoted as saying "Make more loans? We're not going to change our business model or our credit policies to accommodate the needs of the public sector."[1] Other executives were cited as viewing the TARP "as a no-strings-attached windfall that could be used to pay down debt, acquire other businesses or invest for the future."[2] The *Times* also cited seven banks that had already used the funds to acquire other institutions and quoted Christopher Carey, the chief financial officer of City National (the subject of Thorson's audit) as saying that the bank planned to retain the TARP money to build a "fortressed balance sheet" in case the economy got worse.[3]

For us, the article proved two points. First, contrary to Treasury's insistence that reporting on use of funds was impossible or useless, if banks could discuss how they were using the money with the *Times,* they would certainly be able to respond to our survey. The need for such reporting also seemed all the more acute; if the *Times'* anecdotes were representative of what other banks were doing with the money, there was a real danger that Treasury's stated policy goal of increasing lending would be unfulfilled.

On top of this, *Bloomberg* had reported the day before the inauguration that Treasury had sent out its own survey seeking lending data from the twenty largest TARP recipients, which it would then publish on its website.[4] Though I appreciated the gesture toward increased transparency, this survey came nowhere close to meeting our concerns. As the *Times* article indicated, lending was only one potential use of TARP funds, and without reviewing *all* of the potential uses by all 364 banks, Treasury would be getting only part of the story.

We met with Kashkari the day after the inauguration to tell him about the audit, and beforehand I asked Kevin if he thought that maybe we had misjudged him. If Treasury had decided to probe into how much lending the banks were doing, it might be appreciative that we were going out and painting a more complete picture for them.

Kevin told me he thought the Costa Rican sun must have melted my brain.

He was right. When we told Kashkari about the letters, his response was even worse than Kevin had expected.

"You can't do this, you can't," he warned.

When I asked him why not, he rolled his eyes and snapped back, "Because it will destroy the program."

"How will it do that?" I asked.

"Banks will run away from it. Your audit will scare them off," he responded.

I explained to him that it shouldn't be a shock to the banks that a survey like this was coming. After all, I said, Treasury had already sent its own survey, and a bill that had passed the House that day required even more robust reporting than what we would call for in the audit.[5] In addition, the banking regulators, to varying degrees, had also indicated that they would launch some type of initiative to measure uses of TARP funds.

"It's different," he argued. "The banks view you as the TARP special prosecutor. They're terrified of you. They view their regulators differently. They know them. They trust the regulator who is on site all week with them. You are a lot different than the guy who has a beer with them every Friday night."

Unbelievable, I thought. He actually seemed to be arguing that the banks' comfort with their thoroughly captured regulators was a good thing.

Kashkari also, of course, repeated the fungibility argument, saying our survey would be worthless because the banks would easily game it. I told him that we had come up with a number of good ways to require them to account for the uses, but he was adamant about the audit's uselessness and the harm it would cause.

I argued that our audit might also complement some of the new conditions that Lawrence Summers, the new director of the President's National Economic Council, had indicated that Treasury would impose on TARP recipients. In a letter to Congress the week before arguing for the release of the second $350 billion in TARP money, Summers had said that it would require healthy TARP banks to "increase lending above baseline levels" and would "preclude use of government funds to purchase healthy firms rather than to boost lending."[6] Our audit, I said, could help ensure compliance with those conditions.

Kashkari dismissed the point, saying "Those new conditions are purely political. And I strongly suspect, even if they're adopted, the new administration may not want you looking too closely at them." I was somewhat surprised that Kashkari was essentially accusing his incoming bosses of making false promises to Congress just to get their hands on the second cache of TARP funds. But he was ultimately correct; those "commitments" never saw the light of day.

Our audit chief told us that it would take another week for him to get the letters out to the banks, so Kevin and I decided to send an announcement to Congress ahead of time detailing the audit. When we sent Kashkari the draft of the statement later that day, within an hour he called us up to his office and asked us to hold off on sending it out for a few weeks in order to give the likely incoming Treasury secretary, Timothy Geithner, a chance to weigh in. I quickly called Treasury's new chief of staff, Mark Patterson, to see if he too wanted us to hold off, but he was noncommittal, saying that if we wanted Geithner's input we should wait, but otherwise it was up to us.

Kevin and I wrestled with what to do. He was worried about the political risk for SIGTARP. If banks in fact started fleeing TARP, the Obama administration might be inclined to blame us, as Kashkari had suggested. Though we were confident that we wouldn't in fact scare off banks, it certainly was possible that they might start withdrawing from the program for other reasons. Those included the conditions Summers had outlined and the strict restrictions in the bill that had passed the House earlier that day, including one that struck fear into the heart of every banker: eliminating executives' bonuses. Kevin thought the safer course was to stick to our original recommendation, wait it out, and then announce the audit in a few months, after the impact of the House legislation and Summers' letter had blown over.

Ultimately, though, doing what was politically shrewd wasn't our mandate. I thought of my old boss at the Office, Rich Sullivan, whose mantra was always to do the right thing, and I asked Kevin, "Did we uproot our lives and come all the way down to Washington to do the 'safe thing'? Or the 'right thing'?"

"Let's try the right thing," Kevin said with a smile. "Worst thing that happens? They fire us, and we get to go back to New York. At least my wife will be happy to have me home."

We decided that we would always operate in the same nonpolitical way we had as prosecutors in the Office: we'd just focus on the job.

* * *

As we waited for the new Treasury team to arrive, Congress released the second half of the TARP funds. With vast new sums of money available to flood out the door, we were hoping that the change in administration would also bring a greater sensitivity to the growing potential for TARP to be plundered by Wall Street criminals. Not surprisingly, we were already beginning to see some alarming cases of TARP-related fraud.

Soon after I hired Chris Sharpley, he started staffing investigations with experienced federal agents recruited from the law enforcement agencies throughout the federal government that had experience in investigating sophisticated white-collar criminal cases. We needed them, too; we were almost immediately running cases.

Just a month into our tenure, in January 2009, the SEC called asking for help on what would become our first case. It had been investigating Gordon Grigg, a financial adviser based in Tennessee, for defrauding investors through a $10 million Ponzi scheme.[7] The SEC's investigators had found that Grigg had been promoting his investment fund by telling investors that he had access to high-yielding "TARP-guaranteed debt." Through this fictional investment, he offered investors high returns that were supposedly guaranteed by the U.S. government. We told the SEC that no such debt existed, and because as a law enforcement agency we didn't have the ability to charge our own cases, we worked to find a prosecutor that could bring criminal charges against Grigg. Because he lived in Nashville, we worked with the U.S. Attorney's Office for the Middle District of Tennessee.

This wasn't the type of fraud that we had anticipated investigating; we'd envisioned targeting those intent on stealing *from* TARP, not those trying to rip off investors by trading on the TARP name. This case, though, made Kevin and me realize that it was equally important for us to protect the general public from such TARP-related misconduct and then use the publicity that the indictments from those cases generated to deter others from committing similar crimes. We were able to quickly help put together a criminal case against Grigg, and within seven months he had been charged, convicted, and sentenced to ten years in jail.[8]

Also in January, we started assisting in what would become one of the highest-profile investigations related to the financial crisis and TARP. I had seen in the news that New York State Attorney General Andrew Cuomo had launched an investigation into bonus payments made by Merrill Lynch immediately before it had been acquired by Bank of America the previous month. Among other things, Cuomo was investigating whether the bonus payments had been structured to avoid TARP's loose restrictions on executive compensation, which would have kicked in once Bank of America closed the transaction. I was already familiar with Cuomo's team. Shortly before I left for Washington, our mortgage fraud group had opened a joint investigation with Cuomo's office into the possible manipulation of prices in the multitrillion-dollar credit default swap market during the financial crisis. So I called another friend from the Office, Ben Lawsky, who was now working for Cuomo. Within a few days we announced that SIGTARP would team up with Cuomo on the investigation.

We didn't have many people yet on board at SIGTARP, so I immediately got personally involved in the investigation, attending the interviews of Bank of America CEO Ken Lewis (who was as nervous as a cat), Merrill Lynch CEO John Thain (whose arrogance in person matched every public description of him), and Hank Paulson (who displayed remarkable candor and cooperativeness over the course of several interviews on several different audits and investigations). As we conducted interviews and reviewed documents, the investigation soon shifted focus to Bank of America's failure to disclose billions of dollars of losses at Merrill to its shareholders prior to their vote on the proposed acquisition. We also started to look at some questionable statements made by Lewis and others to Treasury and the Federal Reserve in December 2008.

In December, as the losses at Merrill continued to pile up, Lewis had told Paulson and Bernanke that he was considering invoking a clause in their preliminary deal documents that would permit Bank of America to scuttle the deal. Paulson then all but threatened Lewis, telling him that the Fed might replace Lewis and Bank of America's board of directors if they walked away from the deal—a decision that Paulson believed would put Bank of America, Merrill, and the national economy at risk. When Lewis backed down, Paulson agreed to put into motion the process to provide the bank with $20 billion in additional TARP funds and to guarantee a portion of $100 billion of its toxic assets against losses.[9] As Edolphus Towns, the chairman of the House Oversight and Government Reform Committee, later suggested at a hearing, Lewis's actions arguably resembled an "old-fashioned Brooklyn shakedown" of TARP.[10]

During one of my trips up to New York on the case I met with Cuomo. As a veteran of many Washington battles as HUD secretary in the 1990s, he was generous with his advice. He warned that TARP was destined to have problems and encouraged me to resist the inevitable pressure I would receive to keep quiet about my criticisms and recommendations. Colorfully recognizing that he had "seen this movie before," Cuomo stressed that if I kept quiet, Treasury and Congress might try to scapegoat me for TARP's problems. In Washington, he said, being loud was a virtue.

The investigation would go on for a year before Cuomo's office brought civil securities fraud charges against Bank of America, Lewis, and his former chief financial officer, Joseph Price. The complaint, which included allegations that the defendants had made misrepresentations to the government to get additional TARP funds, was still pending in early 2012.

The investigation that would lead to SIGTARP's most important convictions also began in early 2009. I opened the case on a pair of hunches that turned out to be wrong about a bank that had received what was called "conditional approval" for TARP money. After the first nine megabanks were bailed out by CPP, Treasury required the smaller bank applicants to demonstrate that they had enough loss-absorbing capital to qualify for TARP funds. When a bank failed to meet Treasury's standard, Treasury either encouraged the bank to withdraw its application or gave it "conditional approval," which allowed the bank to receive TARP funds only after it raised a specified amount of private capital. Our investigation began after one of our lawyers e-mailed me an article from *The Wall Street Journal* that described how Colonial Bank, based in Montgomery, Alabama, had announced in December 2008 that it had received preliminary approval from TARP for $550 million[11] without disclosing that it would get no money unless it first raised $300 million in private capital.[12] Colonial's stock price shot up by more than 50 percent after the initial announcement and then dropped back down after the bank finally disclosed the capital-raising condition.[13] We thought this might be a case of insider trading, with executives at Colonial misrepresenting the kind of approval the bank had received in order to make a quick profit by selling their stock after the share price surged. We opened an investigation along with the SEC.

We were still in the early stages of our inquiry when another article hit our daily news clip service. In early April, Colonial announced that it would meet its TARP conditions (and therefore qualify for $550 million in taxpayer money) through an anticipated $300 million investment by Lee Farkas, the head of Taylor, Bean & Whitaker (TBW), one of the largest nonbank mortgage originators in the country.[14] Based on what we had already learned about the two companies, something about the announcement didn't smell right. A little more digging made us question how Farkas could get his hands on hundreds of millions of dollars in order to invest in the very bank that was lending *him* money. I was concerned that we were seeing the kind of case about which I had previously warned Treasury: banks misrepresenting the nature of their capital to get TARP money.

This looked like Refco all over again. Every quarter, Refco's CEO, Phil Bennett, had hidden hundreds of millions of dollars of losses by moving them off and then back onto Refco's books through disguised "round-trip transactions." The transactions made it appear that independent third parties, such as hedge funds, had lent Refco money, but Refco had really been, in effect, lending the money to itself.

My hunch was that we might find that Colonial was the real source of Farkas's $300 million "investment," and I told Sharpley to issue SIG-TARP's first subpoenas to Colonial and TBW for documents.

Colonial's outside lawyers were generally cooperative, and they soon initiated an internal review of their client. Counsel for TBW, on the other hand, stonewalled us, raising my antennae. I told the agents to ramp up pressure on both entities and warned Treasury that it shouldn't fund Colonial without checking with us first.

As the agents dialed up the pressure, Kevin got a call from an old friend from the Office who was now a criminal defense attorney in New York. He told us that he had a client who worked at Colonial and had information about another employee who was destroying records called for by our subpoena. He offered to bring his client in to talk to us in exchange for limited immunity from prosecution.

Just as we needed a prosecutor to bring our cases, we also needed one to grant witnesses immunity. I sensed that I was sitting on an enormous case—two banks potentially conspiring with each other to steal more than a half-billion TARP dollars—and I knew I had to be careful in deciding where to go. My preference would have been the Office, but all of the potential criminal acts appeared to have occurred in Florida (where TBW was located and Colonial had a major presence), Alabama (Colonial's corporate home), Virginia (where Colonial's TARP application had been received by the FDIC), and Washington, D.C. (where Treasury had approved the application). I couldn't take the case to New York. I decided to keep the case close to home and take it to DOJ's Washington-based fraud section.

Though I'd had a terrible experience with DOJ on the FARC case, I had gotten to know the new head of the Criminal Division, Lanny Breuer, who was revamping his team. He assured me that any case we brought to his office would become their top priority. So I took a leap of faith and brought Lanny and his team onto the case.

The investigation soon took off. Though my hunch about the source of the $300 million capital raise proved wrong (it was still fraudulent, just not in the way that I'd suspected), we soon uncovered a massive multi-billion-dollar accounting fraud that had somehow gone undetected and uninvestigated for seven years. Part of the fraud involved TBW's Farkas working with Colonial insiders to steal hundreds of millions of dollars of cash from Colonial and essentially replace it with fake and overvalued assets that now sat, still overvalued, on Colonial's books. Working off of the whistle-blower's information, we sent two of our best and most experienced agents down to Florida along with a more junior agent on loan to SIGTARP from the FBI. They almost immediately started flipping and wiring up accomplices and quickly worked their way up the criminal food chain. We got a breakthrough when Farkas drove across Florida on a weekend afternoon to meet a Colonial employee in a parking lot to deliver a thumb drive of what we were told was false accounting data. Unfortunately for Farkas, the Colonial employee was cooperating with us. Within weeks we had gathered overwhelming evidence against Farkas and other coconspirators.

By late July, Kevin and I wanted DOJ to take the case down and arrest Farkas immediately. The agents had already built what we believed was an airtight case against Farkas that included witness testimony, recorded conversations, and incriminating documents. When DOJ pushed back, I ran some of the evidence by my former colleagues still at the Office who couldn't believe that DOJ wouldn't charge the case.

We called a meeting at our office and tried to lean on the DOJ prosecutors and their bosses to bring charges against Farkas. Our pitch was simple: there were a lot of investors out there buying and selling shares of Colonial stock who didn't know that the company had a multi-hundred-million-dollar hole in it, and the best way to stop the fraud was to lock up Farkas.

The DOJ prosecutors continued to push back hard. Their timidity was frustrating; I think that they just didn't have the confidence that comes from prosecuting a series of complex high-profile cases. They wanted more time to acquire ever more evidence to build an impregnable case. Kevin and I pressed on, knowing that we would have charged the case in a heartbeat if we had been the prosecutors (a fact that we annoyingly shared with them over and over again). We also knew that getting the case charged would be a great win for SIGTARP. We had effectively stopped Treasury from throwing $550 million of taxpayer funds into a fraudulent pit at Colonial, but until there were charges we couldn't demonstrate to the public what we had done. Handcuffs on a powerful and wealthy financial executive such as Farkas would send a strong message of deterrence to others who might be contemplating TARP-related crimes, and charges would help give solace to the worried Congress and public that someone was actively policing TARP.

The issue came to a head over the course of several meetings. At one point, Kevin angrily suggested that a high-ranking DOJ official was acting "like a birther" for repeatedly expressing doubts in the face of a mountain of evidence. In a later meeting, I told the same official that he needed to put his "big-boy pants on" if he wanted DOJ to play in the major leagues of securities fraud cases. I complained bitterly to Lanny, who was sympathetic but unable to move his team. We did eventually convince DOJ to seek court authorization to raid TBW and Colonial's Florida offices in early August 2009, which received heavy media coverage after the FBI tipped off the local press (by the way, if you ever wonder why the press shows up at search warrants and arrests, it is always, and I mean always, the FBI that tips them off).

By the time that DOJ indicted Farkas, an interminable ten months after that, we had built an impressive case that involved billions of dollars in losses from different frauds perpetrated by Farkas and his coconspirators. In all, DOJ did a good (albeit belated) job with the case, convicting eight defendants and sending Farkas to prison for thirty years.[15] As of early 2012, it was by far the most significant case to arise out of the financial crisis.

With such cases of fraud already beginning to crop up, I was eager to get off to a good start with the new administration and work protections into the design of any programs that it might implement now that it had access to the additional $350 billion in TARP money authorized by Congress. President-elect Obama had announced on November 24, 2008,[16] that his pick for Treasury secretary was Timothy Geithner, and I was cautiously optimistic.

ONCE NOMINATED, I started paying close attention to the news about who would become the new Treasury secretary, the two likely picks being Geithner, who was then the president of the New York Fed, or Summers, who had served as Treasury secretary under President Clinton. When Obama announced that Geithner would get the job, I was relieved. Though I knew little about either one, the media's description of Summers as being an impossible-to-deal-with bully had made me an unabashed Geithner supporter. To this day my mom still enjoys reminding me that I once championed his nomination.

My enthusiasm for Geithner was dampened, however, after the news broke that he had failed to pay some taxes he owed from his time working at the International Monetary Fund (IMF) from 2001 to 2003.[17] When I first heard the story, I gave him the benefit of the doubt. I too had had a tax issue with the Senate Finance Committee during my confirmation. Unbeknown to me, my accountant had made an error on my 2005 tax return by deducting the modest "Blue Book" value of the 1991 Chevrolet Lumina (less than $2,500) that I had donated to charity instead of the standard $500 deduction. She was unaware of a recent change in the law, and as a result, there was an error in the return that was caught by Senator Grassley's staff. They were fully satisfied with my explanation, and the issue went away after I refiled my return and paid the difference. So I had more than a little sympathy for Geithner as he was being raked over the coals over what could have been an innocent mistake. As the story unfolded, however, it seemed that Geithner's actions might have gone beyond a mere error.

As an employee at an international organization, his payroll taxes hadn't been withheld from his paycheck; instead the IMF had paid Geithner directly both his and the IMF's payroll tax contributions and provided him with forms indicating that he should forward those payments to the IRS.[18] Geithner had instead kept the payments, which was discovered during an IRS audit of him in 2006.[19] The statute of limitations for that type of offense was generally three years,[20] which meant that at the time of the audit, Geithner was on the hook only for 2003 and 2004.[21] He paid the taxes for 2003 and 2004[22] but kept the rest. Prior to formally announcing his nomination, the Obama transition team made sure that Geithner finally paid the amounts for 2001 and 2002 as well.[23]

It was when I heard the second part of the story that I began to have some concern. Geithner's explanation as to why, after being caught by the IRS in 2006, he had paid only for the years for which the statute of limitations had not run out (2003–2004), didn't seem credible to me. Senator Grassley had submitted what are called questions for the record to Geithner during his confirmation process asking for an explanation, and in response he had written,

"At the conclusion of the 2006 audit, I was told what I owed and I paid that amount. It did not occur to me to file amended returns for 2001 and 2002. In November 2008, as part of the transition team vetting process, the errors I made in 2001 and 2002 were drawn to my attention, and I decided it was appropriate to correct the error."[24]

In other words, the president of the Federal Reserve Bank of New York, the most important of the U.S. Federal Reserve Banks and one of the key players in setting monetary policy for the United States, told Congress that it *"did not occur to"* him that if he had violated the tax laws in 2003 and 2004, he might have also done so for 2001 and 2002. I suspected that Geithner and his lawyer were carefully selecting their words to give the impression that he had been unaware of his 2001–2002 obligations, when it was more likely that it "did not occur" to him to pay taxes that the IRS wasn't forcing him to pay.

Geithner, of course, would survive the controversy and be confirmed, but this approach—what I suspected to be a careful and potentially misleading parsing of the truth—would soon characterize many of Treasury's public statements about TARP.

THE SENATE CONFIRMED Geithner on Monday, January 26, and we heard that President Obama and Vice President Joe Biden would be coming to Treasury later that day to swear him in. Amid the excitement of the day, I got a close-up view of some of the elaborate protocols of power in Washington.

First, my deputy chief of staff, Cathy Alix, told me the room where my audit and investigative staff had been working, called the Gallatin Room, had to be vacated. It was right across from the ballroomlike Cash Room, where the ceremony would take place, and Treasury told Cathy that we had to clear out of the room so that the White House could use it as a staging area for the swearing in. My team was under enormous pressure, with our February 5 date for our first report to Congress looming, and I confirmed with Cathy that we wouldn't be able to move our computers to another room. The team would be effectively shut down for a whole day. So I asked Cathy why they had to use Gallatin.

"They say the White House needs the room," she explained.

Cathy had come over to SIGTARP from a high-ranking administrative post at Treasury, and she knew everything there was to know about the building, so I asked her if there was any reason they really had to use our room, as opposed to any of the other ones near the Cash Room.

"Not at all," Cathy told me. "The treasurer's office, which is right next door, is completely empty, and they could easily put all of the necessary equipment in there."

It made no sense to me that we should shut down our operations for no apparent reason, so I told Cathy to tell the Treasury people that we weren't moving and they should use the empty office next door.

Prior to her time at Treasury, Cathy had served in a high-ranking administrative role in the White House and had even helped run the 2004 Republican National Convention. She knew Washington protocol better than any of us, and she understood what I did not: you just don't say no to a request from the White House. But she was a firm believer in Washington hierarchies, and she took the order without blinking an eye, though she later told me that she had been somewhat shocked by my response and that she couldn't recall anyone ever disregarding a White House request.

About an hour later, Cathy brought a Treasury official to my office, who told me that we were going to have to leave the room. "The president wants the room," she said. "You have to move out."

Oh sure, I thought to myself, *now it's the president himself who wants the room.*

I explained that my team was under the gun and again refused. About an hour later, Cathy told me that the advance team had found another room.

When Kevin heard about it, he angrily asked me if I had lost my mind. "Are you actually *trying* to get us fired?" he said.

But I had apparently impressed Cathy with my obstinacy. She later told me she'd been thrilled because we were the exact opposite of business-as-usual Washington. It had been a defining moment for her with SIGTARP, she said, convincing her to stay on board.

When I asked Kevin a little later if he might have taken a slightly different approach, we both burst out laughing. We figured that at least I'd sent an unmistakable message about my view of SIGTARP's independence.

Later that night, I got a stronger dose of Washington's love affair with power. Kevin and I went to the Cash Room to see Biden swear in Geithner as Obama stood next to him. I found the fawning reaction from the crowd toward Geithner unsettling. In the Southern District of New York, though we definitely respected the U.S. attorney, we thought of him or her like any other boss, someone who had to earn your respect. This was different. In Washington, a cabinet official is treated as a cross between Princess Diana, the pope, and Bono. The ceremony felt like a deification.

I had my first two interactions with Geithner over the next two days, and they were also unsettling. As a bureau head, I was invited the next day to Geithner's first senior staff meeting, which was a monthly gathering of the heads of the myriad agencies that made up the Treasury Department. I was one of the last people to arrive and was curious to see how Geithner would address the group, populated mostly by short-time Paulson holdovers and acting heads of agencies waiting to be replaced by presidential appointees. I sat in the back and observed.

Geithner's brusque style struck me as obnoxious. He was speaking to a group of people who had been working their tails off for the past four months trying to keep the financial system from entirely melting down, and he barely acknowledged their hard work and sacrifices. Instead he sternly lectured us, warning us about making stray statements to the press and directing us to minimize any intra-Treasury agency conflicts that might arise. It was bizarre. He spoke about issues that struck me as being fairly trivial and did so in a tone that seemed as if he was angry with us.

The next day I was scheduled to have an oversight meeting with Geithner, which was also to be attended by Gene Dodaro from GAO and Elizabeth Warren and her fellow members of the Congressional Oversight Panel. I requested a private meeting with Geithner, and it was set up for just five minutes before the broader meeting. My plan was to impress on him that I viewed SIGTARP's role as different from that of GAO and COP, which as arms of Congress were necessarily going to be focused on how TARP was being executed *after* the key program decisions had already been made. I thought it was important to clarify that as an agency within Treasury, our job was to protect the programs *before* they were announced, by helping shape them to avoid losses from fraud. But this briefest of meetings made it eminently clear that things had changed dramatically since my last visit to the secretary's office. Whereas Paulson was welcoming and interested in what we had to say, Geithner looked put upon and distracted. I spoke for all of thirty seconds before I was rushed out the door. On the way out, I told Mark Patterson, Geithner's new chief of staff (and a former Goldman Sachs lobbyist), that I needed to find a time to continue the meeting and suggested that we schedule regular meetings, as I knew Paulson had done with his inspectors general.

There was no follow-up meeting. Geithner had no interest in meeting with me on even an irregular basis, and we would have only one other one-on-one meeting over the next two-plus years. Whereas Paulson appeared to view SIGTARP as a potential ally that could help protect TARP and enhance its credibility, Geithner was utterly dismissive.

As I walked with him out of his office and around the corner to his large conference room, we were met by a phalanx of TV cameras, reporters, and photographers. I took a seat between Geithner and Elizabeth Warren, whom I was meeting for the first time.

Geithner gave a short prepared statement to the press in which he launched a "new policy" designed to "increase transparency." Treasury, he said, would now post all TARP contracts on its website.

I was momentarily fazed by the announcement. Given that we had made that recommendation more than a month earlier, it seemed only right that Geithner's team would have let us know they were going ahead with it. I hadn't learned yet to put on a Washington poker face, and my expression of annoyance was captured in a photograph that my dad later pulled down from the Internet and sent to me. While Geithner speaks, with Elizabeth Warren smiling at him, I am glaring at the smiling Neel Kashkari.

After the meeting, I had my first meeting with Elizabeth. Up until that point, all that I really knew about her was that she was a Harvard Law School professor and had already become an outspoken critic of Treasury's lack of transparency in its handling of TARP.[25] Although Kashkari occasionally threw insults my way, it was nothing compared to the hostility that Treasury officials expressed toward Elizabeth, who was described as a self-serving media hound interested only in bringing attention to herself (I would soon be characterized similarly by them). I wasn't sure yet what to make of Elizabeth or the panel she chaired, which was made up of three Democratic appointees and two Republicans. For the first two reports the panel had issued, there had been Republican dissents,[26] and I was worried that the Republicans might seek to discredit the panel's findings by claiming that the Warren-led majority was advancing a partisan political agenda. I was determined that SIGTARP be perceived as nonpartisan, and I wasn't sure how much I wanted to associate with COP. Also, though I instantly liked Elizabeth personally, I wondered if I could trust her. Would she pull punches on the Democrats and maybe even go after me if I criticized the Obama administration?

In general, I had made a career out of reading people, but that day I made two mistakes. I assumed that even though Geithner had been gruff and dismissive, he would be willing to work with us, and I viewed Elizabeth with suspicion. As I would quickly learn, I couldn't have had it more backward.

SIGTARP's FORTUNES SEEMED to take a turn for the better when that same week, we received a letter from Barney Frank,[27] the colorful chair of the powerful House Financial Services Committee. Frank, who was a Democrat, had helped deliver the necessary votes to Paulson to get TARP passed, but he had quickly become a vocal critic of the way Treasury was carrying out the bailout. Frank was unhappy with Treasury's failure to live up to its early promises that it would use TARP to help stem the tidal wave of foreclosures sweeping the country and to spur lending by the banks.[28] With the Democrats now firmly in control of Washington, Frank figured to be a key—if unpredictable—player in our little bailout universe.

The letter, which Frank also sent to the media, was a strong endorsement of our audit of the banks' use of TARP money. Kevin and I congratulated each other. We were doing what we thought was the right thing, we hadn't been fired (yet), and with a similar public endorsement of the audit by Republican Senator Chuck Grassley, we had now garnered public support from both sides of the aisle. That morning I also received good news that Senator McCaskill's bill enhancing SIGTARP's jurisdiction and granting us full law enforcement authority was about to be officially "dropped" (introduced to the floor) and could be voted on as soon as the following week.

Our celebration was short-lived. That same afternoon we received a stark reminder of our inexperience in navigating some of Washington's complex and treacherous waters. The modest press coverage our audit announcement received had apparently been noticed by officials at the White House's Office of Management and Budget (OMB). Shortly after Frank's press release went out, an OMB analyst e-mailed one of our administrators to remind us that under something called the Paperwork Reduction Act, we were forbidden to send out any survey to more than ten TARP recipients without first getting White House approval. The act had been designed to prevent government agencies from needlessly harassing a large number of people or companies with requests for information.

As our counsel described the act's requirements, Kevin and I realized that getting approval could involve a long bureaucratic process. Even if we were lucky, the required procedures would take at least six months to get through before we could send the audit letter out to the banks. The bright side, however, was that we could petition OMB for a waiver, which OMB had just granted to Treasury for its monthly lending survey. We sent the petition letter out first thing Thursday morning as Kevin and I headed to the Hill that day for meetings with Frank and Senator Shelby followed by scheduled meetings at the FBI and the Federal Reserve. Before the day was over, I would be nearly struck by congressional spittle, get caught in a bureaucratic snare, listen to Geithner get yelled at by a member of Congress, and be warned that I was about to piss off the *president*. Just another SIGTARP Thursday.

Shortly before we walked into our meeting with Shelby, my BlackBerry buzzed with the good news from Barry Holman, my audit chief, that OMB had granted the waiver. I was relieved. Although Kevin had warned me that I was being paranoid, I was convinced that OMB was intentionally trying to hang up the audit. I was glad to see that I was wrong.

The meeting with Shelby was like a speed round of *Jeopardy*. Most of my meet and greets with members of Congress were long on small talk and short on substance. Not with Shelby. I probably covered more in fifteen minutes of rapid-fire questions and answers than in most hour-long meetings with other members of Congress. We covered capital injections into the banks, their ability to report on their use of funds, our audit into the same, TALF, and a preview of our upcoming initial report to Congress. Shelby ended the meeting by telling us that he strongly supported our efforts to date, and stressed that I needed to take full advantage of the remarkable opportunity I had been given to serve my country.

I walked out exhilarated. The good feelings for us on the Hill outweighed the difficulties with Treasury. I was feeling that we really were seeing a new dawn for transparency, and with the good news from OMB, it looked as though things might in fact be changing for the better under Obama and Geithner.

Then I turned my BlackBerry back on.

Just seven minutes after Barry had sent his e-mail about us receiving the OMB waiver, he had sent another message that OMB had reversed its decision. "Literally as I hit the send button on my last message," he wrote, "our contact at OMB called me back to say she had misspoken."

Misspoken? So much for my warm fuzzies. I couldn't believe it. When I asked what had happened, Barry said that in his decades of government service, he'd never seen anything like it. He said that our OMB contact wouldn't even say if she had been told by someone to reverse herself. I told Barry to try to get an explanation. I knew that Treasury was strongly opposed to the audit, and this struck me as politics at its worst—it seemed like someone at OMB was carrying Treasury's water.

Frank wasn't happy either. I'd never really followed members of Congress closely before I headed to Washington. Though I knew the New York senators, some of the congressional leaders, and my own congressman, I had never heard of many of the members of Congress that I was now meeting on a regular basis. Not so with Barney Frank. He was a regular on the Sunday talk-show circuit, and seemed to always be in the news. I agreed with his positions far more often than not, and I always enjoyed his brash, confrontational take-no-prisoners approach, so I was excited to meet him. His supportive letter suggested that he would be a powerful ally.

As we walked into Frank's office, he was leaning back in his chair, his suit jacket off and his hair tousled, with his rumpled shirt just barely tucked into his pants. He could not have presented a starker contrast to the neatly groomed and proper Shelby. Frank skipped the usual formalities and mumbled so quickly that I had a difficult time deciphering what he was saying. One of the first questions out of his mouth—accompanied by an impressive spray of saliva that seemed to hang in the air for seconds before settling a good foot beyond the front of his desk—was to ask me if the audit letters had gone out to the banks yet.

For a split second I was unsure what to do. Did I really want to fill him in? Should I be airing our dirty laundry? Would he think I am the dumbest IG in the world for not fully understanding the implications of the Paperwork Reduction Act before first announcing the audit?

I quickly realized I had to tell him what had happened and that I really didn't know when the survey would finally get out to the banks. He didn't respond to me directly. Instead, he immediately picked up his phone, dialed, and barked into the receiver, "Tell him Barney Frank is on the phone." After a short pause, he screamed about the act of obstruction that was inhibiting SIGTARP from carrying out its audit of the banks. I had no idea who he had called, but I assumed that someone's voice mail had just taken a beating. He looked at me and said, "Geithner. That should hopefully take care of it, but if not, make sure you let us know."

I was thrilled that someone as influential and important to the new administration as Frank had picked up our cause but also worried by his choice of target. My complaint, after all, was with OMB, and though someone at Treasury might have convinced OMB to change course, I didn't consider that Geithner himself might be involved. As Kevin pointed out later, that was an important lesson. Anytime you talk to a member of Congress, your issue becomes their issue. They own it, and they'll do whatever they want with it. You can lead the horse to water, but you shouldn't be surprised by who it kicks in the head once it gets there.

The rest of the meeting was terrific. Frank was effusive in his praise for what we were doing, and he asked if President Obama had officially endorsed me as the special inspector general. When I said not as of yet, he said, "You know, the Obama team signed off on you. We made sure that they wouldn't just switch you out."

As Kevin and I walked out, I asked him if he really thought Frank had called Geithner.

He looked at me with a smile and said, "I have no idea. None."

After a sit-down with the FBI about potential cases we could work together, we had to race over to the Federal Reserve. Kashkari had called the meeting to discuss a set of recommendations that we'd made to address the problems we saw with TALF, including its potential expansion to include purchases of mortgage-backed securities, the program's disproportionate reliance on credit-rating agencies, and the complete absence of a compliance regime.

When we arrived at the Fed, we were confronted by what seemed like dozens of Treasury and Fed officials, including Kashkari and Scott Alvarez, the Fed's general counsel. It turned out to be an ambush: they were clearly trying to intimidate us into backing down on the recommendations. After some assurances that they were looking into ways to address our concerns, Kashkari explained the real reason we'd been summoned.

He told us that it would be better if we left the recommendations out of our February 5 initial report to Congress. Treasury and the Fed would work with us to address the issues we had raised, he promised, so why couldn't we just put off the recommendations until the next report, after they had more time? I explained to Kashkari that wasn't how it worked. The whole point of SIGTARP was to make recommendations when we saw fraud vulnerabilities, and that was exactly what we saw in TALF. We couldn't now put the genie back in the bottle; we had an explicit obligation to report to Congress any recommendations we made.

Kashkari raised the ante, telling us that TALF's success was very important to President Obama and that the president wouldn't want the program "harmed" by our public criticisms.

The statement hung in the air. I had gone toe-to-toe with Kashkari a number of times by now, but this was different. It sounded like a threat. He didn't say outright that the request had come from the White House or that there would be consequences if I ignored his request, but the implication seemed clear: if I went forward, I would be taking on the president on an issue that was near and dear to him. The same president, of course, who could fire me with one stroke of his pen.

I told Kashkari that I was open to discussing the recommendations if it turned out some of our assumptions were wrong or would even change them for the report if he convinced us that we were off base, but we weren't going to leave them out entirely.

On the walk back to Treasury, Kevin and I agreed that there was no way that President Obama, ten days into his job, was even aware of our upcoming report, let alone concerned about our TALF recommendations. But we figured that to invoke his name that way, Kashkari must have had permission to do so. Maybe not from the president, but probably from someone pretty high up, who must have been seriously worried about Congress's reaction to our report.

THE NEXT DAY, we still had not received a green light from OMB to go forward with the audit, so Kevin and I, now having learned a little about how things get done in Washington, decided to bring into the loop a friendly staffer from Grassley's office, Emilia DiSanto. She and Grassley had been among our strongest supporters, and I figured she might be interested in helping us out.

A longtime veteran of Washington, Emilia was Grassley's chief investigative counsel. She had once been brutally attacked outside her home after one of the congressional investigations that she led had apparently angered the wrong people,[29] and as a result of her investigative experience, she either shared or was the impetus for Grassley's fierce commitment to strong and effective IGs. After I described the situation, she told me that she thought it was highly unlikely that OMB had acted alone.

"Treasury's fingerprints are all over this. We turn up the heat on their involvement, and this'll go away," she quickly concluded. She also said she'd ask Grassley to raise the issue in a meeting he would be having that afternoon with Peter Orszag, the new director of OMB.

The congressional machinery we had set into motion was soon in high gear. Grassley sent a letter to Orszag describing OMB's conduct as "unacceptable" and questioning whether it was "obstructing" our audit. The letter also called for a report on any communications that OMB had had with either Treasury or the financial industry about our survey. Grassley also sent out a press release calling on "OMB to get out of the way of Special IG for TARP."[30]

Almost immediately, calls from the press started pouring in. *The Washington Post, The Wall Street Journal,* and the *Boston Herald* all asked me to comment, but we referred them back to Grassley. We were learning how to negotiate the press whirlwind.

Grassley's letter clearly riled Orszag's staff. I soon got a message that his chief of staff was trying to get hold of me, and when I called her back, she vented pure disjointed rage, screaming that she and Orszag had been "blindsided" by calls that day from both Frank and Grassley.

When I tried to explain that we had in fact sent our letter to Orszag the previous day, she disparaged the "career people" who worked at OMB and made the bizarre comment "If you want me to care, fine, but otherwise I don't care." I still have no idea what she meant. I just told her that since she was calling me, it only made sense that she should care about getting her facts right.

The next morning, a Saturday, I opened *The Washington Post* and was startled to see a picture of Geithner and me in the Business Section, next to an article entitled "Bailout Fund Letters Are Held Up."[31] It began, "The Obama administration is blocking the chief watchdog of the $700 billion federal bailout of the financial system from immediately sending banks requests about how they are using taxpayer funds."[32] I instantly thought, *Okay, this is it, now I'm definitely going to be fired.* Thankfully, Karen was there. When she woke up, I read the article to her and said, "I'm gone. Done. This is bad. Really, really bad."

I explained to Karen that after all that had happened that week, it was now going to look as though I had run to the press to plant a negative story about the White House. After I told her that I truly didn't think that I would still have a job on Monday, she said she doubted that I would get fired but stressed that we would be okay if I did. Then, as Kevin had said to me a couple of days earlier, she said, "The worst thing that happens, we go back home." That was just one of what would be dozens of times when Karen's calming perspective helped keep me sane while I was in Washington.

My fears eased as the weekend unfolded. Frank went on Sunday's *This Week with George Stephanopoulos,* lauding our bank audit. We also got word from Emilia that OMB was backing down and granting us the waiver. I stopped worrying and started preparing for my first congressional hearing as the head of SIGTARP, that Thursday, when we would release "the book."

7

By Wall Street for Wall Street

"M R. BAROFSKY," Senator Shelby boomed with a grin, ". . . this
is a very important job that you occupy. . . . [Y]ou might be
unemployable after you do this. But you know and I know that these
people have got to fear you and your office. If they do not fear you, they
are going to play with you."[1] I was seated between Elizabeth Warren and
GAO's acting chief, Gene Dodaro, under the bright klieg lights of the Senate Banking, Housing, and Urban Affairs Committee hearing room.

Shelby's comment about my never being able to work again brought
down the house, so much so that Shelby couldn't help repeating it later
in the hearing.[2] Playing along, I turned to Karen, who had moved some
patient appointments around in New York so that she could be there, and
said in a stage whisper, "Not true, we'll be fine."

So kicked off my first of twenty hearings before Congress as TARP's
special inspector general.

In doing a little homework on how the questioning of a panel of witnesses works in such hearings, I learned that senators will either direct a
question to a particular witness or just throw a question out to the entire
panel. When that happens, it's like a game show. Each of the three witnesses has a microphone in front of him or her with an on/mute switch,
and whoever lights up the microphone first by pushing the "on" button
gets to answer the question. My strategy? Speak only when spoken to and
otherwise treat the "on" button as if it were coated with the Ebola virus.

Elizabeth Warren, by contrast, fairly pounced on the questions. Though I still answered more than my fair share, I was so pleased that Elizabeth soaked up some of the trickier policy questions in my maiden hearing that at one point I wrote her a note saying "Thank God you're here."

One of the focal points of the hearing was the ongoing housing crisis. Several senators expressed great frustration with Treasury over TARP's still unfulfilled promise to "preserve homeownership."[3] The committee's chairman, Senator Christopher Dodd, commented on how TARP had not been used to help home owners and said, "Stopping foreclosures must be our top priority."[4] Elizabeth, who at the time was more focused on the issue than I was, confirmed to the committee that Treasury still had done nothing to fulfill its obligations under the statute to stem foreclosures.

The hearing and the press coverage that followed also covered our TALF recommendations,[5] and the reaction from the New York Fed was almost immediate. Shortly after the hearing we got a call from its legal department offering to come down and brief us on its plans to now implement several of our recommendations. We also learned from a Fed official's leak to the press, in advance of the meeting, that the Fed had apparently abandoned Dudley's position that it couldn't be involved in enforcing compliance; it was now planning to launch a "robust compliance program."[6] That was remarkably encouraging, if for no other reason than that it was finally acknowledging our concerns.

It was the first tangible proof (though far from the last) that our friend Stuart Bowen, the inspector general of SIGIR, was exactly right about using the power of the press. Dudley had not completely reversed his position because our arguments had suddenly become more persuasive; the thing that had changed was some press coverage and a little bit of interest from the Senate.

Things were changing at Treasury as well. The following week began with a rumor, which we confirmed with Treasury, that Geithner was considering taking the increasingly unpopular TARP out of Treasury entirely, a plan that a Treasury lawyer told us was still in the "concept phase." Then, on Tuesday, February 10, Geithner held a much-anticipated press conference announcing the official rebranding of TARP as the Financial Stability Plan. I learned that this was a long-standing Washington tactic: if a program is unpopular, give it a new name. After the announcement, for a couple of months no one at Treasury would utter the word "TARP" to us, and they even requested that we replace references to TARP in our next quarterly report with the acronym FSP. We, like the rest of the world outside of Treasury, ignored their silly request.

Geithner described four new TARP initiatives in his speech. First, he announced that Treasury would be conducting "stress tests" to measure the largest banks' ability to withstand a further downturn in the economy. The banks that failed the test, he explained, would have to raise capital to meet any shortfall indicated by the tests, presumably by selling additional shares of their common stock. If they were unable to do so, he promised, Treasury would provide them with whatever capital they needed through TARP. (About half of the banks failed the tests, and all but one, GMAC, were able to raise capital without resorting to TARP funds.)

The next component of the plan was a public-private investment program that would combine money from the Federal Reserve, Treasury, and the FDIC with that of private players to purchase up to $2 trillion of "legacy assets," including residential mortgage-backed securities (RMBS). In connection with the new program, it was announced that the Fed was prepared to expand TALF to include RMBS, against our advice and with no further word about what additional fraud protections, if any, were being put into place.[7] Finally, Geithner promised a long-awaited $50 billion housing program, to be detailed in the coming weeks, which would include what would come to be called the Home Affordable Modification Plan, or HAMP.

Kevin and I watched Geithner's performance from my office. He looked twitchy, sweaty, and obviously nervous. As it became apparent that the speech was long on platitudes and short on details, we watched the stock market ticker in the lower right corner of the screen begin a steep descent, down 4.6 percent for the day.[8] The markets were hoping for detailed programs, and they expressed their disappointment with Geithner's vacuous speech with a large sell-off.[9] The Dow Jones Industrial Average plunged nearly two hundred points during the speech alone.[10] When Geithner was done, we just looked at each other. "Where do we even begin?" I asked.

It was a sobering moment. We had been struggling just to keep up with TARP in its current $700 billion form, and now, over the course of Geithner's twenty-minute speech, it looked as though our job had just increased by trillions of dollars. At $700 billion, we were responsible for providing oversight for a sum larger than the annual economic output of Turkey, which in 2009 was the seventeenth largest economy in the world.[11] Including what had just been announced, the numbers added up to close to $3 trillion, larger than the entire federal budget and all but four countries' annual output worldwide.[12]

We thought we should've at least been given a prespeech briefing. Amazingly, even after the speech, when we asked Kashkari for more information about the new programs, he told us that they weren't yet sufficiently formed to give us anything beyond a short stack of press releases issued by Treasury that day. That became Treasury's modus operandi: first, announcements intended to "shock and awe" the media that made for good sound bites but were not particularly well thought out; then, weeks later, scattered and incomplete details that had to be reworked on the fly. And finally, poor program execution that accomplished little, if any, of the originally announced goals. Several of the programs announced that day followed the pattern exactly.

ONE BRIGHT POINT of Geithner's announcement was the vaguely described housing program. I had already been hearing angry complaints from members of Congress about the absence of a mortgage modification program for months. Many members emphasized that they had voted for TARP only because they had thought it would help struggling home owners, and indeed whole sections of the TARP statute regulated how Treasury would modify the mortgages once it conducted its originally planned massive purchase of troubled assets.[13] So I was looking forward to our scheduled February 13 briefing at Treasury with GAO and COP to hear details of how this new $50 billion housing program was going to work. There was so much suffering around the country, with 2.3 million different properties receiving foreclosure filings and more than 900,000 bank repossessions in 2008 alone.[14] And with the unemployment rate shooting up 2 percent in just the past six months,[15] it looked as if things were only getting worse. Furthermore, after spending two months diving into the comparatively unfamiliar waters of banking, I was also eager to work on something familiar, mortgage fraud.

Mortgage fraud cells across the country had been lying low since the crash; the financial crisis had tightened underwriting standards considerably, and with less overall lending, there were fewer opportunities for fraud. I knew, however, that $50 billion in government cheese was going to draw out a lot of rats, and I was looking forward to building the right traps to catch them.

I was concerned right away when the Treasury presenters explained that the largest mortgage servicers would effectively be running the program on behalf of Treasury, earning taxpayer-funded incentive payments each time they agreed to permanently modify a mortgage. Servicers technically do not have an interest in mortgages themselves, although they are typically subsidiaries of the holding companies of the large Wall Street banks that do. Their primary role, at least in good times, is to collect mortgage payments, which they then forward to the owners of the mortgages, such as the investors who purchased the bonds that were backed by the loans. They're also responsible for any negotiations to modify mortgages for struggling borrowers and for running the foreclosure process when a loan goes bad.

Servicers make money in several ways. For one, they charge the owners of the mortgages a fee based on the total amount of unpaid principal of the mortgages that they service. In other words, servicers add up the total amount of loans under their watch and then take a percentage of that out of the money due to investors. They also earn fees when borrowers are late on their payments and charge for certain foreclosure-related services. Importantly for the servicers, when a home is sold in foreclosure, they are typically paid all of their fees and advance expenses before the owners of the mortgages get any of the proceeds of the sale. As a result, though there is a good chance that investors will lose a significant amount of money in the foreclosure of a home, the servicers are in a much better position to recoup their fees and expenses. In that way, the economic incentives of the investors and the servicers often clash. Though it may be better for an investor if a mortgage is modified, the servicer may be better off if a home goes into foreclosure. Treasury's failure to adequately address this inherent conflict of interest would eventually help cripple its mortgage modification program.

As we started asking the Treasury officials some pretty basic questions about how the program would operate, it became apparent that they had developed only a set of ideas, not an executable program. Frustrated, I asked how far they were from having a plan that they could describe in enough detail so that we could provide meaningful input. After we were told "at least several weeks, maybe more," I suggested that they call us back when they had a better sense of what they were actually going to do.

Even their bare-boned description, however, left me concerned. As I well knew from my work at the Office running the mortgage fraud group, the program would be vulnerable to fraud if it did not include tight underwriting standards, such as requiring written verification of borrowers' residence and income. Treasury also risked inadvertently promoting a version of the advance-fee "foreclosure rescue" schemes that we had prosecuted at the Office. A nationwide program would almost certainly encourage rings of fraudsters, who would charge struggling borrowers large up-front fees in return for empty promises of "guaranteed" government mortgage modifications.

We also saw vulnerability to some new types of fraud. Treasury would be making incentive payments to the servicers per loan put into a permanent modification. That might lead corrupt servicers to try to collect payments for loans that either did not exist or that were so deeply in default that they had no chance of qualifying for the program. Serious, well-crafted protections would have to be put into place in order to assure that the one TARP program intended to help Main Street didn't drown in a flood of fraud.

Driving home that same night around 10:30 (another exciting Friday night of Diet Coke and Trader Ming's noodles in my smelly office), I heard on the radio that the president was going to announce a comprehensive mortgage modification program in Arizona the following Wednesday. I was appalled. Either Treasury had been lying to us about how far along its crafting of the program was, or the White House was being wildly premature. I called Kevin, who'd also heard the announcement, and asked him which he thought had happened.

"I don't know," he replied. "But either way, it doesn't bode well for home owners."

As promised, President Obama announced the program in a sweeping speech at an Arizona high school the following Wednesday. He promised that it would help "3 to 4 million homeowners to modify the terms of their mortgages to avoid foreclosure" and provided some basic details of the program along the lines of what we had heard at the briefing.[16] Surprising us the most was the president's promise that the plan guidelines would be issued "two weeks from today."[17]

That same day, Treasury released additional details about the program, such as the amounts of the incentives that would be paid to home owners, investors, and servicers, and the total cost: $75 billion ($50 billion to be borne by TARP and $25 billion by Fannie Mae and Freddie Mac).[18] Treasury was still silent, though, on the nuts and bolts of how the program would work. I reached out to Kashkari and TARP's compliance officer, but they told me that that they weren't yet ready to provide us with any more details.

Now we were really worried. It seemed inconceivable that they would be able to put together a well-thought-out program in such a short period of time. This once again seemed more like political posturing than an executable plan.

The next day, Kevin and I were meeting in my office while CNBC was playing in the background. We heard some shouting and looked up to hear Rick Santelli, a CNBC anchor, in midrant against the new TARP mortgage modification program. He described it as a plan for "losers" and compared it to Castro's Cuba.[19] At one point, he turned to the roaring traders on the floor of the Chicago Mercantile Exchange and asked, "How many of you people want to pay for your neighbor's mortgage that has an extra bathroom and can't pay their bills? Raise their hands."[20] Finally, in a phrase that would change the landscape of conservative politics in the country, "We're thinking of having a Chicago tea party in July."[21]

Treasury, by rolling out a hurried and poorly thought out mortgage modification program, had just helped give birth to the Tea Party. Santelli's rant, and the political movement it inspired, hung over the program for the rest of my time in Washington.

As more days passed with no details about the program from Treasury, I became increasingly nervous that it was just going to officially roll out the program before we could make our recommendations to protect it from fraud. No one at Treasury had yet engaged with us about our concerns, so on February 26, I sent over to Kashkari a series of recommendations based on the little that we already knew. In addition to the obvious fraud protection measures (written third-party verifications of borrowers' representations about their income and residence), we included some specific to HAMP, including a requirement that servicers must prove that they had collected three monthly payments during a trial period before they received incentive payments. I believed that that would deter servicers from trying to collect large piles of up-front incentive payments for fake or unqualified loans.

Most important, we recommended that Treasury launch a broad and immediate public outreach program that would warn borrowers to stay away from criminals offering fraudulent modification services. As I repeatedly told Treasury officials, only through a high-profile media campaign could Treasury tamp down such fraud schemes. Kashkari told me that our recommendations would be considered as they finalized the details of the program.

When more details of the plan were finally announced, though, they didn't include several of our recommendations, including up-front income and residence verifications. I could also see that the plan did almost nothing to address some of the fundamental problems that plagued the housing market. For example, although the problem of underwater mortgages was and continues to be at the heart of the foreclosure crisis, there was no component in HAMP that meaningfully addressed reducing the amount of principal owed by home owners on their mortgages. Nor was there relief for the unemployed borrowers; HAMP participants needed to demonstrate a minimum income in order to participate.

As I TRIED to draw attention to our concerns about HAMP, I was also becoming increasingly worried about the rollout of one of the other major components of Geithner's speech—the multitrillion-dollar Public-Private Investment Program, or PPIP.

Our primary source of information about PPIP's development came from *The Wall Street Journal,* which seemed to publish a leak from either Treasury or the White House on a daily basis. My weekly meetings with Kashkari started to follow a script: I would complain about being kept in the dark about the program, and Kashkari would claim that because nothing had been decided, there was nothing yet for him to tell us. I told him repeatedly that I had enormous concerns about the leaked structure of the program.

"For some of these ideas, I really don't think there would be anything we could do to protect them from fraud. They may make sense from the markets' perspective, but from my vantage point, you could be looking at Hurricane Katrina–like losses from fraud," I told Kashkari, referring to the massive fraud losses that the federal government had suffered in providing hurricane relief. His response was to assure me that once they had a plan in mind, we would have an opportunity to be briefed and share our views.

That never happened. Instead, late on a Thursday afternoon, March 19, 2009, we were told that PPIP would be announced the following Monday. At the briefing on Friday, Kashkari made clear that the program was going to be announced as planned, regardless of any objections or recommendations we might have.

As Treasury finally walked us through the details of the different programs and subprograms that would form PPIP, the fraud risks jumped out at us. Although it was going to be funded overwhelmingly with taxpayer dollars, PPIP had been designed by Wall Street, for Wall Street. We only later learned, in connection with one of our audits, that at the same time that Treasury had been keeping us in the dark, it had been working on the design of the program with BlackRock and the Trust Company of the West Group (TCW), two of the giant investment houses that would later manage funds under the program and stand to profit from it the most.[22] A third, Pacific Investment Management Company (PIMCO), also participated in program design and applied to run a PPIP fund but then later withdrew its application.[23] When we finally saw the program details, it was obvious why Treasury had kept us out of the loop: there was no way we could have signed off on it.

PPIP was split into two subprograms. The first, called the "legacy loan" program, proposed spending $500 billion to $1 trillion alongside private investors to buy pools of underperforming loans still sitting on bank balance sheets. The program's rules would encourage private investors to put up about 8 percent of the money, with TARP and the FDIC funding the rest. Most of the government's stake would be in the form of nonrecourse loans (the type that the investors could walk away from at any time), and the government would be entitled to only half of the potential profits despite having up to 92 percent of the exposure to losses. In our April report to Congress, we described the program's risks.[24] The FDIC eventually walked away from the TARP piece of the program entirely.[25]

The heart of Geithner's proposal, however, was in the second part, the "legacy securities" program, which was the realization of Lee Sachs's goal back in January to "go big" on the toxic assets still clogging the banks' arteries. The program was to be run by Treasury in tandem with TALF, which was run by the Fed. It would start with a handful of preselected private fund managers, who would raise a sum of private funds. Treasury would then match the private amount raised, dollar for dollar, and then lend additional TARP money through nonrecourse loans to the funds, each of which would be called a Public-Private Investment Fund. Depending on the amount of the loan, Treasury would put in either two-thirds or three-quarters of the money into the fund but again would have rights to only half of its profits. Once fully funded with taxpayer and private money, the private fund manager would be able to use the combined funds as the "haircut" to acquire a far larger nonrecourse loan from the Federal Reserve, via TALF, to buy legacy mortgage-backed securities. In other words, the private fund manager could use one TARP program that was massively leveraged with taxpayer funds and then leverage it again *through another TARP program* that itself was massively leveraged with taxpayer money. That "leverage on leverage" gave Wall Street a huge potential upside for profits while leaving the taxpayer on the hook for massive potential losses.

The rules issued by Treasury as to what assets could be bought were relatively simple; the primary restriction, once again relying on the credit-rating agencies, was that the mortgage-backed bonds must have *originally* been rated AAA, even if they had since been significantly downgraded.[26]

As we pored over the details of the program and asked a few questions, it became clear that Geithner and his team must have been so desperate to get toxic assets off the banks' balance sheets that they hadn't adequately considered the potential for massive taxpayer losses from fraud. As we began to voice our concerns, they returned to their "reputational risk" argument; they seemed to honestly believe that their Wall Street brothers wouldn't take advantage of the flaws in the program to profit at the government's expense.

When I had first voiced my objections to Congress about TALF's potential expansion to residential mortgage-backed securities, it had been primarily because I didn't think the program would be able to cope with the threat from fraud that came with purchasing mortgage bonds that were nearly impossible to value. The proposed PPIP structure increased that risk exponentially. At least under the existing version of TALF, the investors had to meet the small skin-in-the-game down payment *with their own money*. What Treasury proposed here would undermine even that most basic protection by allowing the fund manager to apply TARP money to cover up to *two-thirds* of that haircut. In other words, with a 5 percent haircut, a purely private party had to put $5 up in order to get a $95 nonrecourse TALF loan, which in and of itself presented great dangers. But a PPIP fund could put up just $1.67 of private money to get an additional $98.33 in Fed and Treasury buying power. Even if the haircut were quadrupled to 20 percent, the taxpayer would still be on the hook for more than 93 percent of potential losses.

In addition to this massive taxpayer-provided leverage, we saw other serious problems with PPIP. First, Treasury was conferring upon the managers of the funds the ability to drive up the prices of individual bonds in an otherwise frozen market. With up to $1 trillion in purchasing power, the managers could pick and choose which bond prices they wanted to drive up by buying them and later, by selling them off, which ones they wanted to drive down. For funds that already had those types of bonds in their portfolio—and Treasury stated as one if its applicant criteria that a fund should have at least $10 billion in such "eligible assets" already under management[27]—this created enormous opportunities for illicit profits.

All a fund manager had to do to book instant profits was to use the government-supplied market-moving purchasing power to drive up the prices of the bonds already in his private portfolios. When the prices shot up, the manager could sell off the bonds from other accounts at the inflated price or take home fee income from the paper profits in the private accounts. The taxpayer, however, could eventually lose out, because the manager had an incentive to intentionally overpay for a bond with government money in order to drive up its price. Over time, market forces would eventually push the price back down to the bond's actual value, leaving the manager with profits and the taxpayer with a loss in the PPIP funds. PPIP thus had the potential of giving the fund managers picked by Treasury an unfair advantage over the rest of the market. They could literally pick winners and losers; and for those winners, there would be a tremendous payday.

The program was also ripe for collusion because the buyer and seller of the bonds could agree to an inflated price and secretly split the profits, while the taxpayer was left to take the losses. Or there could even be buyer-buyer collusion, with different PPIP fund managers bidding up prices on behalf of one another to generate profits for other parts of their business, a type of fraud that would be extremely difficult to detect. Yet another potential problem was money laundering. Treasury told us that it didn't plan to check the books and records of the investors in the individual PPIP funds. Kevin, who had been one of the leading money-laundering prosecutors in the country, saw a real danger that Treasury could end up unknowingly laundering money for organized criminal enterprises. If even one PPIP investor was later found to be dirty, the damage to TARP's reputation would be incalculable.

We saw Geithner's Financial Stability Plan for what it was: an unprecedented trillion-dollar playground for fraud and self-dealing. We quickly put recommendations together to address the most obvious flaws in PPIP and the newly expanded TALF. They included requiring the Fed to do its own analysis of each RMBS bond that it lent money against to avoid getting stuck with bonds backed by the most fraud-riddled loans, such as the completely undocumented "liar loans." We also recommended that Treasury require each participating fund manager to erect a strict ethical wall within the firm between the team that was managing the PPIP fund and other parts of the company that dealt with other similar investment funds.

This last recommendation shouldn't have been controversial at all. The Fed often imposed such walls in its own bailout programs, including a remarkably similar program in which it hired fund managers to buy RMBS issued by Fannie Mae and Freddie Mac. Treasury also required walls for the asset managers it hired to oversee its own growing portfolio of TARP assets.[28] In both instances, those who worked on the government projects could not participate in or have access to any other parts of their companies that could be influenced by the market-moving decisions they made with taxpayer money.

Nonetheless, neither that nor many of our other recommendations was received warmly, to say the least. Treasury's tone alternated between condescension and outright anger. It argued that our recommendations would gut the announced programs, but I had little patience for its arguments: I had been warning Sachs and Kashkari for months that I had deep concerns about the programs and that keeping us in the dark about them could result in programs that simply could not be protected from fraud. They totally ignored my warnings, and I wasn't about to bless flawed programs simply because they hadn't come up with workable alternatives.

THE HURRIED ROLLOUT of HAMP would soon bring with it a rash of misconduct and criminal activity, which would become a major part of our work. Treasury's bungling of HAMP and its refusal to heed our warnings and those of the other TARP oversight bodies resulted in the program harming many of the people it was supposed to help.

In late spring 2009, our auditors started doing some preliminary fieldwork, taking a long, hard look at how the program was being rolled out. By early July, we launched a formal audit, as there were already indications that the mortgage servicers on which Treasury so heavily relied were unequipped to carry out the program effectively.[29]

We soon verified what we had suspected: Treasury had failed to ensure that the servicers had the necessary infrastructure to support a massive mortgage modification program. Their business models were built around processing mortgage payments and implementing foreclosures, not modifying mortgages. They had been as caught off guard as we were by the president's February announcement and were completely unprepared for the deluge of requests following his speech. Worse, though Treasury provided various "directives" to the servicers, they shifted constantly, making compliance all but impossible. Documentation guidelines, for example, were changed routinely, exacerbating a quickly emerging problem with the servicers's incompetent handling of borrower documents.[30]

Another big problem was that Treasury kept changing the terms by which servicers had to evaluate borrowers for modifications. These terms were called the Net Present Value (NPV) test, which was supposed to indicate what made more economic sense for the investor who owned the loan, modification (which would result in a test result of "NPV positive") or foreclosure ("NPV negative"). Under HAMP, if the NPV test for a particular loan was positive, the servicer was *required* to offer a modification. But Treasury couldn't figure out the right formula for the test, which was at the heart of its entire program, changing it *nine* times in the first year alone.[31] That led to further confusion and in at least one instance to the doubling of the time necessary for the servicer to run the test.[32]

With the servicers so ill equipped to process and implement the program, it barely got off the ground. The initial low participation numbers caused Treasury officials to panic, making things even worse. They threatened the servicers with public denunciation if they didn't increase their numbers dramatically and called them to Washington over the summer for a very public scolding. They then set a goal of 500,000 preliminary or "trial" modifications by November 1, 2009. To meet that goal, Treasury pressured the servicers to dispense entirely with our paperwork recommendations and turn to the exact same tactic used by the banks in the lead-up to the financial crisis: undocumented "verbal" trial modifications.[33] For "verbals," the servicer could put the borrower into a trial modification based on a single telephone call but couldn't convert it into a "permanent" HAMP modification (at which point Treasury would start paying incentives) until the servicer received and processed all of the underlying documents.[34]

The no-doc liar loans of 2006 might have rightly gone the way of the dinosaurs, but now Treasury was pushing the servicers to issue their 2009 equivalent: no-doc trial modifications. Though we had advocated requiring trial modifications as a way to prevent fraud, we had never intended for Treasury to grant them on an undocumented basis. As we would later discover, that would create a tidal wave of misery for struggling borrowers.

FORTUNATELY, TREASURY'S ROLLOUT of PPIP, unlike that of HAMP, was delayed by months. The Treasury team needed to select fund managers from among the more than one hundred applicants seeking to become one of the lucky nine who would be granted the program's remarkable profit opportunity. That extra time was a godsend. If Geithner's projections for the programs were correct, never in the country's history would the government be pushing so much money out in such a short period of time with so few protections in place. The extra time gave us a chance to appeal to Treasury, Congress, the FDIC, and the Fed to force the adoption of strong antifraud provisions.

Kevin and I wrote strongly worded warnings about the problems in our April report to Congress, and we also went on a press offensive.

At first, I'd been cautious with the press. I'd spoken to only a handful of newspapers and refused all television interviews. Part of my reluctance was due to the warnings I had heard from other IGs; I didn't want to lose credibility by appearing to be a "press whore." But the immediate effect of the relatively moderate press coverage of our first congressional hearing—getting the Fed to take our concerns about TALF seriously—impressed me. Kevin and Kris had been strongly urging me to talk to the press more, and I decided it was now time, as I recalled Bill Burck's advice from my fourth day on the job that I had a "bully pulpit" and a limited window of time in which to use it. Kris set up profiles with *The Washington Post, The New York Times,* and *The Wall Street Journal.* Any reluctance I had totally disappeared when Kris came to me with the following question from a newspaper reporter: "Is SIGTARP oversight preventing banks from participating in and killing the TARP program?" The question had obviously been planted by officials at Treasury, probably to get us to back down. I had to engage.

The *Journal* helped our case—at least with respect to deterring Wall Street criminals—by titling its piece "Mr. Barofsky, the TARP Cop, Gets into Role as Street Tough" and portraying me as something of a crusader, reporting that I kept the FARC bayonet knife on my desk and quoting an anonymous "government official" as saying "He thinks he's Eliot Ness."[35] The article also quoted sources from Wall Street saying, in essence, that my aggressive approach to investigations was scaring the bejeezus out of them.[36] In the *Post* article, unnamed Wall Street executives and Treasury officials described me as "an overreaching zealot scaring banks from joining the financial rescue."[37] And, on the lighter side, the article quoted Kevin's welcome to the reporter who visited our malodorous offices: "I think the Treasury people stuck dead fish in the rafters."[38] (Kevin's wife was less than thrilled that that was Kevin's first on-the-record quote at SIGTARP. I thought it was hilarious.)

The articles proved to be devastatingly effective, helping to convey what Hank Paulson would later tell me was one of SIGTARP's greatest achievements: a strong message of deterrence and letting the public know that someone was on guard protecting their interests.

We began to gather momentum. Sports teams get it. Political campaigns get it. Now SIGTARP had it. With the release of our April report, we decided we'd go truly big with the press about our concerns with Treasury's $2 trillion plans. I did a whirlwind of television and newspaper interviews. Our message was simple: Treasury's desperate attempt to bail out Wall Street was setting the country up for potentially catastrophic losses.

We also highlighted our law enforcement efforts, including a new initiative I'd put together for a TALF-PPIP law enforcement task force, chaired by me and including the FBI, SEC, ICE, IRS, and others. I wanted to let potential fraudsters know that we were bringing out the heavy hitters of white-collar criminal enforcement. Our deterrence message was reinforced by our first arrest on the same night the report came out— April 21, 2009—of the Ponzi-scheming Gordon Grigg.

Congress quickly reacted to our report. The day it was issued, at about 5 p.m., I got word that Democratic Senator Barbara Boxer's staff was introducing a bill that would give us an additional $20 million to investigate conflicts of interest and possible collusion in PPIP and TALF. The bill was introduced the very next day, and although the amount we were getting was reduced to $15 million, it had a bipartisan group of cosponsors, and it looked as though it could pass quickly.

We had a congressional hearing in front of the Joint Economic Committee a couple of days later. I became a bit nervous when it was Representative Elijah Cummings's turn to question me. He had a reputation of being a tough questioner at these hearings (having once suggested that Kashkari was a "chump"), and he seemed to seethe with a boiling intensity as he waited his turn. After I explained the myriad ways in which taxpayers could be victimized and fund managers unjustly enriched under PPIP, Cummings asked me what other types of unforeseen circumstances could flow from the advantages that Treasury sought to confer on its fund managers. I explained that I worried that if PPIP led to fundamentally unfair results, it could result in the American people losing ever more faith and trust in their government. "[I]t could damage the psyche of the American people," I said.[39]

Cummings bore down on me, looking as if he were about to take my head off. He then said slowly, emphasizing each word, "I agree with every syllable that you just said."[40]

Whew! I thought. The rest of the hearing followed a similar course, with the members of the committee expressing deep concerns about the issues raised in our report.

That same night Lori told me that another bill, this one proposed by Republican Senator John Ensign, was about to get dropped. It was essentially a cut and paste of our PPIP recommendations. Lori would work with the staffs of both Senators Ensign and Boxer to combine their two bills, resulting in what became known as the "Ensign-Boxer Amendment," which would eventually be attached to an already pending bill related to housing.

Although our arguments may have convinced Congress, Treasury still wouldn't budge. If anything, as we delivered our recommendations to Treasury in the weeks leading up to the April report, Kashkari and his team only became further entrenched in their positions. They also started to find more mischievous ways to try to undercut our effectiveness, which became particularly pressing as we started our first probe of the bailout of the insurance giant AIG.

8

Foaming the Runway

ON MARCH 14, 2009, the news broke that Treasury had authorized the insurance giant AIG to pay $168 million in "retention bonuses" to employees in its Financial Products division, the very unit whose reckless bets had brought down the company. Taxpayers had put up $170 billion (including $40 billion from TARP) to keep AIG's collapse from precipitating a meltdown of the global financial system, and now the executives from the division that had caused its ruin were going to be paid lavishly.

The news triggered an explosion of outrage. While I was getting coffee early that week in the Treasury cafeteria, I looked up at the television to see Senator Grassley calling on the AIG executives to either quit or commit suicide,[1] and that was probably one of the more muted reactions from Congress. For those on the left, the payments represented more evidence of Treasury's betrayal of the public in administering TARP. While home owners continued to get pummeled by the foreclosure crisis with no meaningful relief in sight, the executives at AIG at the unit most responsible for requiring a taxpayer bailout in the first place were now getting *bonus* payments of up to $6.4 million (with twenty-two executives receiving at least $2 million each),[2] all effectively paid for by the taxpayer. For those on the right, the payments encapsulated everything that they saw wrong about the government's policy of "corporate welfare," which seemed to endlessly reward failure. They were both right.

Although Congress had recently passed legislation that imposed stricter rules limiting bonus payments that could be paid by TARP recipients to their executives, the bill also contained a little noticed clause. It exempted payments, such as those made by AIG, that had already been promised in contracts already in effect when the legislation was passed.[3] Treasury had given AIG the green light, in part, because of this provision.

The team at Treasury was aware that the payments would provoke a storm in the press, but, as was becoming increasingly typical in Treasury's dealings with us, I found out about the payments only after the fact. TARP's compliance officer told me about them on the evening they were made, with a warning that Treasury was bracing for "a lot of negative publicity."

While the public comments by Treasury officials mirrored the anger expressed by Congress, the internal response was far different. When we discussed the payments with Kashkari and the TARP team, they didn't seem to begrudge the AIG executives the bonuses at all. They told us that the payments were necessary to keep the "uniquely" qualified executives in their jobs to do the delicate work of unwinding the enormous mess they had created. As to the reaction from Congress, Kashkari dismissed it as being "political."

By that point, Kevin and I were used to these types of reactions from Treasury. The Wall Street fiction that certain financial executives were preternaturally gifted supermen who deserved every penny of their staggering paychecks and bonuses was firmly ingrained in Treasury's psyche. No matter that the financial crisis had demonstrated just how unremarkable the work of those executives had turned out to be, that belief system endured at Treasury across administrations. If a Wall Street executive was contracted to receive a $6.4 million "retention" bonus, the assumption was that he must be worth it.

The abject fetishization of the lords of high finance became even more apparent as we conducted an audit of the process by which the "pay czar," Kenneth Feinberg, determined the pay for the top executives at AIG, Citigroup, Bank of America, and a handful of other institutions that needed TARP assistance in order to survive. A brilliant lawyer with a thick Boston accent, Feinberg was known as the consummate moderator, and he had been brought in to help mediate some of the nation's most contro-

versial settlements, including determining compensation for the families
of the victims of the September 11 attacks. A colorful character, Feinberg
had a unique way with words, as I learned shortly after Senator Grassley
asked us to review a potential conflict of interest on the part of one of the
lawyers on Feinberg's team. I received a telephone call that the caller ID
indicated came from the Treasury Building. When I picked up the phone
someone with a thick Boston accent declared "Neil, it's fucking McCar-
thyism!" It took me a second to realize it was Feinberg.

He came under intense pressure from the TARP recipients, who
showed no shame in pushing for ever-higher salary awards. More note-
worthy, however, was the pressure exerted by several Treasury officials,
who also pushed to increase the value of the pay packages.[4] Kashkari's
successor, Herb Allison, became particularly involved in Feinberg's delib-
erations over AIG executive pay, speaking regularly with AIG's CEO and
then advancing the company's arguments while lobbying Feinberg to
change his determinations.[5]

The March 2009 AIG bonus payments were the most provocative of
any of the pay decisions the government made. There were immediate
calls for congressional hearings, and the House quickly passed a bill that
called for a 90 percent tax on bonuses for TARP recipients that received
more than $5 billion (it did not pass the Senate).[6] There were even reports
flying around Washington of death threats against AIG executives. Before
long, we received requests from both the House and the Senate to initiate
an audit on Treasury's role in approving the bonuses, and within a week
we were gathering documents and information. When asked at a hearing
if we would determine whether Geithner had known about the bonuses, I
said that we would find out "who knew what, when, how and why."[7] It was
a poor choice of words. I had forgotten that that phrase was a sensitive
one in Washington, invoking memories of Senator Howard Baker asking
similar questions about President Nixon during the nationally televised
Watergate hearings.[8] The press seized on my comment, reporting that
my selection of those words was surely intended to "send a chill up Tim
Geithner's spine."[9]

The controversy provoked by the bonus payments flowed from the
visceral anger about the extraordinary rescue of AIG. The once proud
icon of stability had been felled by the unbridled greed and hubris of its

relatively small and previously obscure Financial Products division. The division, headed by Joseph Cassano, had enthusiastically joined the mid-decade mortgage mania by staking out its own special corner of the financial universe through something called credit default swaps (CDS). Those "derivatives" were financial products whose value wasn't in the form of tangible assets but instead derived from the performance of the credit default obligations (CDOs) at the heart of the crisis.

Credit default swaps were bets on whether CDOs would default or not, that is whether the thousands of borrowers whose mortgages backed any given CDO would continue to make their monthly payments. They were essentially insurance policies for bonds: AIG offered contracts to the megabanks in the United States and Europe providing that, in return for a series of premiumlike payments, AIG would "provide protection" for a particular CDO bond. The contracts required AIG to pay out if "a credit default event" occurred, which would happen only if the CDO wasn't able to make its required payments. In a little-noticed provision, however, AIG's obligations under the contracts would change in the event (unfathomable at the time that they were written) that its own platinum credit rating was downgraded.

When the housing market was booming, AIG thought it was essentially collecting free money from the banks. AIG issued credit default swap contracts only on the highest-ranked AAA portions of the CDOs, and, like the rating agencies and the big banks, AIG's models all indicated that its risk of loss was almost zero. All of the premiumlike fees it charged for the credit default swaps added up to serious profits, with the Financial Products division reportedly booking $2.5 billion in profits in 2005 alone.[10] Cassano even declared as late as August 2007, "It is hard for us, without being flippant, to even see a scenario within any kind of realm of reason that would see us losing one dollar in any of those transactions."[11]

But, of course, there was such a scenario. Whereas insurance policies are subject to tight regulations to make sure that there is plenty of money on hand to pay out in the event of a loss, CDS contracts aren't covered by these regulations. As derivative contracts, they were exempted from regulation by a law passed during the waning days of the Clinton administration,[12] and as a result, AIG had no obligation to keep any given level of cash on hand in case it had to pay out on its contracts.

The problem began to become apparent in the latter part of 2007 when the housing bubble burst. As AIG's financial condition began to deteriorate, the credit-rating agencies initiated a series of downgrades of the company's credit rating. Those downgrades, in turn, triggered clauses in many of AIG's CDS contracts that required the company to pay out cash "collateral" to the CDS counterparties—those with which it had signed the contracts—if the CDOs insured started to lose value. As borrowers across the country began missing their mortgage payments, the previously AAA-rated CDOs began to falter, leading the rating agencies to downgrade the bonds. As a result of those downgrades, along with the CDOs' plummeting market prices, AIG suddenly had to provide massive amounts of cash collateral to its large bank counterparties. As the panic picked up toward the end of 2007, AIG was buried under an avalanche of collateral demands.

The volume of cash required to meet these demands was astonishing. Assume that a bond that had been trading for $100 dropped to $70. AIG would then have to post $30 of collateral. Because the cash was viewed as collateral, not a payout, if the bond's price subsequently rose, the banks would have to send a portion of the cash back to AIG. In 2007–2008, however, CDO prices were headed only down, and with each price drop, AIG had to send the banks more cash. In the year leading up to September 30, 2008, the company was required to post more than $55 billion in collateral to its counterparties.[13] Because of the regulatory loophole, it didn't have to keep reserves against the risk of payout, and as a result it just didn't have the necessary cash to meet the unending demands.

By mid-September 2008, AIG was just about out of money, and with yet another downgrade imminent, an enormous new bill for more collateral payments was about to come due. On the Friday before the same weekend that Geithner, Bernanke, and Paulson were desperately trying to stave off the imminent collapse of Lehman Brothers, New York Fed officials were told that there was a good chance that AIG would run out of money and be unable to make those payments the following week, which would have plunged the company into bankruptcy.[14] After Lehman declared bankruptcy the following Monday, panic swept the globe. Frightened by the consequences for the global financial system if an institution as large and interconnected as AIG was allowed to follow Lehman into bankruptcy court, on September 16, 2008, the Federal Reserve extended AIG an $85 billion line of credit in return for nearly 80 percent of its stock. AIG thus effectively became a ward of the state.

The fact that just six months later individual executives from the very division that had visited this catastrophe on AIG were being paid huge bonuses out of taxpayer funds violated all principles of propriety and fairness. It was no wonder that Congress asked us to investigate. My auditors threw themselves into the job, and they were preparing for their interviews of Treasury personnel when we were struck by a direct assault on our status as an independent agency.

With Hoyt gone, Geithner and Obama had no permanent Treasury general counsel, and a series of lawyers cycled through the job as acting general counsel. One was an affable career attorney named Bernie Knight, who stopped by my office one afternoon.

"So, Neil, do you think SIGTARP is inside or outside of Treasury?" Knight asked.

Kevin was in my office, and we shot each other quizzical looks. *What now?* I wondered.

"In, obviously. Just look at our badges and the official Treasury seal on our reports," I said. "Of course we are part of Treasury. Why do you ask, Bernie?"

"Well, you said at a hearing recently that you report to Congress, not the secretary." Bernie responded.

"That's true, Bernie. We're required to provide reports to Congress, but that doesn't put us outside of Treasury," I said.

"But do you view yourself as under the secretary's supervision?" Bernie asked

"I'm not sure what that means. But the answer is no if you're asking me if I report to him. I think Congress was pretty clear that I'm independent. But does it really matter? Why do you ask?" I said.

"Well, we were thinking that if you don't report to the secretary, then you may not be in Treasury." Bernie then explained that if we were outside of Treasury, he was worried that providing us with privileged information might be used as a rationale for others to get access to protected documents and communications.

"But we're in Treasury, and we're entitled to full access to *any* material, privileged or otherwise," I responded.

"Okay, thanks," Bernie said as he left my office.

"What the fuck was *that* all about?" I asked Kevin. Kevin just shook his head. We chalked it up to just another odd moment on planet SIGTARP. We soon found out the reason behind Knight's visit.

I got an e-mail from him on the night before our auditors were scheduled to interview the lawyer at Treasury responsible for handling the AIG bonus issue. I had earlier been told that Treasury was seeking to postpone the interview, and in his e-mail Knight repeated his concern about Treasury not being able to protect privileged information disclosed during SIGTARP's interviews of Treasury personnel if we were in fact not part of Treasury. Knight explained that he had decided to seek clarification from the Department of Justice as to whether SIGTARP was within Treasury, and, if so, whether I reported to the secretary.

I blew a gasket. I couldn't believe that Treasury was actually trying to avoid answering questions about the bonus payments by using this ridiculous theory. I was even more concerned about why it was suddenly also seeking clarification of whether I "reported" to Geithner. I fired off an e-mail to Knight, threatening to notify Congress that Treasury was using an absurd argument to obstruct our audit into the bonuses. Treasury quickly backed down on the interview but still insisted on going to DOJ to get a ruling on our status. I directed my chief counsel, Bryan Saddler, to prepare a response and asked him to figure out what the implications would be if DOJ ruled that I "reported" to Geithner.

When Bryan sent over the relevant provisions of the Inspector General Act, I quickly saw what Treasury was up to. Unlike many other departments, Congress gave the secretary of the Treasury a special power with respect to the Treasury IG, and if DOJ ruled that I was subject to that provision, it would mean that for those audits or investigations that "could reasonably be expected to have a significant influence on the economy or market behavior," I would be considered fully "under the authority, direction and control" of Geithner.[15] Even worse, Geithner could kill anything I was working on if he deemed it necessary to "prevent significant impairment to the national interests of the United States."[16] He could make the case that nearly every single thing we did fit under those vague contours.

In other words, if he won his appeal to DOJ, he could potentially direct the conduct of our investigations and the writing of our audit and quarterly reports. Worse still, he might be able to veto nearly every subpoena and report we issued.

Kevin, Bryan, and I all chipped in to write a response to the Department of Justice's Office of Legal Counsel. Kevin and I had filed enough legal briefs between the two of us to know when we had a slam-dunk case, and this was one of them. We cited the statute that had created SIGTARP itself, which we believed clearly established our independence, and also the statements of Senator Baucus while the bill was still being debated. After all, Baucus had written the bill, his committee had jurisdiction over Treasury, and he had said at my confirmation hearing, "You are special. . . . You are independent. You are fully independent."[17]

"Why do you think Bernie is picking this fight with us?" I asked Kevin.

He laughed. "Bernie? There's no way that Bernie is behind this. This is coming from the third floor," he said, referring to the floor where Geithner and some of his senior staff sat.

"But if we lose this, won't Congress rally to our side and just fix the law?" I asked.

"Maybe, but maybe not. In the meantime, they can really screw with us," Kevin observed.

As DOJ continued to drag its feet on its ruling, I started getting increasingly anxious that it might actually decide against us. I called Bill Burck, who had left the White House with the change of administration and was now working at a Washington law firm, to get his take on how serious this was.

"They are totally trying to fuck you," he warned. "Geithner or someone very close to him got it in his head that he can cut your balls off with this and make your life hell. You need to move fast. Before DOJ fucks you, because they will."

He advised that I mobilize Senator Grassley.

We got the word to our friend and Grassley's right hand on oversight issues, Emilia DiSanto, and she asked me to send all the information that I had on the issue. We soon received a similar request from Representative Issa.

Grassley sent a letter to Geithner asking for all documents relating to the matter, and within what seemed like minutes of our sending the information over to Issa, he issued a press release entitled "AIG Investigation Must Move Forward Without Interference from Treasury."[18] The press had a field day. Even the *Wall Street Journal* editorial board weighed in, this time in a sarcastic call to "Abolish the Inspector General,"[19] accusing the administration of hypocrisy in seeking control over SIGTARP.

Grassley was relentless in pursuing the issue, using his perch as top Republican on the Senate Finance Committee to tie Treasury's nominee for general counsel, George Madison, in knots with waves of questions about whether, if confirmed, he would respect SIGTARP's independence. As the Senate went into its summer recess with Madison still not confirmed, Treasury finally withdrew its request to DOJ. Of course, no one at Treasury or DOJ bothered to tell us, and we only found out about a month later from a member of the press.[20]

Unfortunately, that was hardly the only way in which the Treasury team tried to interfere with our efforts.

WE HAD SOME moderate hope that our relations with Treasury might improve after Kashkari stepped down in late April. He was gracious in his departure, stopping by our Gallatin conference room to pick up extra copies of the bound reports and complimenting us on how comprehensive they were. Though I'd had my run-ins with Kashkari, I found myself surprisingly conflicted about his departure. Sure, he was combative, not always forthcoming, and excessively deferential to Wall Street, but Kashkari had generally been straightforward with me. I don't think he ever flat-out lied to me, which in Washington put him into rarefied air. I have no idea if he felt similarly, but I had a grudging respect for him. I thought of our disagreements as just that: differences of opinion passionately held by two people with very different worldviews. But I never questioned his deeply patriotic commitment to his job. He had made great personal sacrifices, and as he left Treasury, I congratulated him on his service and for his significant role in helping to prevent a complete collapse of our financial system.

I even felt empathy for him after a front-page *Washington Post* piece appeared about eight months later. The article—accompanied by a photograph of a wild-eyed Kashkari chopping wood while building a cabin near Lake Tahoe—painted him as a scarred victim of post-traumatic stress disorder from his days in Washington.[21] Kashkari, of course, landed on his feet and soon announced that he was taking a high-level position at PIMCO. (The revolving door between Treasury and the giant investment funds and banks just never stops spinning.)

In any event, we thought his replacement, Herb Allison, might be a considerable improvement.

Allison was in many ways Kashkari's opposite. Unlike us thirty-some-things who had been running TARP and SIGTARP, Allison, at sixty-five, was at the end of his career. He was a lifetime product of Wall Street, having spent twenty-eight years at Merrill Lynch, where he served as its treasurer, chief financial officer, chief operating officer, and president. He left Merrill in 2002 to become CEO of the giant pension manager TIAA-CREF, and retired in 2008 as a very wealthy man. Allison's retirement was cut short in September of that year, however, when Paulson offered him the job of CEO and president of Fannie Mae as Treasury put it into conservatorship. Allison accepted and served in that job until President Obama nominated him to run TARP.

Though Allison certainly wasn't going to provide any diversity from the Wall Street echo chamber at Treasury, he was at least an adult. We were also hopeful that his many years on Wall Street might provide him with a degree of skepticism about his former colleagues' motives that was sorely missing at Treasury. It was also clear that he wasn't going to be using his TARP service as a springboard to a job on Wall Street; he had already retired from that life.

Allison opened our first meeting by telling me how my name was regularly trashed at Treasury but emphasizing that he was ready to rise above all that and start with a clean slate. His plan was to bring more discipline to TARP: he wanted to "out-SIGTARP SIGTARP." I responded by reviewing some of the problems with Kashkari that we hoped to avoid.

Whatever hopes I took away from the meeting about establishing better relations were soon dashed. In May, I headed off on my belated honeymoon to South Africa, which had been rescheduled as part of my negotiated settlement with Karen when I took the job. When I landed, I got the good news that the Ensign-Boxer amendment on PPIP and TALF had passed the Senate, 96–0[22] and that it now very clearly stipulated that Treasury would have to consult with SIGTARP on our concerns about PPIP.[23]

I smiled as I read the message. Though the requirements of the statute were mostly advisory, Congress was nonetheless *forcing* the Treasury team to consult with us before issuing new rules or regulations for the program. It could still reject our recommendations, but the bill required it to explain to Congress why it had done so. The bill still had to pass the House, but Lori reported that its prospects looked good.

Then Treasury leapt into action. Knowing that I was on the other side of the world, Treasury officials started to work their contacts on the Hill to try to kill or amend the bill. Lori, again proving that putting her in charge of our legislative affairs was one of the best decisions I'd made at SIGTARP, was able wrangle from the staffers Treasury's pitch against the bill.

The complaints came straight out of the big banks' lobbying playbook. When the Wall Street lobbyists descend on Capitol Hill to work against regulation that might rein in their ability to earn rapacious profits, they stick to a pretty consistent script. A key tactic is to argue that issues relating to high finance are so hopelessly complex that it is nearly impossible for mere mortals to understand the unintended consequences of the legislation. The advocates of such regulation, the argument goes, just don't have the requisite experience to understand the complex markets and the negative unintended consequences that would supposedly flow from their proposals. Those arguments were advanced when Wall Street convinced Congress to prevent derivatives from being regulated,[24] and they were repeated in the debates over financial regulatory reform under the Dodd-Frank Act.

Given that Geithner had hired former Goldman Sachs managing director and "top lobbyist" Mark Patterson to be his chief of staff,[25] it should have been no surprise that Treasury rolled out the tactic to try to shoot down the Ensign-Boxer amendment. The staffers told Lori that Treasury's chief complaint was that it didn't want to have to be forced to work with us "because SIGTARP does not understand financial markets." Treasury also argued that our office was made up of "rogue cop types" and that we didn't have the ability to understand the complex concepts that they had tried, unsuccessfully, to explain to us. When I asked Lori to find out who was making this pitch, she responded that her contacts had said that it didn't matter who the Treasury official was, "because they are just relaying information from higher up." Lori interpreted this as meaning that the directions were coming from Geithner himself, although she didn't know for sure.

A delegation of Treasury officials was heading to Capitol Hill the next day for a meeting with staffers to argue against the amendment, and Lori was able to wrangle an invitation to the meeting so that we could defend ourselves. Kevin would go on my behalf, and the staffers in charge of setting up the meeting weren't going to tell Treasury we'd be there. If the Treasury team thought they could take advantage of my absence, they were in for a rude surprise when they ran into Kevin. Underestimating me was understandable, but underestimating Kevin was just stupid.

As expected, Treasury's representatives were seriously thrown off by the fact that Kevin was there to respond to their arguments. Kevin's cogent defenses of the positions that we had taken reassured the staffers that we had experienced and sophisticated lawyers on hand who knew Wall Street and understood how the markets work. After we agreed to a few minor changes, the amendment passed Congress and was signed into law a few days after I got back from South Africa.

I was furious that Allison had sent his officials to Congress to trash us behind our backs; I felt it was a bad-faith attempt to take advantage of my absence. It was one thing to engage in a spirited and respectful debate over important issues, I told Allison in our first meeting after I came back, but running to the Hill and calling us names while I was out of the country was juvenile. Allison didn't even try to defend the political maneuvering, saying that because the Senate had not yet confirmed him, he hadn't been able to control the situation. Unfortunately, things did not change much after his confirmation, and the intransigence that Treasury continued to show toward our efforts to limit the potential abuses in TARP, even as problems continued to bubble up, seemed to marry a callous indifference toward the public interest to an almost slavish bias toward Wall Street.

At least the new law forced Treasury to work with us on antifraud and conflict-of-interest provisions for PPIP and TALF, and the urgency was made all the more apparent by the mess we were continuing to see unfold following our far more limited input on those issues in HAMP. After just a few months, we were already seeing a rash of just the kinds of abuses we had feared, and even as a program that was supposedly designed to stem foreclosures unleashed a new wave of misery on home owners, none of our urgings could make the Treasury team make a serious effort to address the program's obvious failings.

My understanding of the duplicitous nature of the world I now inhabited further sharpened when I ran into one of Treasury's legislative officials in late May while walking down one of Treasury's spiral staircases, fuming from my latest scrimmage with Allison. The official stopped me and gave me a lengthy discourse on how he had learned—confidentially, of course—just how much Elizabeth Warren hated me, was jealous of me, and was plotting my demise. I knew that not a word he was saying was true, but I just thanked him for the heads-up and took off.

It was revolting. This was clearly an attempt to drive a wedge between Elizabeth and me. Much as Treasury had leaked negative stories about me "scaring away" banks from TARP, such stories had recently sprung up about Elizabeth, suggesting that she was a "Cassandra" whose criticisms of TARP "could undermine already tenuous support" for the bailouts.[26]

That incident extinguished the last shred of hope that I had for better dealings with the new administration. If anything, this group was proving to be far worse. Kashkari and his crew might have driven me nuts, but at least when they had attacked me, it was generally head-on. The first thing I did when I got back to my office was to arrange for a call with Elizabeth. If Treasury was spreading lies like this about her to me, God only knew what messages they might be sending about me to her.

We exchanged congratulations on our respective recent reports and commiserated about the "anonymous" comments about us in the press and how little change there had been between the Paulson and Geithner regimes. We also discussed Treasury's obstinance on different transparency issues, including our common cause of getting Geithner to require banks to report on how they were using TARP funds. I proposed that we work on a joint project, and Elizabeth agreed that it was a good idea. We decided to do a review of how Treasury was dealing with selling back to the banks warrants—options that allowed it to purchase shares of the banks' common stock at a certain price—that it had received from the banks as part of the CPP transactions. The project was an ideal collaboration: it would bring together the panel's access to academics and economists, to determine if Treasury was getting a good price for the warrants, with our ability to dig into the internal processes used by Treasury. It would also give us an opportunity to send Treasury a strong message that its attempt to create a split in their oversight bodies had failed miserably.

As we were saying our good-byes, Elizabeth told me that I should be paying closer attention to HAMP; she was worried that Treasury didn't know what it was doing and that the program would do little to address the enormous and growing foreclosure crisis.

Treasury's pressure on the mortgage servicers over the summer of 2009 to goose their numbers through hundreds of thousands of unverified "verbal" trial modifications was beginning to produce horrifying results.[27] Our ongoing reports would eventually detail how Treasury's pressure to loosen their up-front documentation requirements had led to the victimization of many home owners.

The flood of trial modifications caused the servicers' systems to first buckle and then break as borrowers seeking to make their modifications permanent flooded the underequipped servicers with millions of pages of documents. The servicers' performance was abysmal: they routinely "lost" or misplaced borrowers' documents, with one servicer telling us that a subcontractor had lost an entire trove of HAMP materials.[28] Borrowers routinely complained that they'd had to send their documents to their servicers multiple times—a survey by ProPublica found that borrowers had to submit documents *on average* six times—but the servicers would still claim that the documents had never been received and then foreclose.[29] The sheer volume also meant that fully qualified borrowers got lost in the storm; servicers would later confess to us that the sheer volume from Treasury's verbal trial modification surge made it nearly impossible for them to separate the modifications that fully qualified and had a chance to be successful from those that were hopeless.[30]

By disregarding our document and verification recommendations, Treasury had needlessly complicated the transition from trial to permanent modification. In order to ensure that the modifications weren't scams, we had proposed trial modifications that would automatically convert to permanent status after three payments over three months. Treasury, however, allowed trial modifications to drag on for an extended period, and it was not unusual for borrowers to be stuck in trials for more than a year. Servicers could put just about any borrowers they chose into verbal trial modifications to pump up their numbers and then could refuse to convert them to permanent status as long as just a single document was supposedly outstanding,

Aggravating the problem was that the design of the program potentially rewarded servicers who "lost" documents: it could be more profitable for a servicer to drag out trial modifications and eventually foreclose than to award the borrowers quick permanent modifications. Mortgage servicers earn profits from fees, particularly late fees, and under HAMP, Treasury allowed mortgage servicers to charge and accrue late fees for each month that borrowers were in trial modifications, even if the borrowers made every single payment under their trial plans. (The rationale was that by not making the full unmodified payment, the borrowers were technically "late" on each payment.) If the modifications were made permanent, Treasury required the servicer to waive the fees, but if the servicer canceled the modifications (say, for example, for the borrowers' alleged failure to provide the necessary documents), the servicer could typically collect all of the accrued late fees once the homes were sold through foreclosure. In other words, servicers could rack up fees by putting home owners into late fee–generating trial modification purgatory and then pulling the rug out from under them by failing their modification for "incomplete documentation," which they did in droves. Indeed, even though Treasury eventually changed its practice of allowing undocumented trial modifications, by early 2012 there were still more HAMP modification failures than successes.

As a further incentive for bad behavior, Treasury gave the servicers permission to take all the preliminary legal steps necessary to foreclose at the exact same time that they were supposedly processing the trial modifications. Though servicers technically weren't supposed to actually foreclose while a trial modification was pending,[31] they reportedly were doing so anyway.[32] Servicers were also apparently demanding up-front payments before putting borrowers into modifications and requiring them to waive all claims and defenses before considering them for one, both blatant violations of program rules.[33]

The abuses didn't stop there, though. One particularly pernicious type of abuse was that servicers would direct borrowers who were current on their mortgages to start skipping payments, telling them that that would allow them to qualify for a HAMP modification. The servicers thereby racked up more late fees, and meanwhile many of these borrowers might have been entitled to participate in HAMP even if they had never missed a payment.[34] Those led to some of the most heartbreaking cases. Home owners who might have been able to ride out the crisis instead ended up in long trial modifications, after which the servicers would deny them a permanent modification and then send them an enormous "deficiency" bill. They were charged for the difference between the modified monthly payments and the original amount of their payments for all of those months, which could be a crippling amount, and were also slapped with a host of late fees. Borrowers who might otherwise never have missed a payment found themselves hit with whopping bills that they couldn't pay and now faced foreclosure.[35] It was a disaster.

Making matters even worse, Treasury all but paved the way for outright fraud by ignoring my recommendation that it kick off HAMP with a broad nationwide television and radio advertising campaign that would educate home owners about program details and warn them of the dangers of program-related fraud. I had begged Treasury to at least run public service announcements in the cities that had seen the highest incidents of fraud in the run-up to the financial crisis, warning that dormant mortgage fraud cells would soon reemerge. They failed to do so, and, as I had predicted, the chaos of HAMP lured a host of criminal predators running fraudulent advertisements for "guaranteed Obama modifications" from coast to coast.

We began doing our best to crack down on them, and one of our earliest criminal convictions came from a case in San Diego brought against the principals of a company called Nations Housing Modification Center. The defendants, who later pled guilty, were charged with running a telemarketing firm that used a mailing address on Capitol Hill and official-looking letterhead to give the impression that they were affiliated with

HAMP. They charged borrowers $2,500 to $3,500 each and did absolutely nothing in return for the close to $1 million that they stole.[36]

Another case took me back to New York to announce charges against the principals of American Home Recovery, which operated a similar scheme in which they were accused with not only charging up-front fees but also telling borrowers to forward to them, instead of to the banks, partial "mortgage payments," which they then pocketed.[37] We helped obtain similar charges in cases around the country.

Our investigation team worked tirelessly, building those cases and working with other agencies to shut down as many of the scams as we could, but it was a game of whack-a-mole that we could never win. A broad early public awareness campaign was the only thing that would have given us a chance to combat the fraud, but Treasury didn't listen about that until it was far too late, not airing its first commercial until the middle of 2010.[38]

Treasury also failed to take action against the servicers themselves. Because most of the abuses we saw coming into our hotline involved accusations that servicers had violated their contracts with Treasury, those fell under Treasury's jurisdiction and there was little we could do other than refer them to Treasury. We did what we could to get the borrowers the help they needed, but ultimately any action against the servicers would have to be brought by Treasury, not us. Treasury, however, demonstrated no interest in taking even the most modest steps to punish them. That was unconscionable, given the pain being inflicted on so many home owners.

One all-too-typical story, reported by David Dayen of the online news site Firedoglake, captures the horror that HAMP visited on so many borrowers.[39] Dayen wrote about Jeremy Fletcher, a swimming pool builder from California. Dayen explained that Fletcher's business had been booming before the housing bubble burst, and in 2007 he moved into a $900,000 home in California. When the housing market crashed, people stopped buying pools, and Fletcher's sales dropped from $250,000 in 2007 to $40,000 in 2008. Dayen reported that by early 2009, Fletcher was broke, "paying for his $4,200 mortgage out of savings and barely hanging on."

After HAMP was announced, Fletcher called Citi Mortgage, his servicer, but Citi rejected Fletcher, telling him that he was not in default. Then, in the summer of 2009, just as Fletcher was considering selling and downsizing, Citi called him out of the blue, offering a HAMP trial modification that would cut his monthly payments nearly in half, to $2,170. As Dayen wrote, "They signed him up over the phone, he made his first payment by ATM card, and that was it. Within a few days, they sent over a modification package that put it in writing: if Fletcher made his trial payments for 90 days, and sent in his application with a full income statement that qualified, 'we will give you a permanent modification.'"

Despite sending in the documents and making all of his new trial payments for a full year, Citi never provided Fletcher with a permanent modification. When Fletcher called the bank, Citi told him that everything was on track and that he should just be patient. Then, without warning, Fletcher got a call from Citi "telling him that he was 12 months due on his loan and owed $15,000." Citi had dropped him from the modification. Though no one that Fletcher spoke to at Citi could explain why, they could tell him that if he didn't pay up in thirty days they were going to take his home.

Fletcher couldn't afford a lawyer but found a friend who agreed to help him out for free. After the lawyer poked around, Fletcher got a call back from someone at Citi who told him that there had been no valid reason for cancelling the modification, he'd "just got lost in the cracks."

Next Citi demanded that Fletcher resubmit his HAMP application paperwork, which he did. Two days after being told by Citi that his paperwork was in order and the modification was about to go through, Fletcher was contacted by Saxon Mortgage, then a subsidiary of Morgan Stanley, which told him that Citi had sold Saxon the loan. It demanded that he make all of the past deficiency payments immediately.

After making a series of calls to Saxon, he found someone who was able to pull up "the history of the now-16-month modification process in her computer." The specialist acknowledged that Saxon had made a "mistake" and told Fletcher to make the modification payments. But a couple of months later, Saxon dropped Fletcher from the HAMP trial modification, wouldn't accept any further payments, and was about to foreclose.

Dayen's article also brought to life the psychic toll that the dehumanizing process often took on borrowers. "'This eats at me every waking moment of every day," Fletcher told him. "The kids wake up every day wondering if they'll have to leave. I think about it when I'm working, when I'm not working I'm on the computer, writing letters, making phone calls. Even when I'm surfing, that was my one respite, now when I'm in the water, I start thinking about it."

The collateral damage went beyond Fletcher's mental state. The servicers reported Fletcher's "delinquency" to the credit-rating agencies, and as a result "his contractor bond could not be renewed because of the credit history. When he finally found an insurer to renew, they charged him 6 times what he had paid before."

The damage HAMP had inflicted on the Fletcher family was astonishing. As Fletcher summed up, "I was thinking, if we didn't get the help from Citi, we could sell the house, we still had savings, a good credit history. We had options." But after the HAMP nightmare, his savings account was drained, his credit history was shot, his home value had plummeted, and his hope had faded. "'It's in the waiting for the modification that everything got bad,' he said."

I REMARKED TO Kevin at one point as the abuses were flooding into our hotline that it seemed as though Treasury simply didn't care about the suffering of so many borrowers. Instead, Treasury officials seemed too busy congratulating themselves on the trial modifications the program was raking up. "The only ones benefitting from this debacle are the banks," Kevin astutely observed. We would eventually discover that that was no mistake. Helping the banks, not home owners, did in fact seem to be Treasury's biggest concern.

We learned that when, later that fall, we were invited to another oversight meeting with Geithner, GAO, and the COP. For a good chunk of our allotted meeting time, Elizabeth Warren grilled Geithner about HAMP, barraging him with questions about how the program was going to start helping home owners. In defense of the program, Geithner finally blurted out, "We estimate that they can handle ten million foreclosures, over time," referring to the banks. "This program will help foam the runway for them."

A lightbulb went on for me. Elizabeth had been challenging Geithner on how the program was going to help home owners, and he had responded by citing how it would help the *banks*. Geithner apparently looked at HAMP as an aid to the banks, keeping the full flush of foreclosures from hitting the financial system all at the same time. Though they could handle up to "10 million foreclosures" over time, any more than that, or if the foreclosures were too concentrated, and the losses that the banks might suffer on their first and second mortgages could push them into insolvency, requiring yet another round of TARP bailouts. So HAMP would "foam the runway" by stretching out the foreclosures, giving the banks more time to absorb losses while the other parts of the bailouts juiced bank profits that could then fill the capital holes created by housing losses.

All of a sudden, bits and pieces of conversations that I had had began to fall into place. Allison had used the phrase "helping them earn their way out of this" during part of a more extended conversation that summer about his worry that the banks could still collapse. HAMP was not separate from the bank bailouts; it was an essential part of them. From that perspective, it didn't matter if the modifications failed after a year or so of trial payments or if struggling borrowers placed into doomed trial modifications ended up far worse off, as long as the banks were able to stretch out their pain until their profits returned.

Geithner's revelation (he apparently similarly told bloggers in 2010 during an off-the-record conversation that HAMP had succeeded in extending out the foreclosure crisis)[40] also helped explain one of the odder aspects of HAMP. For many borrowers, the modifications weren't really all that "permanent." Instead, after five years, the interest rate would be permitted to rise, much like the resetting adjustable rate mortgages of the financial crisis. This meant that within a handful of years after the "permanent" period of HAMP expired, the average borrower whose interest rate had been reduced to the minimum rate during his modification would eventually see his monthly payments rise by 23 percent, possibly putting him once again at risk of default.[41] Though that policy might undermine the long-term success of the program from the borrowers' perspective, it made perfect sense if an immediate "foaming of the runway" for the banks was Treasury's primary goal. For the banks, five years was an eternity.

Unfortunately, once I got a chance to speak, the allotted time for the meeting was running down. I used the time I had to impress on Geithner that the administration was losing credibility through its administration of TARP and that that was a self-inflicted wound that could be healed by being more open and forthright with the public. As we wrapped up the meeting, Geithner came across the room to our side of the table to engage in a round of handshake good-byes. When he approached us, he pointed at Kevin.

"This guy, Kevin, he was glaring at me the whole time. I was getting nervous," Geithner said with more of a smirk than a smile.

As Kevin gave his best fake laugh, I replied with a smile and said, "You should be, I never go anywhere without my muscle."

Unfortunately, my warnings to Geithner at the meeting went unheeded. Treasury's failure to be forthright with the American people would only increase in the coming months, along with the blowback against anyone who tried to challenge what was becoming an increasingly misleading narrative.

9

The Audacity of Math

ONE OF THE most infuriating features of the government's management of the bailouts was the condescension expressed toward the public about the right to know exactly how our money was being used. In my own direct dealings with Treasury, I constantly ran into the view that the public had to be spoon-fed TARP news, usually with an artificial sweetener, because they couldn't possibly be expected to take the time to understand TARP's complexities. I was even told, when I asked for information about how the investment funds set up under the PPIP program were performing so far, that we shouldn't publish the results because the public just wasn't sophisticated enough to understand that they were only preliminary numbers. I couldn't have disagreed more with that patronizing attitude. Just from the remarkable interest we'd seen in our SIGTARP website, I knew that people would and could take the time to wade through complicated reports to see what was happening with *their* money. Our site was by no means fancy; we just put up all of our reports so anyone who was interested could find them.

One day about five months in, I asked Kris if she could find out how many hits we'd had. Kevin suggested that we all make bets about what the number would be, and I declared that *The Price Is Right* rules were in effect. Whoever got closest without going over would receive the meaningless title of "SIGTARP employee of the week." Kevin guessed 15,000, Lori guessed 10,000, Kris guessed 25,000, and I bullishly bet on 50,000.

The next day Kris came in with the actual number: 12 million. When she first told me, I looked at her as if she were Wilt Chamberlain claiming that he had slept with more than 10,000 women. Kevin joked that the URL must be one letter off from a porn website, recalling that one of our candidates for a toll-free number had in fact been an active sex line. But the number was correct. Clearly people were deeply interested in the inner workings of TARP, and by the time I left SIGTARP, we had more than 50 million hits and 3.6 million downloads of our quarterly reports.[1]

One of the most important misconceptions among the public, I felt, was that TARP was the only big government bailout, when in fact its $700 billion was just a drop in the ocean of bailout programs propping up the financial system. As the effort to enact reform began to emerge in the late spring of 2009, I felt it was increasingly important for the public to get a fuller view of just how massive a response had been required to rescue the system. After all, Paulson and Geithner hadn't just saved the banks, they'd also preserved a status quo that was dangerously broken, and in so doing they might have actually increased the danger lurking in our financial architecture. For example, by encouraging the largest banks to acquire one another, they had made the too-big-to-fail banks even bigger, with the top five bank holding companies more than 20 percent larger in terms of assets than they had been before the crisis.[2]

Meanwhile, at the mere hint of reform, the banks' lobbyists reawakened from their brief bailout-induced siesta.[3] Given the success of those lobbyists in recent years in gutting regulations that might otherwise have mitigated the size and scope of the crisis, there was a growing concern that history was about to repeat itself. Instead of meaningful financial reform, we could end up with more of the same, setting the stage for the next crisis.

The first step in making real changes to the system, I thought, was to shed light on the truly extraordinary nature of *all* of the bailouts. Getting a better understanding of the astonishing magnitude of the support necessary to stabilize the system this time around would provide a much-needed preview of the likely costs the next crisis might inflict in the absence of meaningful reform. Exactly how big were the bailouts? I'd never heard a definitive overall number. To the extent that at least some in the media had tried to answer this question, the numbers were all over the map, differing by trillions of dollars. When I asked a member of my team to track down an official government estimate of total financial industry support, I was only slightly surprised to find that there wasn't one. I thought that it was vital that we use our July 2009 quarterly report to Congress to fill that hole in the public's consciousness.

I told my team to dig into how many programs had been put into place and how much money had been spent by each so far. We would include only programs that directly or indirectly supported financial institutions, so that would exclude, for example, the massive stimulus programs. I also wanted my team to find out how much in total the government had decided it would have to commit to each of these programs to make them credible to the participants and the markets, regardless of whether or not all of the money actually ended up being spent.

I thought it was important to understand the extent of those commitments to appreciate what's truly required to staunch a panic. For example, I knew that the government had made a pledge of support of up to $3.36 trillion to guarantee the money market industry.[4] That was because during the heat of the crisis, after Lehman failed, one of the supposedly superreliable money market funds had paid investors who cashed out less than the amount of their initial investment, which had triggered a run on many of the other funds as investors pulled their money from money market accounts. After that run threatened to cut off a major potential source of funding for the banks and the rest of the financial system, Treasury had effectively ended the run by guaranteeing the funds in return for a fee. Fortunately, the program had worked, calming the markets, and Treasury had not had to pay out a single claim. But I thought it was important to convey to the public the magnitude of the government's intervention in that and so many other areas as it tamped down the global panic. If just that single program involved trillions of dollars of guarantees, I wanted to reveal to the public how many other such weak spots there were in the system.

The results of our research were staggering. We counted thirty-five programs and found that astonishing amounts of money had been committed or spent over and above the $700 billion of TARP. For example, a Federal Reserve program pledged $1.8 trillion to prop up the commercial paper market, through which companies borrow money over a short period of time.[5] With credit markets freezing, companies were having a hard time finding private financing, and in, January 2009, the Fed had an outstanding balance of $349.9 billion under the program.[6] In other words, half as much as the total for TARP had been spent on just that one part of the financial system.

We found that the programs had maxed out at $4.7 trillion. As loans were repaid and programs were successfully wound down, the amount outstanding by the time we conducted our review was $3 trillion. The total of the amount that had to be *committed* by the government for the programs, though, was truly shocking.

Kevin came into my office one day and just said, "It's $23.7 trillion."

"What is?" I asked.

"Total government commitment, it's $23.7 trillion."

I really didn't believe the figure until I saw the backup documents that had been provided by each of the agencies themselves. This total commitment was almost double the entire annual economic output of the United States. If there were ever a single number that demonstrated the panic felt by the regulators during the financial crisis, it was that $23.7 trillion.

In processing that figure, it's important to understand that much of the money would never have had to actually be spent. For one thing, some of it was backstopping loans that were already backed by collateral, such as mortgages or valuable securities, so a good portion would certainly be recouped. Further, for some of the programs, it was highly improbable that all of the committed money would ever have to be spent. For example, the entire money market industry would have had to be wiped out to draw down the full $3.36 trillion that Treasury had committed to save it. There were also some assets that the government had backstopped in more than one program, such as when the Federal Reserve purchased a bond that was guaranteed by another governmental agency.

This is why when we announced the findings, I took pains to clarify what the $23.7 trillion really represented and what it did not. To help avoid confusion, I ordered the team to remove the word "exposure" from the introduction of the figure in the draft of our report, because that word implied that it was a definite calculation of potential losses. In truth, the total amounts that were at risk for loss were incalculable, as everything depended upon how the crisis played out. Unfortunately, when Representative Issa broke our press embargo on the report a day early by releasing a statement about our findings, he put the spotlight almost exclusively on the $23.7 trillion rather than on the $3 trillion actually outstanding. Never one for understatement, Issa put the figure in a biblical context: "The potential financial commitment the American taxpayers could be responsible for is of a size and scope that isn't even imaginable. If you spent a million dollars a day going back to the birth of Christ, that wouldn't even come close to just $1 trillion—$23.7 trillion is a staggering figure."[7] As helpful as Issa so often was to us, his emphasis on the $23.7 trillion, along with the release of information drawn only from the report's executive summary, misdirected the initial press coverage.

All hell broke loose in the press, and the meaning of the number was widely misconstrued as an estimate of total potential *losses* instead of *commitments,* in part because of two mistakes we'd made. In the short executive summary that Issa cited in his release we didn't give the details about what the $23.7 trillion figure really represented, instead stating that "the total potential Federal Government support could reach up to $23.7 trillion." In retrospect, we should have included the caveats from the body of the report that painstakingly explained what the number meant, but we hadn't anticipated that the summary would be looked at by itself; the press usually worked from a full report.

The other mistake was that our editors had failed to delete the word "exposure" from the heading of the section that described what the $23.7 trillion represented, further compounding the problem.[8] I was angry, mostly at myself, for missing the mistake in my final review of the report before publication.

We took an initial beating in the press about the figure. *The New York Times* ran a critical story about what had become the headline number after Treasury's spokesman issued some statements criticizing our use of the word "exposure" as inaccurate and describing our estimate as "inflated"[9] and "distorted."[10] Of course, he and the rest of the Treasury team well knew that we had provided a detailed explanation of the number's meaning in the report, and also that Treasury had in fact supplied many of the supposedly "inflated" numbers. As Kris and I reached out to the media to walk them through the report, however, the coverage began to calm down and more accurately portray its contents. Before the day was out, though, the *New York Post* ran a hilarious graphic, which my father-in-law cut out and sent to me. It was a half-page photo of me testifying at my confirmation hearing, with my head Photoshopped onto the body of Dr. Evil, complete with his pinky at the corner of my mouth. The caption of the photo said "Mr. Doom" and had a bubble with me saying "We need $23,700,000,000,000."

The reaction to the report was an important lesson about the nature of spin in Washington and the elaborate gamesmanship involved in the release of information to the public. I understood why the press initially seized on the story the way it did, and I was unfortunately all too aware by that point of why the Treasury team had jumped on the opportunity to go after us about it. But given the explanations we'd quickly followed up with and the extensive description we had provided in the full report we sent to Congress, I was disappointed by the reaction a couple of days later of one of the Congressmen we'd come to view as an ally.

I had two hearings after the report came out. The first went well, with representatives from both sides of the aisle commending us for releasing the figures. But I received a far different reception the following day, July 22, as I waited my turn to testify in front of a House Financial Services Committee subcommittee. Barney Frank suddenly came storming into the waiting room. I hadn't seen him since our meeting in late January.

"Mr. Chairman!" I said cheerfully. "Will you be sitting in on the hearing today?"

"No," Frank said brusquely, once again dispensing with introductory pleasantries. "I'm here to see you," motioning to a door off to the side of the room. His scowl suggested that he wasn't there to buck up my spirits before testifying.

As I followed him into a private hallway, Frank pounced. "You can't do what you did," he said. "It was irresponsible. You can't just throw a number like that out there, $23 trillion. You have to be smarter than that."

I knew that Frank was one of the most important Democrats in Congress. His support had been instrumental to SIGTARP, and I knew that he could make my life miserable. But I had already gone to pains to make clear what the number meant. I also wasn't quite sure what he was saying: whether we should have been clearer about the figure or that we shouldn't have released it at all. If he was saying the latter, I wasn't going to agree with him. Doing so had raised awareness about the dangers still lurking in the financial system in just the way I'd hoped.

I asked him if it wasn't a good thing that we'd figured out how much was really being spent, how much had been committed in bailouts, and how many different programs had become necessary to save the financial system.

"You agree that's a good thing, right, in the interests of transparency?" I said.

"Of course, but that's not all you did," Frank said.

"Right, then I added them up," I said.

"You shouldn't have done that," he fumed. "There was no reason for you to do so. Let others add them up. Let the Republicans add up the number, twist it the way they want to, misrepresent what you said. But you don't do their political dirty work for them."

Math, I thought to myself, *I am getting yelled at by Barney Frank for doing math that anyone with a calculator could have easily done.* I told him that I took his point but that I thought it was important to get the facts out there.

"Well, don't do anything like this again," Frank said.

"Trust me, Mr. Chairman, I will definitely take into account what you're saying next time," I responded.

"Good," Frank said, hurrying out the door.

I did learn from the experience. The following year, we updated our research and found that the total amount outstanding had increased from $3 trillion to $3.7 trillion. That time, I made sure that all of our caveats were included in the executive summary as well as in the body of the report.

IN ADDITION TO describing the true extent of the bailouts in that same quarterly report, we reported on our ongoing problems in getting the Treasury team to be more transparent about how TARP money was being spent. Though I had expected the report to generate a congressional response to those criticisms, which it did, I had not imagined that the president would be publicly confronted with our concerns.

The night after the second hearing, I'd collapsed on the couch at home with Karen to split a bottle of wine, and as I was catching her up on all of the craziness of the week, including my conversation with Frank earlier that day, I suddenly remembered that the president was having a prime-time press conference that evening on his health care initiative. We came into the conference late, and only about two minutes after I turned the television on, a reporter from the Chicago Tribune asked Obama, "Also, the TARP inspector general recently said that your White House is withholding too much information on the bank bailouts. So my question for you is, are you fulfilling your promise of transparency in the White House?"[11]

"What did she just say?" Karen exclaimed.

"Shhhh!" I said. "Let's hear his response."

The president fumbled over the answer. "Let me take a look at what exactly they say we have not provided. I think that we've provided much greater transparency than existed prior to our administration coming in. It is a big program. I don't know exactly what's been requested. I'll find out, and I will have an answer for you."

I looked at Karen and said, "I am definitely, definitely getting fired tomorrow."

But at least I knew that our concerns about the lack of transparency had now been conveyed loud and clear to Obama.

Kevin called almost immediately. "You watching?" he asked.

"Yep," I said.

"I think it was the only non-health-care question asked," he pointed out.

I hung up the phone and looked at Karen. "Definitely getting fired tomorrow."

The next day, Issa issued a press release saying "The fact that President Obama doesn't even seem to be aware that the TARP Inspector General has reported that the Treasury Department is obstructing transparency is simply staggering."[12] Chris Sharpley told me that he had heard the question and answer replayed on the radio as he was driving in that morning. If we hadn't been before, we were now squarely on the White House's radar screen.

I hoped that the White House would follow up and reach out to me to hear more fully about our concerns, but that, unfortunately, never happened. Nor did I see any shift in Treasury's dismissive attitude toward our recommendations, although we had seen a significant change from the Federal Reserve.

AFTER THE ENSIGN-BOXER amendment passed, we began slogging it out with the Treasury team to get it to address our concerns about potential abuse in the PPIP and TALF programs. We were able to come to compromises on a number of key provisions that vastly improved the safety of the programs, but there were two critical problems that we couldn't resolve. One was the need for strict ethical walls between the fund managers getting PPIP money and the rest of their firms, so that they couldn't game the system and unfairly drive up the prices of the securities that they already held. The other was what we referred to in "Fedspeak" as the "leverage-on-leverage" issue—the need to prohibit the PPIP funds from borrowing TALF money on top of the money they had already borrowed from Treasury. We felt that this "double dipping" gave them a perverse incentive to take on excessive risk at the taxpayer's expense. We felt those two issues were worth a war, and we continued to wage it for months.

In an endless series of meetings, Herb Allison repeatedly told me that the fund managers that had already been selected by Treasury—including firms such as BlackRock, Wellington Management Company, TCW, Invesco, and Angelo, Gordon—had said that they would pull out of the program if Treasury required walls. I pointed out to Allison that they might be crying wolf, given that three of the nine selected managers—BlackRock, Wellington, and AllianceBernstein—had already agreed to walls in their participation in other government programs, such as the Fed's nearly identical mortgage bond–purchasing program. The fact that the Fed had also considered walls important made no impression. Allison had no convincing substantive response, other than to argue that PPIP was "different" and that, as Neel Kashkari had similarly claimed, a wall requirement would destroy the program.

Allison's credibility on that point was somewhat undercut months later when I learned that one of those same fund managers, AllianceBernstein, had decided to impose an ethical wall of its own accord for its PPIP fund because it thought it was the best practice.[13]

I knew the Fed understood the issue, and I tried to enlist the New York Fed's chief of compliance, Martin Grant, in my effort. As I filled Martin in on our discussions, he shared my concern with Allison's insistence on going forward without walls. As someone who ran compliance over a similar program, he understood that although walls alone were insufficient to protect against fund managers' unfairly profiting, they were an essential starting place. Ultimately, I begged Allison to send his PPIP team to New York to meet with Martin so that he could explain why the walls were so important. He agreed, but Martin told me after the meeting that "they just didn't get it." I could sense him shaking his head on the telephone.

After each conversation, I would call Martin to get his take on Treasury's arguments, both to commiserate and to make sure that I wasn't missing anything. At one point, after I quoted Allison verbatim, Martin joked, "It sounds like Larry Fink [the CEO of BlackRock] is talking, and their mouths are moving."

The back-and-forth with Allison became progressively more heated, and at times our arguments would stray from the topic at hand. Once, in what seemed like a complete non sequitur, the beet-red Allison exclaimed, "And I am personally offended that you, as a senior government official, would mock the secretary of the Treasury while giving a speech! Something that *he's* not happy about."

At first I was totally confused. "I have no idea what you're talking about, Herb."

"The clips from *Saturday Night Live*?" Allison responded.

Ahhh, the PowerPoint, I thought. Included in my standard speech at public events were clips that I had acquired from *Saturday Night Live* of a skit in which one of the cast members, playing Geithner, reviewed the results of the "stress tests" of the too-big-to-fail banks. I explained to Allison that I had used only two short clips and that they had made fun of the banks, not Geithner. I also told him that I had used the clips only after I saw an interview in which Geithner said that he thought that the skit was hilarious and that I was sure he didn't mind.

"Well, he does mind. And what do you think he's going to say to the press?"

I told Allison that I had intended no offense and would take it out.

In the end, Treasury wouldn't budge. The only wall I ever got from Allison was a copy of Pink Floyd's CD *The Wall* as a gag holiday present.

I realized the best I could do was to police the fund managers rigorously, and I formed an internal group at SIGTARP to keep on top of them and let them know that we were watching their every move. Even so, by January 2010, we had opened an investigation into one of the fund managers for the exact type of conduct that I had warned would occur without a wall. The fund manager had sold a recently downgraded mortgage-backed bond out of one of the private accounts that he managed to a broker and then almost immediately repurchased the bond back from the broker for the PPIP fund at a higher price.[14] The investigation was ongoing when I stepped down.

WE HAD MUCH more success with the Fed in getting it to limit the proposed $800 billion expansion of TALF to include loans made for the purchase of residential mortgage-backed securities. The Fed had originally agreed to Geithner's plan to expand TALF, but ultimately Fed officials came around to appreciating the concerns we had raised.

After we issued our report detailing the potential problems, a team of economists and compliance personnel came to our offices to discuss our recommendations. During the meeting, every time Kevin or I spoke, our guests would all furiously take notes. At one point, they asked me to interpret one of the comments in our report on TALF. As I gave the answer, half of the room seemed relieved while the other half shook their heads.

"What?" I asked.

"Sometimes we have these Talmudic-like discussions about the meaning of certain parts of your reports. And as you can see, we were split on this one," one of the economists said, laughing.

"Guys," I said. "Just call. We're happy to talk anytime." (Later Kevin would comment that it felt as though we had just lived out a scene from the movie *Revenge of the Nerds*. I responded that it was rare indeed when I was one of the cool kids in the room.)

As we went through the different pitfalls, one of the Fed employees shook his head, commenting that he thought there was a good chance that they were never going to find a way to safely implement the program. He was right; they never did. They realized that TALF just couldn't be safely adapted to include those toxic bonds.

The Fed also eventually agreed with us on our concerns about the leverage-on-leverage issue and how little skin the fund managers would have in the game, eventually telling Treasury that it couldn't support its proposal. In a remarkable call, the Fed official handling the issue told me that while at first they hadn't seen the problem, once we had clarified it, they changed their minds. That call was the only time I heard those words said in Washington. We were wrong, thanks for pointing it out, and now we'll fix it.

With that, what was left of Geithner's $2 trillion Financial Stability Plan was gutted. The FDIC had effectively shut down the first part of the PPIP plan, and now the other core parts of PPIP had been neutered by the Fed.

In the end, less than 6 percent of the proposed $2 trillion was actually expended.

It was a somber moment for Kevin and me. We felt that we had done our jobs in protecting the taxpayer's interest, but the programs' all but total demise meant that there was still no government solution for the toxic assets that continued to pollute the banks' balance sheets, and we certainly didn't feel like celebrating. Though we knew that we had not been responsible for the reckless program design, we felt a degree of responsibility for there now being no effective program for getting the assets off the banks' books. It was frustrating. Rather than stonewalling us, Treasury could have consulted with us *before* the programs were announced and we could have worked together in finding a solution that would assist the banks but also adequately protect the taxpayer.

Geithner and his Treasury Department, however, were not terribly interested in working through many of the issues we continued to raise about TARP's failures, as I found out during a meeting in October 2009 that I had requested with Geithner to plead my case.

SHORTLY AFTER THE oversight meeting Geithner had held with Elizabeth Warren, Gene Dodaro, and me in October, in which I had hardly any time to express my concerns, I had a follow-up meeting with him.

As Kevin and I approached Geithner's office, I couldn't help but think back to my first day on the job. What a difference ten months made. We were no longer the wide-eyed newcomers hesitantly walking laps around the building searching for the secretary's office. Back then, we had been the newest people in the building, and it had seemed unlikely that we would ever close the chasm between our experience and those with whom we were meeting. For this meeting, however, Kevin and I were the longest continuously-serving Treasury officials in the room, and we weren't lacking confidence.

When we walked in, I took a seat next to Geithner. Kevin, Allison, and Geithner's new general counsel, George Madison, arranged themselves around the room, but this was to be an almost exclusively two-person conversation.

I told Geithner that TARP's deep unpopularity was avoidable but that so long as people felt that Treasury was hiding the ball by not striving to provide full, accurate and complete information about TARP and how the banks were using TARP funds, the criticism was going to continue. I said that I thought our capacity as a nation to deal with what could be a continuing financial crisis was being undermined by a loss of faith in government. If people didn't believe in their government, I said, they wouldn't be willing to support the extraordinary measures necessary to engineer a similar rescue when the next crisis inevitably struck. Then I said that the current loss of government credibility could be traced to Treasury's mishandling of TARP. Fairly or unfairly, the popular view was that it had transferred wealth from taxpayers to Wall Street, and that Treasury officials, including him, were perceived as too closely aligned with Wall Street.

Geithner got dramatic. "Neil, you think I don't hear those criticisms? I hear them. And each one, they cut me," he said, pausing and then making an emphatic cutting motion with one hand as he said "like a knife."

I made sure not to look at Kevin, as I wasn't sure if I could keep a straight face if I did. The gesture was so extreme.

"But Mr. Secretary, this is avoidable," I said. "These are failures that you could have avoided, and they can be fixed. But it starts with more transparency."

All of a sudden, an angry Herb Allison chimed in. "I am personally offended that you are suggesting that the secretary of Treasury has been less than fully transparent with the American people." He had unbelievably once again trotted out the "personally offended" line. I didn't even look at him.

"To be clear, Herb," I said, talking to Allison but maintaining my gaze on Geithner, "I am not *suggesting* that the secretary has failed in transparency, I am *stating* it. Mr. Secretary, you've failed to be sufficiently transparent, and that is one of the reasons why people are so angry. But you can still fix it."

Up until that point, Geithner had seemed cordial, although I could sense an underlying tension and disdain in his voice. Now he erupted.

"Neil, I have been the most *fucking* transparent secretary of the Treasury in this country's entire *fucking* history!" he boomed, moving forward in his chair. "No one has ever made the banks disclose the type of shit that I made them disclose after the stress tests. No one! And now you're saying that I haven't been fucking transparent?"

Geithner's proclivity for profanity was no secret, but I was still taken aback for a moment. A year earlier, when I had been just a prosecutor in New York, I never would have imagined that one day one of the most powerful government officials in the world would be dropping f-bombs on me.

"Mr. Secretary, you've done some good things, to be sure," I responded, and after a pause, I said slowly, "but you could do so much more."

Geithner looked as if he was going to get out of his chair and throttle me, when Madison intervened to calm things down.

After I suggested that an important first step would be to adopt our recommendation and finally require the banks to report on how they were using TARP money, Geithner gave me a lengthy lecture about the fungibility of money, with a "you're a smart guy, you've got to know you're full of shit on this issue" tone.

I then walked Geithner through the results of our audit on how the TARP banks had used the money, pointing out that although the quality of the answers certainly varied by bank, many had been able to give us a good deal of insight into what they did. Some of the smaller banks, for example, had described individual projects that they had initiated with TARP funds.[15] A number of midsize banks had used TARP to repay lines of credit that had been shut down by other financial institutions.[16] Some of the larger banks had used the TARP funds to gobble up their competitors, including PNC's controversial acquisition of Cleveland's National City Bank,[17] and Citi and Bank of New York Mellon were among the dozens of banks that reported that they segregated or specifically tracked their TARP funds.[18] Geithner was still skeptical, explaining how easy it would be for the banks to manipulate their numbers.

As we parried back and forth, Geithner repeatedly reached a pitch of anger, regaling me with detailed expletive-filled explanations that established my apparent idiocy. He would then calm himself down and give me a forced, almost demonic smile. I had argued to enough juries to know when my arguments were falling flat, so I finally changed course, making one final pitch to try to convince Geithner to adopt our use-of-funds recommendation.

"Mr. Secretary, let's say you're right, and I'm completely wrong. What's the harm of just doing it anyway? What's the downside? Congress and it seems like every editorial page in the country agrees with me. If you commit to do this, no matter what the results are, you'll shut me up. We can even do a joint press release in which I will herald your commitment to transparency. It's an incredibly easy win-win," I said.

"Worst-case scenario, you guys are right and we waste a little time. But if I'm right, we bring important transparency to the American people. Either way, we both get to move on. Because otherwise, we're just going to be back here having this same conversation next year." I said.

I got the sense that unlike my other arguments, that one might have resonated with Geithner. He didn't have to believe in the project, he just needed to recognize that he was causing himself unnecessary pain by not playing along. As we wrapped up the meeting, he said that he would give it serious additional thought.

As we walked out, he stopped me. "You know, Neil, you really did scare a lot of people away from TARP," he said.

I couldn't believe he was going back to that old line.

"But that was probably a good thing," he said. "A very good thing."

I was impressed. Geithner was recognizing something that I had argued ad nauseam to Kashkari and Allison: that to the extent that enhanced oversight and fraud prevention scared away bad players from seeking taxpayer money, it was a net positive for the program. I thanked him for the compliment and for his time, and as we walked into the anteroom, Madison took us aside. "Neil, give me a call. We're going to get this worked out for you. No promises, but I think we can get this resolved." (Eventually, Treasury did relent, partially, conducting a voluntary one-time survey in 2010, after most of the major banks had left the program.)

It was the weirdest meeting of my life.

Kevin and I left Geithner's office at around seven in the evening, our steps echoing loudly off of the marble floors in the deserted block-long hallway. After what seemed like ten minutes (but was probably no more than thirty seconds), Kevin stopped and looked at me.

"What the fuck was that?" he asked.

We both burst out laughing, releasing the incredible tension that had built up over the meeting. "Shhh," I said. "Wait until we get to the car."

"In all honesty, I think he was about to come out of his chair and beat the living shit out of you," Kevin said.

"What? You don't think I could take Geithner?" I asked, laughing back.

"Probably not, but if I ever had any question about whether coming down to Washington was the right choice, that alone made it worth it. That was fantastic. And by the way, he *really* hates you," Kevin said.

"Good day for SIGTARP," I said, getting into the car.

"Great day for SIGTARP," Kevin replied.

As KEVIN AND I shortly started to receive more of the results of our audit investigations, including those of the AIG, GM, and Chrysler bailouts, Geithner's approach of playing his cards close to his vest and keeping us out of the decision-making process began to make sense. The hurried decisions, lack of transparency, and unquestioning deference to Wall Street that characterized the approach to the PPIP, HAMP and CPP programs were hardly isolated incidents; it became clear to us that they were part of an emerging pattern that no secretary would want exposed.

10

The Essential
$7,700 Kitchen Assistant

A S OUR PRESS OFFICER, Kris Belisle, had warned me when I interviewed her, shading of the truth was an accepted part of doing business in Washington. I still found it frustrating, however, whenever I identified to some of the beat reporters one or another misleading half-truth being touted by Treasury's press office about TARP and their reaction was to just roll their eyes. I kept trying to unwind the spin anyway, and the further we dug into the way TARP was being administered, the more obvious it became that Treasury applied a consistent double standard. In the fall of 2009, as I began receiving the results of three of our most important audits, the contradiction couldn't have been more glaring. When providing the largest financial institutions with bailout money, Treasury made almost no effort to hold them accountable, and the bounteous terms delivered by the government seemed to border on being corrupt. For those institutions, no effort was spared, with government officials often defending their generosity by kneeling at the altar of the "sanctity of contracts." Meanwhile, an entirely different set of rules applied for home owners and businesses that were most assuredly small enough to fail.

Nowhere was the favoritism toward Wall Street more evident than with the government's approach to AIG, where inviolable contract terms were cited to justify the absurd executive bonus payments as well as far richer payouts provided to the megabank counterparties to AIG's CDS deals, honoring even their most reckless bets.

For home owners and small business owners, though, contracts went from being sacrosanct to inconvenient irrelevancies. So when mortgage servicers blatantly disregarded HAMP contracts by trampling over home owners' rights, Treasury turned to a seemingly endless series of excuses to justify its refusal to hold them accountable. Similarly, for more than two thousand auto dealerships, Treasury's auto bailout team sought to *void* the contractual rights granted them under state franchise laws to shut them down.

SHORTLY AFTER MY swearing in, Hank Paulson gave the go-ahead to lend up to $13.4 billion in TARP funds to GM and up to $4 billion to Chrysler to help them stave off bankruptcy. That was an initial outlay, and it was left for the new administration to determine if it would provide any additional funds.[1] As a condition of the funding, Paulson required the companies to submit restructuring plans to the Treasury secretary to prove that they could achieve "long-term viability."[2]

On February 17, 2009, with Geithner now in the job, the companies submitted their "viability" plans, outlining the steps they intended to take if they were awarded more TARP money. They included closing plants, reducing the number of employees, eliminating brands, and reducing the number of their dealerships. GM planned to close an average of 325 dealers per year over the next five years, which, it explained, was a continuation of a downsizing effort that dated back decades. Chrysler cited similar plans to downsize its dealerships, although it didn't provide specific numbers or a time frame.[3]

The plans were reviewed by Treasury's auto team, which Geithner and the administration assembled to administer the bailouts. Led by Steven Rattner, the head of a Wall Street private equity firm, and Ron Bloom, a former investment banker and head of collective bargaining for the United Steelworkers Union, the auto team had plenty of Wall Street firepower but did not include in its ranks anyone with experience in the automobile industry.[4] On March 30, 2009, the team rejected GM and Chrysler's viability plans, identifying five key "highlights" about the problems they had found with the proposals.[5] They included the cost of employee pension and health care plans, improvement of the companies' product mix, and a concern that GM's proposed pace of closing dealerships was too slow.

Following the team's rejection of the viability plans, both GM and Chrysler entered into managed bankruptcies funded by TARP and overseen by the auto team. By the time they emerged several months later, they had shed billions of dollars in debt. In total, Treasury committed $49.5 billion of TARP funds to GM and $14.9 billion to Chrysler,[6] and the government ended up with a 60 percent stake in GM. It had worked out other ownership arrangements for Chrysler.

We had been tracking the auto bailouts in our quarterly reports, but as of the summer of 2009, we had not yet initiated an audit. The Congressional Oversight Panel and GAO were already doing broad reviews, and I didn't want to replicate their work. Then, in July 2009, after it was announced that GM and Chrysler had used the bankruptcy process to terminate more than two thousand of their dealerships, several members of Congress cried foul. Senator Jay Rockefeller, for example, said it was just plain wrong to "leave it to local dealers and their customers to fend for themselves with no real plan, with no real notice, with no real help."[7] Meanwhile, pundits on the right began to speculate that the administration had executed the bailouts to reward their Democratic supporters in the unions and to punish the largely Republican-owned auto dealerships.[8]

Kevin and I saw this as an important issue and decided to dig into it. Although we gave little credence to the conspiracy theories, we wanted to give a definitive answer to a question that neither one of us fully understood: why was the closing of thousands of sales outlets necessary for the ongoing survival of GM and Chrysler? Our audit team went to work, reviewing documents and interviewing officials at GM, Chrysler, Treasury, and some of the dealerships. Toward the end of 2009, they gave me a draft report. As I read through it, I became dismayed and angry.

The auto team had pressured the companies to close the dealerships, and as a result, both companies had dramatically accelerated their terminations. GM had cut off more than 1,400 dealers from receiving new GM vehicles (but gave them until October 2010 to wind down), while Chrysler had shut down nearly 800 dealerships immediately, about 25 percent of its overall dealer network.[9] According to several analyses, those decisions had put up to 100,000 dealership jobs into jeopardy.[10] Fortunately, fewer jobs were ultimately lost because Congress enacted legislation that gave the terminated dealers access to binding arbitration. As a result, hundreds of dealerships that had been terminated were offered reinstatement (apparently without interfering with the companies' turnaround).[11]

The draft report indicated that relatively little thought had gone into Treasury's determination that the dealership closings had to be immediate. Because it had little expertise about the business, the auto team instead solicited views about the companies' original termination plans from a bevy of Wall Street analysts, including those from UBS, JPMorgan Chase, Deutsche Bank, and Barclays Capital, all of which weighed in in favor of closing dealerships, although not necessarily with the swiftness directed by Treasury. Treasury ignored one of the few non–Wall Street sources that it consulted, a representative from the nonprofit Center for Automotive Research who warned that deep cuts could actually do the companies far greater harm than good.[12] The auto team also seemed to give no consideration whatsoever to the widespread job losses that might be caused by the accelerated closings. Finally, it appeared that GM and Chrysler's termination process had been done completely without oversight, resulting in arbitrary terminations.[13]

I found it outrageous that Treasury would push to shutter thousands of small businesses as quickly as possible while unemployment was marching toward 10 percent without having conducted a deeper analysis.[14] But I told my team that we needed to firm up the findings before we could express those concerns to Congress. I sent them back to work, with instructions to nail down exactly what had gone into Treasury's decision-making process.

AROUND THE SAME TIME, we were uncovering a far bigger mess in the execution of the bailout of AIG. We found a pattern of rash decisions, bad management, and, once again, the placement of the interests of the too-big-to-fail financial institutions and their executives above those of the taxpayers funding their bailouts.

Shortly after the blowup over the AIG bonus payments, Congress requested that we review two decisions: first, Treasury's acquiescence to AIG's payment of the $168 million in bonuses and second, the New York Fed's authorization of government dollars being used to effectively pay AIG's large bank counterparties more than $60 billion to buy bonds that were worth less than half of that amount.

The AIG bailout saga began on Friday, September 12, 2008, when AIG officials alerted the New York Fed that the company was in trouble: it didn't have enough cash on hand to meet its obligations in the coming days to post billions of dollars in additional cash collateral to the banks.[15] Although the warning was dire, we found that the New York Fed officials, including Geithner, who was still serving as its president, had initially done little beyond monitoring the situation.[16] With their hands full trying to find a way to rescue Lehman Brothers, which was also on the brink of collapse and would enter into bankruptcy the following Monday, they instead hoped that ongoing negotiations for a deal involving AIG and the private equity firm J.C. Flowers & Co. would prove successful.[17] When Geithner was told the following Monday, September 15, that those talks had failed, he outsourced AIG's problem to Goldman Sachs and JPMorgan Chase, asking them to lead a consortium of banks to put together $75 billion in financing so that AIG could continue to pay its bills.[18]

By the following day, the banks told Geithner that there would be no private deal.[19] Goldman and JPMorgan had prepared a term sheet that laid out the terms under which they would lend AIG up to $75 billion but balked at actually closing the transaction. A JPMorgan executive later told us that they had walked away once they realized that the amount of money AIG needed was greater than the total value of its assets. In other words, JPMorgan and Goldman didn't want to lend money to what they believed was essentially an insolvent institution.[20]

Faced with the prospect of AIG defaulting on tens of billions of dollars of payments to the largest banks in the United States and Europe, and having failed to prepare a Plan B if the private-sector solution fell through, the New York Fed found itself painted into a bailout corner.[21] Having no time to craft their own plan, the officials just stepped into the role of the banks and adopted the terms of the aborted term sheet that JPMorgan and Goldman had crafted. The only meaningful change, they told us, was in the amount of the loan, which increased from $75 billion to $85 billion.[22] In return, the New York Fed received nearly 80 percent of the common stock of AIG.

It quickly became clear that the terms of the transaction were flawed, and within days the New York Fed's general counsel realized that the deal would need to be redone.[23] The 11 percent variable interest rate set by the banks was too high, causing additional pressure on AIG's balance sheet, and the loan did nothing to stem the flow of billions of dollars out of AIG to meet ongoing collateral demands. The necessary restructuring of the deal occurred in November, 2008, this time involving $40 billion in TARP funds, which went directly to the Fed to pay down a portion of the $85 billion line of credit it had originally extended to AIG. Five months later, Treasury would add another $30 billion in TARP cash to AIG's tab.

A second part of the November deal covered the ongoing problem of the cash payouts required each time AIG was downgraded or the prices of the CDOs covered by AIG's credit default swap contracts plunged lower. Geithner and his team decided to terminate $62.1 billion of AIG's contracts with the banks. The deal had two parts. First, the counterparty banks were paid the approximate market value of the CDOs covered by the credit default swap contracts, about $27.1 billion in cash, which was provided almost entirely by the New York Fed in return for the CDOs themselves. For the second part of the deal, AIG and the New York Fed agreed that the banks could keep all of the previously posted collateral, approximately $35 billion, in return for the banks agreeing to rip up the credit default swap contracts. As a result, the bleeding of cash was staunched and the taxpayers became the proud owners of a mass of ill-conceived CDOs.[24] For the banks, between the cash they received from the Fed and the collateral they had previously received from AIG, they had essentially been paid 100 cents on the dollar for $62 billion in CDOs that were actually worth far less than that.

The deal was a gross distortion of the normal functions of the market. In a bailout-free world, instead of being saved by the government, AIG would have been unable to make its cash collateral payments to the banks and gone into bankruptcy. As a result, the banks would have been left with the CDOs and stuck with their continued declines in value. Those losses would have punished the banks for what had been bad and risky bets—i.e., assuming that AIG would be able to meet all of its obligations. In market parlance, each of the banks would have borne the "counter-party risk" of doing business with AIG and suffered the consequences of betting on the wrong counterparty. Instead they were paid out in full.

In that respect, Geithner's opening of the spigot of taxpayer cash for AIG was more of a bailout of the banks than it was for AIG itself. The government thereby sent Wall Street a very dangerous message: counter-parties who do business with financial institutions whose collapse could have devastating consequences for the entire financial system needn't do due diligence or worry about their counterparty risk. Instead, they can rely on the government to bail them out.

That is the crux of the too-big-to-fail problem. The failure of giant financial institutions that are so big and have built up so many obligations *to one another* could cause a domino effect that could take down other major players and eventually the entire financial system. If the govern-ment had not stepped in to save AIG, major banks in the United States and Europe would have potentially suffered tens of billions of dollars of losses at a time when neither they nor the system could withstand such a further shock. The government felt it had no choice, and perhaps that was correct, but as long as there are financial institutions of such size and with so many interconnections, future massive crises—and bailouts—are all but inevitable.

THOUGH THE GOVERNMENT likely had to bail out AIG in order to save the financial system, whether it had to authorize the bonus payments to AIG's Financial Products executives was another story.

Back in the fall of 2008, the New York Fed tried to get a handle on AIG's various bonus agreements, but it wasn't terribly concerned with the details of who would be paid what. The bonus commitments were consid-ered simply in terms of getting a full accounting of how much cash AIG needed. When you are on the hook for $85 billion and counting, as the New York Fed was, $168 million in bonus payments may well seem like just a drop in the bucket.

But as the later reaction to the payments showed, Treasury should have had different priorities. The TARP legislation required that Treasury include executive compensation limits in its contracts, and Treasury had done so with AIG. Executive compensation had already become a hot-button issue with the public, particularly by the beginning of 2009, when news came out that the bailed-out Wall Street banks were issuing tens of billions of dollars in bonuses. But other than sending some Treasury officials over to AIG in November 2008 for a quick review of the compensation structure for its top executives (but not the Financial Products executives), Treasury took a hands-off approach toward AIG's compensation issues, doing little to oversee the taxpayers's $40 billion investment.[25]

As a result, Treasury was caught flat-footed, finding out about the bonus payments only a couple of weeks before they were due. Had Treasury officials been more effectively monitoring the government's investment in AIG and more concerned with accountability and basic fairness, they might have helped prevent the blowup. For example, they could have forced AIG to renegotiate the terms of the contracts as a condition of the additional $30 billion in TARP funds that they had announced several days *after* learning about the imminent bonus payments.[26] They could have refused to allow AIG to make the payments and dealt with the legal consequences that might have followed. At the very least, they could have alerted Congress and the public before making the payments. Instead, with no notice, Treasury and Geithner stood behind the "sanctity" of the executives' contracts.

Meanwhile, the rationale Neel Kashkari had given me for making the payments—that the bonus recipients were essential personnel necessary to wind down AIG's complex transactions—didn't quite wash. When I asked my audit team for a breakdown of the bonuses by position, I saw that although the overwhelming majority of the payments had gone to a small group of executives, every single employee at the Financial Products group seemed to have received *some* payment, including $7,700 to a kitchen assistant, $700 to a file administrator, and $7,000 to a mail room assistant.[27] Though I was skeptical that the executives were so essential, I was pretty sure that those lower-level employees receiving taxpayer-funded bonus payments had nothing whatsoever to do with the supposedly complex work of resolving AIG's positions.

* * *

GEITHNER AND TREASURY'S failure to adequately oversee AIG and subsequent bungling of the bonus payments had deep consequences for the public's assessment of the bailouts. Though likely born more from incompetence than corruption, the mishandling of the situation nonetheless helped solidify the popular perception that I had warned Geithner about—that TARP was little more than a massive transfer of wealth from taxpayers to undeserving Wall Street executives.

Even worse than the bonus payments, at least in terms of financial cost, was the subject of our other AIG audit, which explored the reasons for Geithner's agreement to effectively pay full value to the banks for the CDOs the government purchased from them. These beneficiaries included Société Générale ($16.5 billion in CDOs bought), Goldman Sachs ($14 billion), Deutsche Bank ($8.5 billion), Merrill Lynch ($6.2 billion), UBS ($4.3 billion), Wachovia ($1 billion), and Bank of America ($800 million). Our audit sought to find out why Geithner hadn't negotiated a lower price on behalf of the public.

On its face, it seemed unfair and unnecessary that the government would so grossly overpay for the bonds, particularly to those banks that had already received so much TARP money. The New York Fed, obviously aware of this problem, did initially seek some concessions from the banks, asking them to take less than full payment for the bonds. But we found that those negotiations were halfhearted at best and demonstrated a characteristic deference to the banks, taking an almost apologetic approach. It was as if the New York Fed found the whole process of negotiating unseemly.

The lack of seriousness with which Geithner approached the discussions stood in stark contrast to the far tougher approach that he, Paulson, and Bernanke had taken just a few weeks earlier when they had launched the Capital Purchase Program. Then they had summoned the CEOs of nine of the largest banks to Washington with no advance notice of the subject matter of the meeting. After they were all assembled in one room, Geithner, along with Paulson and Bernanke, forcibly pressed the CEOs to take $125 billion in TARP money. Although acceptance by the banks was

nominally "voluntary," the CEOs understood how adamant the government officials were, and they accepted on the spot with very little push
back. One CEO even told us that he actually thought that he "did not have
a choice in the matter."[28] The government made it clear that it wouldn't
take no for an answer, and, not surprisingly, no one said no.

If Paulson, Geithner, and Bernanke's discussions with the banks over
CPP were a lesson in Negotiations 101, Geithner's approach to concessions in the CDO purchases was Neville Chamberlain–esque. Instead of
gathering the CEOs of the banks together in one room and personally
explaining that it was "good for the country"[29] and necessary to ensure
ongoing support for the bailouts to negotiate a deal that fairly protected
the taxpayers' interests, Geithner handed the job over to midlevel New
York Fed staffers. The staffers were then required to use a prepared script
that emphasized, up front, that any concession made by the banks would
be "entirely voluntary." He also put the staffers into negotiating straitjack-
ets: they were prohibited from suggesting that they would pull the plug
on AIG and leave the banks high and dry; and they were prohibited from
using their leverage from being the regulator of several of the entities.[30]
That approach resulted in a departure from the normal workings of the
marketplace, where concessions on debts owed by struggling companies are not uncommon. For example, in 2008, the bond insurer Ambac
reportedly settled claims on $1.4 billion of mortgage-related CDOs that
it had insured for Citigroup for about 60 cents on the dollar,[31] and later
settled with a number of other counterparties on $3.5 billion in mort-
gage-backed debt exposure for just $1 billion.[32]

Geithner's team also undercut any chance of getting relief for the taxpayer by deciding that no one concession would be accepted unless all
of the banks agreed to the exact same percentage reduction.[33] The New
York Fed officials told us that for this reason, after the regulator overseeing AIG's French bank counterparties told them that it would be against
French law to accept less than full value for the bonds, the negotiations
effectively ended.

With all of those constraints in place, Geithner admitted that the
negotiating strategy had little likelihood of success when my team asked
him about his strategy.[34] He did not, however, offer any reason why he
didn't try harder. He was the president of the most powerful of the Fed-

eral Reserve Banks and easily could have called in help from Paulson and
Bernanke. He could have personally gotten involved in the negotiations
and appealed to the banking CEOs with whom he already had regular if
not daily conversations. In other words, he could have made it clear that it
was a big deal to him and to the country that they agree to some discount.

Unfortunately, even getting Geithner to sit down and talk to us about
it was a challenge. His staff ignored numerous requests for an interview,
and I finally raised our need to interview him for the audit during our
October 2009 meeting. He assured me that he would soon meet with us,
but his staff nonetheless continued to ignore our e-mails. Finally, about
a week later, I sent Geithner a direct e-mail, and after three more days
passed without an interview being scheduled, I threatened to report his
failure to meet with us to Congress. Only then did we get an interview
booked.

Toward the end of the audit an issue arose concerning the issue of
whether one of the banks had agreed to a concession. In an interview in
The Washington Post, the New York Fed's general counsel, Thomas Baxter,
claimed for the first time that the New York Fed's decision not to accept
any concessions from any of the counterparties unless all of the banks
agreed to the same was based in the banking laws.[35] He hadn't told us
that before, so Kevin and I called him and I asked, "Tom, I know that it
didn't happen, but are you saying that even if one or two of the banks had
agreed to take a haircut, you would've turned that down?" Baxter said
I understood his position correctly, and although we were unconvinced
that he was interpreting the law correctly, we included his explanation in
the draft version of our report that we sent to Treasury and the New York
Fed for review.

To our great surprise, however, the New York Fed officials reviewing
the draft suddenly told my auditors that, contrary to my conversation
with Baxter, one of the banks *had* offered to take a discount during the
negotiations. I was furious that Baxter hadn't told us about it, but I soon
received a call from Baxter, who was apologetic. He said that he personally hadn't known about the concession offer, which had come from UBS,
and he sounded genuinely mortified by the New York Fed's apparent failure to disclose the information earlier. He also told me that although it
was true that UBS had agreed to a modest haircut of 2 percent, the bank

had said its acceptance was conditioned on all of the other banks agreeing to the same discount. He said that since the others had already refused, the talks had gone nowhere. Baxter also confirmed that the Fed staff had consulted with Geithner about UBS's offer and that, instead of telling them to negotiate further, Geithner had given the order to effectively pay the banks full price for the bonds. We were stunned. Rather than pounce on UBS's apparent willingness to negotiate and use that as leverage with the others, he had simply folded the tent.

Geithner had said nothing about that in our interview, and I e-mailed his chief of staff to say that we needed at least five minutes of his time to go over the UBS issue. Geithner was on a plane to Asia, and I heard back by e-mail the next day that although he did "not recall" UBS's concession, he didn't challenge the New York Fed officials' account of what had happened.

We later found out, months after the report was issued, about other information that had not been provided to us. The House Oversight and Government Reform Committee subsequently subpoenaed documents that we had previously asked for during the audit, and, included in the hundreds of thousands of pages provided by the Fed were many documents that we had never seen before. Included in these were handwritten notes of the New York Fed's negotiations with the banks that we had repeatedly been told by a New York Fed official did not exist. As other documents related to the bailout were leaked to the press, we opened an investigation into whether the Fed had purposefully obstructed our investigation. That inquiry, which we publicly disclosed, was still ongoing when I stepped down from SIGTARP.

Worried that fundamental aspects of our already issued audit might be inaccurate, I decided to check out some of the other facts provided to us, including the New York Fed's claim that the French government had "forcibly" rejected any concessions from its banks. I arranged for a Saturday afternoon call with the French regulator. Although she said she wouldn't answer questions about certain details of her conversation with New York Fed officials, she was willing to offer us the "French perspective" on the negotiations. In doing so, she emphasized that she had not "slammed the door" on negotiations and had been more than ready to engage in them with the Fed so long as they were at a high level and universal. But she told us that the Fed officials had never seriously pursued that option, commenting that she had been surprised when the Fed officials had never called back. When I asked her about the Fed's assertion that it would be illegal under French law to agree to a discount, she said that the French government could have waived that restriction. "Which we could have done," she said, "if appropriate negotiations took place. But with no negotiations, no waiver." The reaction to our report might have been even more heated had we known about this "French perspective" before we issued it, but it still provoked a dramatic reaction.

WE SENT THE final version of the report to Treasury, the New York Fed, and the board of governors of the Federal Reserve for formal comments in early November 2009, and I soon received a number of complaints. They objected to the "inflammatory" nature of our conclusions, including our view that the handling of the AIG bailout had been haphazard overall and had shown a lack of effort by Geithner and the New York Fed in conducting the negotiations with the banks.

The report also concluded that despite Geithner's claim that the intent of the bailout had been to protect AIG's insurance policy holders, not the banks on the other side of its CDS contracts, the effect had been that tens of billions of dollars of government money had been funneled directly to the banks. We therefore labeled the deal what it was, a "backdoor bailout" of the banks.[36]

That final point drew the most heated objections, and we were asked to change our language. The Federal Reserve's general counsel, Scott Alvarez, was the most aggressive by far. He called me on the Friday before the report was to be released, losing his composure and yelling at me to make changes. I told him that we would be issuing the audit the following week as it was written and that he was free to send a response letter, which we would include in the report.

I was worried that the issues covered in the report were somewhat arcane, and I was happy that Lori had scheduled a hearing about it in front of the House Oversight and Government Reform Committee. That would afford me the opportunity to give an extended explanation of our findings. We were also scheduled to testify before that same committee early in the week to discuss our previously released audit on Bank of America. But on the same Friday that Alvarez yelled at me, Lori came into my office, looking a little shaken.

"What's up?" I asked.

"The hearings, they're gone. The Democrats have canceled both hearings for next week," Lori said.

"Both? Why? What did they say?" I asked.

"Nothing. The official word from the committee is that there is no explanation. But I did some digging," Lori said.

"Treasury!" I said. "Treasury got them to cancel?" I asked.

Lori looked at me pitifully. "No, not Treasury, they don't have that type of influence. Nobody came right out and said it, but the suggestion was that this came from the White House. I got the impression that someone high up in the White House doesn't want SIGTARP on the Hill next week."

Although Lori asked for a formal explanation from the committee, they never provided one. It was all part of the cloak-and-dagger routine in Washington. Hearings are canceled at the last minute, but no one will tell you why, leaving it to you to read the tea leaves and to infer from cryptic off-the-record comments what happened. Lori's hunch might have been right that it was the White House trying to protect Geithner, or it could have been that the chairman had gotten theater tickets to *Cats*. Congress might have been demanding transparency, but it certainly didn't always practice what it preached.

If the intent was in fact to tamp down attention to our report, it didn't work. When I got into work on the November morning the report went out, I took off my jacket, stirred a Splenda into a giant vat of Au Bon Pain coffee, and fired up my computer. Checking out what the Huffington Post was reporting, as I did on almost every report day, I almost dropped the coffee into my lap. The whole top half of the page was a photograph of Geithner with the headline "HOW CAN GEITHNER SURVIVE THIS? Scathing Report Singles Out Treasury Chief for Bungled AIG Bailout."[37] That headline more or less summed up the wall-to-wall coverage of the report as the day went on. In the coming days and weeks, the articles were followed by a smattering of members of Congress from both parties calling for Geithner's resignation for having cut such a lousy deal for the taxpayer.[38]

Although the coverage was brutal, it probably would have blown over in a day or so had Geithner not violated what Bill Burck had told me was one of the cardinal rules in Washington: "Don't punch down," which, as Bill explained, meant that you never publicly attack someone who is lower than you on the political totem pole—you risk raising them and simultaneously lowering yourself. Geithner, though, just couldn't help himself.

When he appeared at a press conference that afternoon with the attorney general on an unrelated matter, he was asked a question about the audit. Losing his cool, Geithner said sarcastically:

It's a great strength of our country, that you're going to have the chance for a range of people to look back at every decision made in every stage in this crisis, and look at the quality of judgments made and evaluate them with the benefit of hindsight. . . . Now, you're going to see a lot of conviction in this, a lot of strong views—*a lot of it untainted by experience.*[39]

When Kris saw the quote getting press coverage, she said to me, "Thank you, Secretary Geithner. He just gave us another three days of coverage. There are a lot of folks out there who wouldn't have covered this who are now going to pay attention."

As always, Kris was right. Geithner's slight toward me became a ministory in itself, and articles about the audit kicked around for weeks. One of the best commentaries came from Paul Krugman of *The New York Times,* who weighed in with a column entitled "The Big Squander." He noted that the rescue at 100 cents on the dollar had been neither necessary nor fair, condemned the choice made not to negotiate more aggressively, and, echoing my own warnings to Geithner just a few weeks earlier, he said that "the public has lost faith in the government's efforts, viewing them as little more than handouts" to Wall Street executives. He concluded "that by treating the financial industry—which got us into this mess in the first place—with kid gloves, they have squandered that trust."[40]

The hangover from the report continued for months. Ben Bernanke was clobbered by questions about the AIG negotiations in his reconfirmation hearings that December,[41] and both Democrats and Republicans bloodied Geithner at a House Oversight and Government Reform Committee hearing in January.[42] I joked to Kevin as we watched Geithner testify, sitting in the committee's lounge waiting my own turn to testify, "Look at us, we've brought the parties together."

When Democrat Stephen Lynch asked Geithner the $62 billion question—why didn't he try harder to cut a better bargain for the American people?[43]—Geithner dodged, and to this day I haven't heard him give any sort of serious answer to it.

After another congressman called for Geithner's resignation at the hearing,[44] for the first time I heard the rumor that Geithner might have asked the White House to fire me. (Though I heard such rumors from time to time, I don't know if there was any truth to them, although *Time* magazine did note when I stepped down that Geithner had "reportedly repeatedly tried to have [me] fired, or at least have [my] role downsized.")[45]

Nervous, I called Bill Burck, the person who understood Washington better than anyone else I knew.

"Bill," I asked, "am I in trouble here? This thing has really blown up. A bunch of members, both Republicans and Democrats, are calling for Geithner to step down. This can't be good for me. Can they fire me?"

Bill, as always, cut through the Washington bullshit and gave me his assessment. "You better pray that Geithner keeps his job. As long as he's there, you're untouchable. They can't fire you without it looking like retribution. They might've been able to do it earlier, but not now," Burck said. "If they fire you now, they'll make you *famous,* and not in a way that's good for them."

"And if he goes?" I asked.

"You would probably have to think about stepping down. If Geithner quits, there's no reason for them not to get rid of you too. It would probably be better to go out on your own terms rather than wait for them to fire you. Like it or not, you're now linked to him," Burck told me.

Geithner and I both survived. As President Obama walked to the podium to deliver his State of the Union address, just hours after the House Oversight hearing that had triggered my worried call to Burck, he stopped to embrace Geithner, which was widely perceived as a signal of his ongoing support.

Though I was once again relieved not to be fired, I also had to expect that things were only going to get more heated from then on, and I kept thinking about how John Angell had joked to me so many times about how eventually my allies in Congress would turn on us if they came to see SIGTARP as a political liability. But I'd learned a great deal by now about the power of the "bully pulpit" I had been given at SIGTARP, and, given the continuing neglect by the administration of the increasingly out-of-control housing crisis as well as the ongoing threat posed by the still-too-big-to-fail banks, I wasn't about to stop using it. I decided to turn my attention to trying to force some substantive changes on those two key issues.

11

Treasury's Backseat Driver

MY ORIGINAL AGREEMENT with Kevin was that he would work at SIGTARP for a year to help me build the agency. That period of time had passed in a blink. Fortunately, for me, he later agreed to stay on through the end of July 2010, but at the beginning of the year he relocated to our newly opened New York City office. We had formed a new investigative group there to handle the onslaught of cases we'd opened looking into TARP-related crimes perpetrated in Wall Street's backyard. The new office paid quick dividends, delivering within months of its opening the first criminal charges against a bank CEO who had tried to steal TARP funds, Charles Antonucci of Park Avenue Bank. Antonucci had tried to fraudulently dress up his bank's balance sheet in order to trick Treasury into giving him $11 million in TARP funds, and our agents worked with prosecutors from the Southern District of New York to bring him to justice.

Although Kevin still came down to Washington about once a week, I missed being able to walk into his office at all hours to talk about the daily craziness of SIGTARP. Over the course of our first thirteen months, we had probably laughed every single day about the absurdity of Washington and about how we, a couple of New York prosecutors, were romping around town with all of these *famous* people paying attention to us.

As he cleaned his office, I told Kevin something he already knew:

"I never would have survived without you, you know. SIGTARP wouldn't have survived without you."

"Fuck you," he answered lightheartedly. Sentimentality was not our strong suit.

I WAS ESPECIALLY appreciative to still have Kevin working with us as we confronted Treasury's latest parlor trick regarding the disastrous HAMP program. Nothing more emphatically attested to the double standard Treasury applied to its handling of the crisis than its incompetence in addressing the foreclosure crisis. As familiar as I had become with HAMP's failures, I had not really fully appreciated the cynicism behind the program's execution until Kevin and I started finalizing an audit report on it in early 2010. After we sent a draft to Treasury, Allison made the absurd claim to us that the program had never been intended to help the 3 to 4 million home owners that the president cited in his speech announcing the program actually stay in their homes through permanent modifications. Instead, he said, the goal had always been to make 3 to 4 million *offers* for *trial* modifications. That claim of such a meaningless standard for HAMP seemed particularly callous given the damage being done by the worsening foreclosure crisis. During 2009, HAMP's first year in operation, another 2.8 million properties received foreclosure filings, up from 2.3 million in 2008, and 2010 was already on pace to exceed 2009. Bank repossessions were also on the rise, increasing from 820,000 in 2008 to 918,000 in 2009, with estimates that 2010 would pass the symbolic one million mark.[1]

It is Government 101 that when setting goals for a program you must make them clear and measurable, so that if they're met or even exceeded, the program can be unambiguously judged a success. On the other hand, if performance falls short, the best practice is to acknowledge the shortfalls and change the program. Treasury was instead doing the opposite, seemingly changing its goals to meet HAMP's anemic results.

In the president's announcement, he had clearly said that it would "enable as many as 3 to 4 million homeowners to modify the terms of their mortgages to avoid foreclosure,"[2] and Treasury's announcement of the program's guidelines described HAMP as "a national modification program aimed at helping 3 to 4 million at-risk homeowners."[3] Even Treasury's website described HAMP as "a $75 billion loan modification program to help up to 4 million families avoid foreclosure."[4] With only 70,000 permanent modifications completed by the end of 2009, the program had a long way to go.[5] Kevin and the audit team were livid about Allison's response and its suggestion that the obviously struggling program was well on its way to meeting its goals. They were convinced that he was recharacterizing HAMP's core goal to an easy to meet but ultimately worthless standard for purely political purposes. I was struck more by the implications of his position.

"Kevin, do you realize what this means?" I asked.

"That they're dishonest?" he answered.

"Yes, of course," I said, "but also that they've no intention of actually fixing the program so that it *can* help three to four million people. Why else make this preposterous claim?"

I looked at Treasury's maneuvers as going beyond mere politics or spin. With $50 billion already earmarked to support HAMP and hundreds of billions of TARP dollars still available to be obligated and spent, Geithner and Allison had more than enough firepower to do something bold about the ongoing crisis. I viewed their ridiculous claim that "offers" were the true goal of HAMP as their signaling that they had no intention of doing so.

When we confronted Allison about it at our next weekly meeting, he defended Treasury's position: "How can we control what happens after a borrower gets an offer? We can't force them to accept it. The only thing we can control is the offer itself."

"Herb, how can you say that?" Kevin responded. "If you make 4 million offers but the offers are so bad or the program is so poorly run that only three people accept, would you then say that the program had met its goals?" Kevin further explained that because Treasury had complete control of the attractiveness of the terms that it offered home owners and servicers, it in fact had a great deal of control over what happened after the offer was made.

In finalizing the audit, in addition to stressing the importance of having meaningful goals, I wanted to paint a clear picture of the program's failures and then try to pressure Treasury to make substantive changes. One area I hoped we might be able to make headway on was the ongoing danger of redefault, where borrowers are unable or unwilling to continue to make payments even after their mortgage is modified. We decided to focus a recommendation on what has often been described as the greatest leading indicator of default, when a borrower is "underwater," meaning he owes more on his mortgage than his home is worth. Despite being widely considered as one of the best ways to stem foreclosures, no incentives had been crafted in HAMP to induce reducing principal (lowering the amount owed on the loan). Even the economists at the New York Fed acknowledged that "a loan modification program that lowers the principal balance on a mortgage will do more to support home ownership than a program that simply eases the terms of the loan."[6]

Principal reduction is considered effective because it both increases the affordability of mortgages and gives underwater borrowers hope that they will one day regain equity in their homes. We thus recommended that Treasury reconsider its approach to underwater mortgages along with other aspects of HAMP that could lead to borrowers' redefaulting on their modifications.[7]

The Treasury team rejected the recommendation, saying only that it would "study ideas that will enhance, albeit modestly, program outcomes" for underwater borrowers.[8] We had expected Treasury's intransigence. Geithner had already made his position clear: when Elizabeth Warren had pressed him during a 2009 hearing, Geithner had said that he had chosen to avoid principal reduction in HAMP because he believed it would be "dramatically more expensive for the American taxpayer, harder to justify, [and] create much greater risk of unfairness."[9]

We released our report on HAMP in March 2010 at a House Oversight and Government Reform Committee hearing at which Allison was called upon to explain the program's failings. He was hammered by both parties, and the Oversight Committee's chairman, Edolphus Towns, closed the hearing by urging that Treasury pursue principal reduction.[10]

The next day, Treasury seemingly caved in to congressional pressure by announcing the outlines of two potentially broad principal reduction programs.[11] The first was a $14 billion TARP-funded refinancing and principal reduction program that would be run through HUD and promised to help up to 1.5 million underwater home owners.[12] The other was part of HAMP and promised to pay incentives to lenders to lower the principal on underwater loans.

At first I was elated. As an agency, we had brought about a change that could potentially lead to hundreds of thousands if not millions of home owners keeping their homes. My euphoria, however, was short-lived. After Treasury finally briefed us on the details of the new programs, in the words of Yogi Berra, it was déjà vu all over again. The new initiatives bore the marks of being hastily rushed out for political purposes: they were incomplete and poorly thought out, and the Treasury officials charged with implementing them couldn't even explain how certain aspects of them would work, including answering basic questions about the HAMP incentive payments.

I told Kevin after the meeting that I thought that the $14 billion HUD program would never get off the ground. I was wrong, but only slightly. As of December 31, 2011, just 646 had been helped by the program, compared to the up to 1.5 million heralded by HUD.[13]

The principal reduction program seemed to have more promise, but my enthusiasm was similarly dampened when I learned that Treasury was going to defer entirely to the *servicers* to decide which borrowers, if any, would benefit from it. That was a complete departure from HAMP's usual practice. Under program rules, servicers had always been *required* to modify any eligible mortgage so long as Treasury's net present value test indicated that doing so was in the best interest of the holder of the loan.[14] With the newly announced Principal Reduction Alternative, however, even if Treasury's test indicated that it was far better for both the investor and the home owner to reduce the principal of the loan, the servicers could still decide not to do so.

Because servicers get paid based on the total outstanding principal of the loans that they service, with a voluntary principal reduction program, the servicers would now have the following choice: they could either modify the mortgage under the traditional but potentially less effective HAMP (by lowering the interest rate to 2 percent and extending the term of the loan to 40 years) and suffer no reduction in their fees; or reduce the principal on the loan, thereby directly taking money out of their own pockets. Why on earth, I asked, would a servicer choose the path that would leave it with fewer profits?

When I pressed Allison about why Treasury wasn't doing more to push for principal reduction, he cited "moral hazard" and argued that doing so would be unfair to "responsible borrowers" who stayed current on their payments.[15]

Though there was a some element of truth to the contention that any mortgage modification—principal reduction or otherwise, voluntary or mandatory—had an element of unfairness to home owners who did not also receive a modification, we viewed Treasury's position as reflecting a remarkably myopic and politicized view of the current crisis. The housing crisis wasn't just about individual home owners; it was also hindering economic recovery.[16] As the conservative economist and former chairman of President Reagan's Council of Economic Advisers Martin Feldstein later argued in a *New York Times* editorial, the large number of underwater mortgages slowed recovery by increasing the risk of borrowers defaulting on their mortgages, inhibiting the necessary increases in consumer spending, preventing workers from moving to areas where there were greater employment opportunities, and restricting the ability of individuals to tap home equity to start up and expand businesses. Although principal reductions were somewhat unpopular, Feldstein explained, the costs to all Americans of not addressing the problem of underwater mortgages should override those sentiments.[17]

I also found it beyond ironic that Treasury was now emphasizing moral hazard with respect to home owners. Though some home owners might try to take advantage of the program by intentionally not making mortgage payments in order to qualify—that risk paled in comparison to that created by Treasury by the way it had rescued the too-big-to-fail banks. Rather than requiring those executives to suffer the consequences of their failures, Treasury had handsomely rewarded those who had failed to do their jobs, saving their banks and making sure that almost all of them kept their jobs and the enormous bonuses that they had taken home before the crisis struck. As the AIG bailout demonstrated, the government had even sent a clear message that there was no such thing as a bet too outrageous for the government to guarantee as long as the institution making it was deemed too big to fail. The same government that had already jumped into the deep end of the moral hazard pool when it came to bank executives was now using the same concept as an excuse not to fulfill its original promise to use TARP to help struggling home owners.

I argued those points doggedly with Allison, but my arguments fell on deaf ears. He wasn't even interested in discussing how moral hazard could be limited.[18] I was at first puzzled by the response, but Kevin suspected that it was election politics at play. "I bet that they're absolutely terrified that going into the midterms the Republicans will dig up the HAMP equivalent of 'welfare queens'—home owners who refinanced to add a pool or extra bathroom and then received HAMP principal reductions—and make them the focus of a nationwide advertisement. Better to have an ineffective program than to take on that political risk."

As Kevin and I had suspected, once we discredited Treasury's stated HAMP goal of 3 to 4 million modification "offers," it continued to move the goalposts and seemingly adopted a new HAMP goal every month. In its "Two Year Retrospective," released in early October, 2010, for example, Treasury declared that the nearly 700,000 *failed* trial modifications (compared to just 467,000 successful ongoing permanent modifications at the time) were *successes* because "every person" who had received a trial modification was "getting a significant benefit" through temporarily reduced mortgage payments.[19]

In our October 2010 quarterly report, we called out that claim for what it was—a "cynical attempt to define failure as success"[20]—and chronicled examples of families (such as the Fletchers in the Firedoglake article) who had been victimized by HAMP trial modification failures.[21] We also tried to focus attention on the need for Treasury to deal with the broken incentive structure in HAMP. Any government program that relies on third parties, such as mortgage servicers, must have a system of rational incentives (carrots) balanced by strict penalties for noncompliance (sticks). HAMP had neither. As Geithner himself acknowledged in Senate testimony in early 2011, HAMP's incentive payments to servicers "were not powerful enough."[22] The numbers proved that to be true. Though HAMP had around 521,000 ongoing permanent modifications by the end of 2010, the housing market was still hemorrhaging, with 2.9 million homes receiving foreclosure filings and the banks repossessing more than one million homes, building off of the already historic numbers of 2008 and 2009.[23]

Treasury, however, continued its spirited defense of the status quo. Within days of Geithner's admission that HAMP's incentive structure was flawed, a Treasury official reportedly told a roomful of cheering mortgage servicers that they would not "see any major new programs coming out" and that instead Treasury would only "tweak around the edges" of HAMP.[24] What was even more infuriating, however, was the ongoing refusal to hold servicers accountable for their incompetence and abuse of home owners. Despite overwhelming evidence of servicer abuses, Treasury did nothing. Back in November 2009, Treasury threatened that servicers who failed to meet "performance obligations under [the HAMP contracts] will be subject to consequences which could include monetary penalties and sanctions."[25] But after that stern warning, it took no meaningful action.

Not that they didn't offer excuses. Treasury officials first confessed to the Congressional Oversight Panel in October 2010 that they were afraid that if they imposed sanctions, the servicers would run from the program,[26] and then backtracked even further at a hearing in January 2011, in which TARP's acting chief claimed that Treasury didn't have "the tools" to effectively penalize the servicers.[27] I sent Treasury a memo about that claim, asking for the legal justification for what seemed like a dramatic shift in its position, but I didn't receive a response before I left.

Treasury's failure to live up to its side of the legislative bargain to use TARP to preserve home ownership was ultimately a choice. Under Paulson, Treasury chose to bail out the largest banks without insisting that they effect meaningful mortgage reform. Under Geithner, that original sin was compounded by a series of further choices in program design (to "foam the runway" for the banks) and execution (refusing to penalize servicers) that always seemed to put home owners' interests second. The simple truth is that Geithner and Treasury chose to never treat the foreclosure crisis, or their promises to Congress to help home owners, with the same seriousness and resolve that they applied to rescuing the banks. By the end of 2011, Treasury had spent only $3 billion of the $50 billion originally allocated to HAMP.[28] In other words, nearly three full years after HAMP was launched, home owners across the country had benefited less from TARP than the credit card company American Express, which received $3.89 billion in CPP funds. With hundreds of billions of untapped TARP funds still available in 2010, Geithner and Treasury had numerous opportunities to fulfill their promises to the American people. Instead, they chose the banks.

THE STRUGGLE OVER HAMP did little to improve my already strained relations with Treasury, but the release of our findings on the auto bailouts pushed things to a whole new level.

In April 2010, GM reemerged in the news when it announced that it would soon be paying back a multibillion-dollar TARP loan. In a congressional hearing shortly after the announcement, I clarified that GM would be paying back that loan with other money it had received from TARP. As I explained, a good portion of the total $49.5 billion that Treasury had provided GM had been placed in an escrow account that GM couldn't tap without first getting permission. The announced loan repayment was being made out of that account, with Treasury's consent.[29] I made clear what Treasury and GM did not, that although it was undoubtedly good news that GM's improved performance since exiting bankruptcy meant that it no longer needed the billions of dollars sitting in the escrow account to survive, it was not as if the source of the repayments was the proceeds from car sales. As Senator Tom Carper said at the hearing, GM was really "taking money out of one pocket and putting it into the other."[30]

The payment was made the next day to loud cheers from Treasury and the White House: Vice President Biden cited it as a "huge accomplishment,"[31] the White House made it a focus of its daily press briefing,[32] and Geithner issued a statement trumpeting the repayment.[33] GM was even more enthusiastic, with its CEO announcing in a television advertisement that "we have repaid our government loan, in full, with interest, five years ahead of the original schedule."[34]

Geithner, however, made no mention that the source of the repayment was other TARP funds, and GM claimed that it had been able to repay the loan "because more customers are buying vehicles like the Chevrolet Malibu and Buick LaCrosse."[35] Senator Grassley issued a release complaining about Treasury not being straightforward with the American people,[36] and as the story started to pick up steam, I got word that Treasury's press office was telling the press that my testimony was wrong, so I quickly released the backup documents. As a result, Allison ultimately had to send a letter to Senator Grassley admitting that the money had come from the TARP-funded account.[37] Once again, an otherwise positive story became a public relations disaster that harmed the government's credibility. As *The New York Times'* Gretchen Morgenson noted in her article on the controversy, "employing spin and selective disclosure is no way to raise taxpayers' trust in our nation's leadership."[38]

The response was modest, however, compared to the reaction to the results of our audit of Treasury's decision to close so many of GM and Chrysler's dealerships so quickly.

We released our report in mid-July. Since our last meeting, the audit team had dug further into Treasury's decision-making process, interviewing many of the same experts that Treasury had consulted as well as others, including representatives from J. D. Power and Associates, the National Automobile Dealers Association, and a former deputy CEO of Chrysler.[39] The auditors found remarkably little support for the auto team's determination that the viability of GM and Chrysler depended on their closing so many dealerships so quickly. Instead, the closings appeared to be more of a matter of convenience; because the companies *eventually* needed to shutter dealerships, they might as well use bankruptcy to accomplish that task more quickly to void the otherwise valid contracts that the dealers had with the companies.[40] As Treasury officials explained, federal bankruptcy had given them a "unique opportunity" to trump the tough and "restrictive state franchise law[s]" that otherwise governed GM and Chrysler's agreements with their dealers.[41]

The auto team's justification for the accelerated terminations was based on its view that GM and Chrysler should follow the "Toyota model," which included fewer dealerships that sold far more cars per dealer.[42] As a result, the theory went, the fewer remaining dealers would each be more profitable and, in turn, would invest more in their facilities. Nicer-looking dealerships would in turn lead to happier customers, which would create more brand equity for GM and Chrysler. With more brand equity, they could offer fewer incentives to car buyers, which would lead to higher car prices and higher profits.[43] The auto team received that analysis mostly from its Wall Street–based analysts.[44]

Although nearly all of the experts that we consulted agreed that the total number of GM and Chrysler dealerships should be reduced over time, there was substantive disagreement about where dealers should be closed and how quickly it needed to be done. For example, though there was a general consensus that the companies had too many dealerships in certain "metro," or urban, areas, several of the experts we consulted felt quite differently about rural dealers. They cited the distinct advantage that GM and Chrysler had in those areas over foreign competitors and the risk of ruining the "historic relationship" that the companies had with local residents in small towns if they terminated the local dealerships. Although it appeared that GM might have initially agreed with that assessment by including in its original viability plan an estimate that just 18 percent of its dealer closings would be in rural areas, that number jumped dramatically after Treasury directed it to accelerate the closings, with rural dealerships making up nearly half of the dealerships slated for termination.[45]

Moreover, the representatives from the Center for Automotive Research, J. D. Powers, and the National Automobile Dealers Association all asserted that given the recession and overall declining sales, it was precisely the *wrong* time to massively cut GM's and Chrysler's sales outlets.[46] Even an analysis obtained by Treasury five weeks *after* it made its decision on the dealership closings indicated that it would take years for GM and Chrysler to recover from the sharp drop-off in sales that the accelerated closings would cause.[47]

Finally, our auditors confirmed that my worst fear was true: no consideration whatsoever had been given to the job losses that would be caused by the accelerated terminations, with no study even being prepared until weeks *after* the decision had already been made. Even then, that report's estimate that an average of fifty jobs could be lost per dealership closing (up to 100,000 total jobs) was not considered by the auto team.[48]

The auditors also interviewed the current head of the auto team, Ron Bloom, and asked if immediately closing down the dealerships was truly necessary for the companies' survival. Bloom agreed that it was not, commenting that they "could have left any one component [of the restructuring] alone."[49] Even GM's CEO, Ed Whitacre, acknowledged that GM might have tried to cut too many dealerships and that the cuts were "not necessary."[50] He noted that "if you had more good dealers then you can sell more good cars, and that is what we are in the business of doing. I still believe that it is a much better idea to have more good dealers."[51]

The report had a distinctly unforgiving tone. As lifelong Democrats, Kevin and I worried on the eve of the report's release that it would be viewed as a gut punch to President Obama. Just three months before the midterm elections, with unemployment near 9.5 percent,[52] we were essentially going to say that his team had unnecessarily directed the shutting down of thousands of small businesses across the country, putting up to 100,000 jobs at risk, all based on a not particularly well-researched theory and without giving even the slightest consideration to those who could lose their jobs as a result. As always, the choice was clear: our job was to ignore the politics and report the facts on what we believed was a terribly flawed decision-making process.

We were not the only ones who saw the potential political impact of the report. We put it out on embargo on Sunday, July 18, 2010, for public release the following day, but within two hours Representative Issa once again shattered our embargo by issuing a scathing press release that concluded with the comment that "The Obama Administration made a conscious decision to accelerate a plan that jeopardized the jobs of tens-of-thousands of American workers."[53] Harsh though Issa's statement was, unlike many of the broad pronouncements that often come from members of Congress, it was unequivocally accurate.

As the criticism of the administration mounted throughout the day, the White House held a conference call conducted by what the press described as an "administration official" (we were later told it was Bloom). Rather than dispute the facts of the report (which he could not; I had verified every fact, section heading, and even the table of contents with Treasury), the "official" erected a straw man, claiming that we were suggesting that Treasury should have let GM and Chrysler collapse. He also accused us of engaging in hindsight and claimed that we were "tak[ing] the situation dramatically out of context."[54]

Bloom's complaints echoed Treasury's official response to the report, which was to create a false dichotomy: either you supported every aspect of every decision made by Treasury in the auto bailouts, or you were a sworn enemy advocating that the government should have let them collapse. Nothing could have been further from the truth. It would have exceeded the scope of the audit for us even to have addressed that broader question in the report, but I personally believed that Paulson and later Geithner had made the right decision to rescue GM and Chrysler from oblivion, given the fragility of our economy at the time. Although I certainly disagreed with Treasury's management of the bailouts and recognized that they would cost the taxpayer dearly, I believed that the alternative would have likely been far worse and that the country is better off today because of the turnaround of those two icons of American manufacturing.

Though I wasn't happy that the White House had convened a Sunday-afternoon conference call to attack our report in such a misleading manner, I also wasn't really concerned that the characterizations would stick; anyone who read the report would clearly see that we were challenging not the bailout itself but the bad process behind the dealership closings.

Then I turned to the editorial page of *The Washington Post* early that Tuesday morning. The lead editorial, referring to me, was titled "Treasury's Back-Seat Driver," and the text seemed to mirror, word for word, the talking points from the White House conference call, only far nastier. It accused me of engaging in "remarkably unfair and unrealistic" hindsight and described the report as a "rehash of familiar dealer complaints." It then adopted Treasury's false dichotomy, claiming that "The alternative [to the accelerated terminations] was *zero* jobs for everyone—either immediately, if the companies were allowed to collapse, or eventually if they were not credibly restructured."[55] The editorial also suggested that I had come under the spell of the corrupting influence of lobbyists.

I was shocked by the harshness of the language and by how far off the characterizations of the report were from what it actually said. In addition, the piece fundamentally misunderstood the role of inspectors general. It was our *job* to be backseat drivers. We weren't politicians second-guessing decisions for political gain, we were auditors analyzing a decision-making process to see if it was flawed. As I said to Kevin, noting the political tone of the attack, "Don't they realize that we're fucking *Democrats*?"

I went into the bedroom and showed the editorial to Karen, telling her for the umpteenth time, "I think this is it." Herb Allison and I had met for our "the gold or the lead" conversation not long before this, when he had advised me that if I didn't change the tone of my reports I risked ruining my long-term career prospects. This seemed like follow-through; they were going to try to destroy my reputation before they fired me. I pointed out to Karen that the *Post* was not attacking the report itself as much as it was attacking me personally. "It's just one newspaper," she said reassuringly. "No one will care."

When I went to work, I hid how rattled I had been by the editorial, telling my staff, "No such thing as bad press, just means more people will read the report." But I really was worried that it finally spelled the beginning of the end for me at SIGTARP.

When I called Bill Burck for his perspective, though, he told me not to worry. "Everyone knows that the *Post* is in the White House's pocket, and no one cares what they say. If anything, it's a badge of honor."

As the day went on, I kept looking for follow-up coverage, but none came. The editorial was largely ignored, and, if anything, other editorials supported our conclusions.[56]

Although I was somewhat relieved, I knew the real test would come Wednesday morning, when I was set to testify before the Senate Finance Committee. If the Democrats on the committee came after me, I was definitely in trouble.

I GOT TO the hearing room early and saw Elizabeth Warren, who was also scheduled to testify. I wasn't the only victim of Tuesday's *Washington Post*, which also included articles questioning her ability to run a new Consumer Protection Bureau that was being created by the Dodd-Frank reform bill, which was about to be signed into law. The articles cited her supposedly ideological bias and her alleged management inexperience. As a sure sign of where the articles had come from, they also suggested that Elizabeth had "antagonized" Treasury and that Geithner's apparent in-house pick to head the agency might be a better choice.[57]

I had gotten to know Elizabeth better over the past months, having had a number of informal lunches with her, and I saw that she'd had to deal with some of the same hostility from the Treasury team that it had directed at me. Over the prior months, the constant backlash from Treasury officials had become increasingly personal toward me, and some of the comments were over the top, even by Washington standards. One Treasury official had accosted one of our employees at a cocktail party and berated her for working for "a fascist." I also heard that a lawyer in the general counsel's office had described me as "the walking embodiment of evil." They had also started to try to chip away at my credibility by suggesting that I was carrying water for the GOP, describing me as "a closet Republican" and telling reporters that I was planning on switching political parties to run for New York State attorney general as a Republican. Elizabeth seemed to be facing similar blowback.

She and I had had one of our occasional lunches just a few days before the hearing, and with Kevin in New York, I'd found it was helpful to have someone to commiserate with. The lunch was a refreshing break, and I knew it was an exciting time for Elizabeth, as she'd been advocating for the new Consumer Financial Protection Bureau for years. She had first pitched the concept in a paper years earlier and had fought vigilantly for it during the drafting of the Dodd-Frank act. The talk for months had been that she would be named its inaugural director, and I thought she rightly deserved the post.

Part of the setup of the new bureau was that it initially would be housed in Treasury, meaning that it would be under the supervision of Geithner. Elizabeth, who is a gifted questioner, had routinely tortured Geithner during his occasional testimony before the Congressional Oversight Panel, and there was open speculation in the press that he was opposing her appointment as director.[58] A couple of weeks before our lunch I had watched her absolutely pummel Geithner at a hearing. I had thought she might go lightly on him with the Consumer Protection Bureau job still up in the air. After all, she was making no secret of her desire for the job, and the White House had to be watching her every move. But she just lit him up, attacking HAMP's design as ineffective and pointing out the damage that had been inflicted on families who had suffered through failed trial modifications.[59] I thought it was a remarkably principled act, the exact opposite of what any other person in Washington angling for a high-profile job would have done.

At lunch Elizabeth and I talked about how frustrating and frightening HAMP's failure had been and how appalling it was that Treasury still refused to acknowledge its failings and start doing something to help the legions of suffering families. When I suggested that it appeared almost as if Treasury was actively undermining the program, she commented that we shouldn't be surprised, given Geithner's "foam the runway" explanation in our meeting back in October.

Elizabeth then lowered her voice. "Can I ask you a different question?" she asked.

"Sure," I said.

"Do you find Herb Allison to be very"—she paused—"angry?"

I laughed. "Absolutely! I thought it was just me."

"I had him in for a hearing on HAMP and asked him some very tough questions, and it got a little heated because he just refused to answer them," Elizabeth explained. "We then had a meeting over at Treasury, and he takes me into a room, just the two of us, and starts yelling at me."

Lowering her voice even further, Elizabeth started impersonating Allison: "'I am personally offended by the way that you spoke to me . . .'"

I cut her off with a howl of laughter. "That's his favorite line!" I said. "If there's one thing about Herb, he's always personally offended!"

BEFORE THE HEARING STARTED, I greeted Elizabeth, and we chatted in the lounge behind the hearing room.

"Looks like Geithner had a busy day with the *Post* yesterday," I said, smiling, although I could see that she was upset.

Our old friend John Angell, Max Baucus's staffer, walked into the back room. I figured John would give us an honest appraisal of where we stood with the chairman.

"Congratulations," John said. "Baucus can't stop talking about the dealer report."

A weight was lifted off my back. As I continued to chat with the staffers, I realized that once again Burck had been dead on. If anything, the staffers were amused and even a little impressed by the *Post* editorial.

When I made some crack about Treasury writing it, one senior Democrat staffer laughed and said that it was more likely to have come directly from the White House.

I might have actually let out an audible sigh of relief when Senator Baucus opened the hearing by citing the auto dealer report as an "independent analysis that has brought critical transparency to the TARP program."[60]

The most surprising support, however, came from my old nemesis, Senator Bunning, who told me, "We want you to do everything in your power to make them accountable. That is why we voted you into that position. And so far, we are pretty pleased with what you are doing."[61]

After the press died down, it seemed as if Allison and his team gave up on any pretense of cooperatively working with us. They started making it more difficult for us to access documents that we had up until that point been routinely receiving, relenting only when I resorted to my now customary threat to report their obstruction to Congress. Meanwhile, with Kevin officially leaving SIGTARP on July 31, things became a lot less fun and a lot more work. I began, for the first time, to think about leaving. Before I did, though, I was determined to keep pushing for better protections to be put in place so that a TARP and a SIGTARP would never be necessary again.

12

Happy Endings

GENERALLY SPEAKING, up until the fall of 2010, Treasury was respectful of our investigative role and stayed out of our way. As our relations further deteriorated after the release of our auto dealers and HAMP audits, though, even our attempts to pursue criminals became fair game. In the middle of September, Kris began receiving calls from reporters, including those at Reuters and *The Wall Street Journal,* asking pointed questions about our opening of a number of satellite offices for our Investigations Division. Our investigations chief, Chris Sharpley, had built a strong law enforcement agency that was hitting on all cylinders, and we had recently opened regional offices in San Francisco, Los Angeles, and Atlanta in addition to New York. Our strategy was paying off, and by the time I stepped down, in March 2011, we had secured criminal convictions of eighteen individuals for TARP-related crimes, with fifty-four more charged either civilly or criminally as a result of our investigations. Thanks in no small part to the Farkas investigation, we had prevented more than $550 million in taxpayer dollars from being lost to fraud and assisted in the recovery of more than $150 million.[1]

Our first investigative priority was banks that fraudulently applied for or received CPP funds, which accounted for just under half of our ongoing investigations. In addition to tips from our hotline (which had more than 20,000 hits) and referrals from prosecutors' offices and other law enforcement agencies, we also developed cases by putting together one of the most sophisticated computer forensic teams in the country. They in turn designed and launched what we called "the CPP Project," scouring databases and filings to search for potential red flags of accounting fraud among TARP-applicant banks. By the time I left, we had already secured civil charges against Bank of America and its CEO, Ken Lewis, as well as criminal charges against executives at Colonial Bank (as part of the Farkas case) and Park Avenue Bank (against Charles Antonucci), and we would soon be announcing indictments against bank executives in various states across the country, including two at United Commercial Bank in San Francisco who were alleged to have successfully stolen nearly $300 million from TARP, all of which had been lost. The majority of our remaining cases arose out of the Sisyphean task of trying to lock up fraudsters who were exploiting Treasury's mismanagement of HAMP to prey on struggling home owners through advance-fee mortgage modification scams.

Though I was thrilled with the progress we'd made, I had some frustrations as well. We had no jurisdiction over criminal activity that predated TARP's enactment and therefore couldn't look at the big banks for potential criminal activity leading up to the financial crisis. Further, DOJ's lack of aggressiveness in the Farkas/TBW investigation reappeared in cases with various prosecutors' offices across the country, particularly after the November 2009 acquittal of two Bear Stearns hedge fund executives for securities fraud. The loss seemed to send a chill down DOJ's spine, making it more and more difficult to get our cases charged.

Given our successes and the obvious importance of prosecuting those who attempted to criminally profit off of TARP, I was disappointed by Treasury's tactics with the press. The questions the reporters were asking Kris started with questions about our new offices, and then later shifted to suggestions that we were wasting taxpayer resources by providing our agents with basic protective equipment, such as guns, ammunition, and bulletproof vests. The reporters had also been given confidential information about a budget request we had recently made to Treasury. When pressed, different reporters told me that "Treasury officials" had been the sources of the questions and the supposedly confidential budget information.

I was incensed. For one thing, it was a hard-and-fast rule, published by OMB, that leaks to the press about budget proposals were forbidden. Further, characterizing necessary expenses as wasteful struck me as outrageous. I explained to the reporters that we were opening new investigative offices in order to avoid the skyrocketing travel costs that were eating through our budget and that we were actually saving money by opening them, as reflected in our request for a smaller budget.

I also explained that white-collar criminals kept guns too and emphasized the importance of making sure that our agents had the necessary safety equipment when forcibly entering premises on a search warrant or arresting individuals in their homes.

We were able to beat back most of those stories, but the leaks would continue, and mocking stories about our agents and the costs of their equipment started popping up in *The Washington Post*.[2] That was despicable; it was one thing to go after me; I had learned that such attacks were just part of the job. But challenging the right of law enforcement agents to have the necessary protective gear was a new low.

Those leaks were just the latest in what had become an openly adversarial approach toward SIGTARP, which included regular refusals to provide us with information. Among other things, Treasury had refused to give us information about some small-business loan-backed bonds that it had purchased with TARP funds, information relating to GM's initial public offering, and even copies of documents necessary to evaluate whether certain TARP recipients were following executive compensation restrictions. Although we were eventually able to get all of the documents after I threatened to go to Congress, it was becoming like Chinese water torture.

Things became even worse, however, after Herb Allison stepped down in September 2010, ceding the leadership of TARP to his combative chief counsel, Tim Massad.

Fortunately, I had a fantastic new deputy by this time, Geoff Moulton, who helped me cope with the frustrating war of attrition that Massad and Treasury seemed to be waging against us. Geoff had been a career federal prosecutor, rising to the number two position at the U.S. Attorney's Office in Philadelphia. During the Clinton administration, Geoff had been detailed to Treasury, where he had been the staff director for the high-profile review of and report on ATF's botched operation in Waco, Texas, against David Koresh. He had then become a law professor at Widener Law School in Delaware, and at the time that I interviewed him, he was serving as the chief counsel for Senator Ted Kaufman.

Kaufman, a lifelong staffer for Joe Biden who had assumed Biden's Senate seat after the inauguration, had been one of the leading critics of the big banks during the regulatory reform debate. Notably, he had been the vocal cosponsor of the Brown-Kaufman amendment to the Dodd-Frank bill, which would have put a hard cap on the size of the banks in order to address the threat they posed by continuing to be too big to fail. I was an advocate of the amendment, which would have forced the breakup of the largest banks, and I was impressed that Geoff had worked for Kaufman.

My diligence on Geoff indicated that he was well liked and remarkably well respected by seemingly anyone who had ever come into contact with him, including both Democrats and Republicans. He would be the perfect follow-up to Kevin and an ideal successor for me if I got bounced from SIGTARP. (Unfortunately, Geoff declined to succeed me when I stepped down, instead returning home and ending what had become a multiyear commute from Philadelphia.)

At Allison's last and Geoff's first SIGTARP-TARP meeting, I congratulated Allison on his tenure and thanked him for his patriotism and public service. He had been difficult to deal with, but I still respected that he had come out of a comfortable retirement to take the job. Massad was running the meeting, so it was him I asked about some rumors that had been swirling around in the press that Treasury was about to announce an imminent restructuring of its bailout of AIG. Massad dismissed my concerns, telling us that although there were always ongoing discussions about AIG, we shouldn't put too much credence in what we were hearing in the press. Massad assured me that he would let us know if anything developed. On that same day, however, Treasury officials apparently briefed the press on the details of a massive restructuring that would be announced within two days.[3] We were not briefed in advance.

The new deal provided that if AIG met a series of conditions over the next few months, Treasury would convert about $49 billion of its existing TARP investment in AIG preferred stock to AIG common stock. When added to the 80 percent of AIG's common stock already received by the Federal Reserve, the government's overall ownership of AIG would increase to 92 percent.[4]

Massad's apparent dissembling about the restructuring was irresponsible, but shortly thereafter, the Treasury team pulled a stunt that flat-out misled the public about the progress of the AIG bailout. On October 5, Treasury released a *Two Year Retrospective* report about TARP, and a featured highlight was the announcement that it now anticipated that TARP losses on AIG would be just $5 billion.[5] At first that seemed like remarkable news, representing a $40 billion drop in anticipated losses in just six months.[6] But when I took a closer look, it seemed as if the drop in losses resulted merely from a shift in accounting rather than from a $40 billion improvement in AIG's business performance. In a subsequent meeting, the Treasury officials handling the accounting acknowledged what I had suspected.

Up until publishing its *Retrospective,* Treasury had calculated its potential losses for AIG based on a formula required by GAO. For the *Retrospective,* however, that methodology was put aside, and instead the loss was calculated according to a formula that presumed that the AIG restructuring would be successful and that Treasury would be able to sell its AIG shares at the current market price.[7] I asked if they didn't have to still use the GAO-approved formula for their annual financial statement, due in mid-November, and the officials said they did. I also confirmed that for the Retrospective, AIG was the only TARP recipient for which they engaged in this type of accounting.

So why the different calculation now? I realized that the *Retrospective* had come out about a month *before* the midterm elections, while the annual financial statement wouldn't surface until two weeks *after* the elections. It looked as if they were trying to pretty up TARP by using an accounting gimmick to make tens of billions of dollars in TARP losses disappear just in time for the midterms. Sure enough, Treasury released the *Retrospective* as part of a press blitz that included Geithner citing the drop in anticipated TARP losses in a piece in *The Washington Post.*[8]

It wasn't so much that Treasury's new calculation bothered me; it was the failure yet again to be transparent about AIG. Earlier in 2010, Treasury's press office had issued an equally misleading statement regarding potential losses for AIG—this time with respect to the government's effective purchase of CDOs from AIG's counterparties at 100 cents on the dollar. In a statement to the media, a press officer claimed that the transaction was "above water" for the taxpayer by citing only to the New

York Fed's purchases at market value while ignoring the other half of the transactions, the tens of billions of dollars that were lost by agreeing to allow the banks to keep all of AIG's collateral. These losses, of course, would be borne by taxpayers as part of the overall projected losses for TARP's investment in AIG.[9]

Now, nine months later, Treasury was again shading the truth for political advantage, and I proposed a simple fix to the *Retrospective*: I suggested to Geithner in a letter that he simply reissue the report with a disclosure explaining the change in accounting and adding the information about what the loss would be under the usual methodology. The proposal was quickly rejected. In a heavily lawyered letter from Massad, the nonsensical response was "Simply stated, there has not been any change in our established methodology."[10]

When we raised the issue in our October 2010 quarterly report, it provoked another minicrisis that Treasury could easily have avoided. Members of Congress quickly condemned Treasury's obfuscation, and the press jumped on it. *The New York Times,* for example, entitled its article "Treasury Hid A.I.G. Losses, Report Says," while *The Atlantic*'s headline read, "So Much for Treasury's [REDACTED] Transparency?"[11]

On the day the news broke, Kris began hearing that Treasury officials had been making threatening calls to the press, telling them either not to cover the story or to make their coverage critical of us. I later also personally heard from reporters of some of Treasury's activities that day, including one anecdote involving very senior Treasury officials going to very senior executives at one newspaper and threatening to withhold access from that newspaper's reporters to Treasury personnel going forward if they did not kill the story.

At first I viewed the swirling controversy as just another SIGTARP tussle. I'd become hardened to the internecine Washington warfare waged in the press by that time and was getting to the point where I could give as good as I got. The next morning, though, I was astonished to see that the White House had joined the fray. It posted on its website and blasted out to the press an article full of mischaracterizations and inaccuracies entitled "The Facts of AIG," written by deputy White House communications director Jen Psaki. Psaki savaged me in the post, saying that I was trying "to generate a false controversy over AIG to try and grab a few, cheap headlines" and was "stuck in a time warp." Suggesting that I had an anti–White House bias, Psaki also questioned my independence, stating "Any truly independent observer would say that Treasury's stake in AIG will be worth more than taxpayers originally invested in that company."[12] She even suggested that I didn't "like movies with happy endings."

When I called Bill Burck to get his take, after the requisite joke about my love of "happy endings," even he couldn't quite believe the venom of the attack. "It's bizarre," he said. "I can't think of an administration ever going after an IG like this. After all, you work for them, and if they think half of what's in there is true, they should just fire you. They are treating you like a political enemy instead of as an employee."

Thankfully, I had been well prepared for that day. Kris had predicted in her job interview that one day our credibility would be attacked, and over the previous twenty-two months, she had slowly built up our standing with the press so when the day came, "no matter what they hear, the press will come to us first and believe us, because we'll prove to them that we tell the truth." Lori had done the same with Congress, and the strategy paid off. The White House posting was all but ignored. It seemed as if the only follow-up coverage came from a handful of bloggers who weighed in on the absurdity of the Obama White House feuding with its own IG.[13]

When I went home that night and told Karen what had happened, she predictably asked, "Aren't you afraid you're going to be fired?" After all of the times that I had whined to her about getting the ax, in some ways the White House attack appeared to pose the most serious threat yet. But I told Karen I was no longer afraid, I was just too exhausted to care anymore.

It was dispiriting. Though we had battled with Treasury from day one, we were still able to have a positive impact, and Herb Allison had once told me, after I had complained about being ignored by Treasury, "You have more influence over TARP decisions than I do. You might not be there in person, but you always have a seat at the table. It seems like every time we're discussing a policy, someone is asking 'What would SIGTARP do? What would SIGTARP say?' Trust me, your voice is heard."

I no longer believed that was true, at least not in a constructive way. As I told Karen that night, "I'm just sick of this town."

"Maybe it's time to go?" she asked hopefully.

I knew for sure that Karen was right when, in January 2011, I testified alongside Massad at a hearing. After the introductions, Representative Issa, now the chairman of the House Oversight Committee, said, "The normal rule of committee is that we go in order of rank. Mr. Massad, I believe you would, by protocol, be first."[14]

I saw red. Massad had not yet been confirmed by the Senate, which meant that I outranked him. During a break, I took Lori aside, irate. "Tell Issa's staffer that there are one hundred senators that would disagree that an *acting* assistant secretary outranks a presidentially appointed, Senate-confirmed inspector general. Tell him now that his boss is chairman, it's his responsibility to make sure that Issa understands basic fucking protocol," I said, fuming.

When I told Karen later what had happened, she burst out laughing. "Why would you possibly care?" she asked.

I started to explain the deep significance of the humiliating slight but then also started to laugh. "Oh, my God," I said. "I'm turning into everything that I hated about Washington."

I had been infected. I'd gone from making fun of and often trampling over Washington's silly protocols to being incensed about testifying second at a hearing. I was becoming one of *them*.

That night I started working on my resignation letter.

I DECIDED THAT before stepping down, one way in which I could use the SIGTARP bully pulpit was to contribute to the effort to focus more attention on the serious limitations of the Dodd-Frank Act, which had been passed by Congress with the explicit intent to end all future bailouts of the too-big-to-fail banks.

Kevin and I had dived into the too-big-to-fail problem earlier, recognizing that the banks that engaged in the manipulative, reckless, and unethical behavior that had helped bring down our economy needed to be fundamentally changed before the cycle of boom, bust, and bailout repeated itself yet again. As reform was beginning to be seriously debated in early 2010, we highlighted in a report what we, and many others, saw as one of the greatest costs generated by Treasury's administration of TARP: the failure to limit the moral hazard created by bailing out the largest banks. As a result of the consolidation of the financial industry, the largest banks had become significantly bigger, led by JPMorgan Chase, which grew by 36 percent, from $1.56 trillion in assets at the end of 2007 to $2.12 trillion at the end of 2010; Wells Fargo, which more than doubled in size to $1.26 trillion; and Bank of America, which grew by 32 percent, from $1.72 trillion to $2.27 trillion.[15] As then Kansas City Fed President Thomas Hoenig explained, the banks had also somehow grown more powerful[16] and had "even greater political influence than they had before the crisis."[17]

With a government guarantee made all but explicit by the bailouts, the executives of those institutions still enjoyed all of the short-term profits and benefits of taking outsized risks backstopped by the government. Worse still, the presumption of bailout made the banks more attractive to creditors, who continued to extend credit at prices that did not fully account for the risks that the banks were taking and, as a result, failed to provide the necessary market discipline to rein in excessive risk-taking. This "heads I win; tails the Government will bail me out" incentive system was still firmly in place. One of the best measures of moral hazard, though, was the metric that matters most to Wall Street executives, their pay. And rather than being scaled down in proportion to their epic failures in risk management, compensation for the top twenty-five Wall Street firms in 2010 actually broke records at $135 billion.[18]

After ticking through several of those concerns,[19] in a line that would be widely quoted, Kevin and I had argued that "even if TARP saved our financial system from driving off a cliff back in 2008, absent meaningful reform, we are still driving on the same winding mountain road, but this time in a faster car."[20] (That line, however, was Kevin's sole act of gross insubordination as my deputy. In every draft, I had added the phrase "with faulty brakes" to the end of the sentence, and each time Kevin took it out. I realized he had done so in the final version only when I saw the quotes in the newspapers.)

Given the severity of the crisis and the need for immediate action, Paulson and Geithner may have been right to temporarily put moral hazard to the side when rescuing the banks. We argued that now, however, was the time to enact tough protections. As the regulatory debate picked up, though, the banks and their lobbying machines kicked into gear, engaging in a relentless campaign to water down what would become Dodd-Frank.

A slender reed of hope had briefly emerged in the Brown-Kaufman amendment, which would have forced the handful of largest banks to slim down to more manageable levels. But despite drawing bipartisan support from several top Republicans, including Senator Shelby, Geithner opposed the bill, and it was eventually voted down. A "senior Treasury official" was quoted in the press as explaining that Brown-Kaufman "would have broken up the six biggest banks in America" and that "[i]f we'd been for it, it probably would have happened. But we weren't, so it didn't."[21]

Instead of taking the Brown-Kaufmann meat cleaver to the banks, Dodd-Frank gave the regulators a scalpel and directed them to attempt to carve up the power of the largest banks through an enhanced and mind-numbingly complex 848-page-long regulation regime. In many ways, the act is too big to succeed.

The centerpiece is a brand-new supercommittee called the Financial Stability Oversight Council (FSOC), made up of ten voting-member financial regulators including its chairman, the Treasury secretary. Congress left the tough decisions about how to rein in the largest banks to FSOC and its members. Among the regulators' many assignments were designing and implementing rules to limit banks' ability to gamble with their capital in proprietary trading (the Volcker Rule), implementing broad regulation of the derivatives markets, addressing the ongoing conflicts of interest at the credit-rating agencies, and setting bank capital requirements.

As for the largest and most dangerous financial institutions, the act directed the regulators to set up a resolution system, called the Orderly Liquidation Authority, that would theoretically allow a too-big-to-fail financial institution to be shut down without a bailout. To accomplish that goal, the act required the regulators to gather from the banks "living wills" that would set forth how each institution could be wound down in an orderly fashion. The act did give the committee some strong tools to effect meaningful change. Among other things, if they found that the living wills were not credible, they could compel major alterations in the structure of the banks, including breaking them up, but only by a two-thirds vote of the committee, which is an obvious constraint on this power.[22]

Dodd-Frank thus put all of its eggs into the financial regulators' basket, the approach championed by Geithner and the White House. This did not seem to me like a recipe for effective reform. After all, one of the most important lessons that should have been learned from the financial crisis was the remarkable fallibility of the regulators. They had been blind, or willfully blind, about the signs of the coming financial crisis, and their track record with respect to previous crises was no better. Lax regulation and supervision had permitted the broad excesses that had led to the inflation of the housing bubble, and a remarkable lack of awareness had prevailed as it began to pop. For example, Bernanke had famously testified before Congress on March 28, 2007, that he was confident that "the problems in the subprime markets seem likely to be contained,"[23] and a couple of months later, Geithner had given a speech in which he lauded the "financial innovation" (e.g., the CDOs and CDSs that would eventually exacerbate the crisis) that he said had increased the "resilience of the market in the face of the latest shocks."[24]

The act also failed to recognize that the regulators often lacked the political will necessary to successfully regulate the largest banks. As recent history has repeatedly shown, through massive campaign contributions, relentless lobbying, and multimillion-dollar payouts awaiting government officials who join Wall Street firms, no legislation can confer the necessary fortitude upon the regulators.

Finally, the act concentrates incredible responsibility and control in one person, the secretary of the Treasury. As chairman of the FSOC the secretary is responsible for the final order to force a megabank into liquidation and for overseeing the required two-thirds vote of FSOC's members to compel material changes in the banks' size and structure.[25] Therefore, even if an individual regulator shows a heroic resistance to being captured by the big banks, the key Dodd-Frank decisions will still rest with a political appointee whose job is to carry out the political interests of the governing administration.

Whether Democrat or Republican, given the political resources at the banks' disposal, it is almost inconceivable that *any* Treasury secretary will be able to make the tough decisions necessary to finally address too-big-to-fail by chopping the banks down to size. And from the front-row seat that I enjoyed during my tenure at SIGTARP, Treasury was and continues to be an institution that has been captured by Wall Street's core ideology. It is simply inconceivable that, having crusaded against Brown-Kaufman's attempt to slim down the megabanks, the current Treasury Department would then turn around and seek to accomplish a similar result through the impossibly burdensome processes set forth in Dodd-Frank. The same political and procedural barriers make it similarly unlikely that a future administration will seriously challenge the structure—and therefore the power—of the largest banks. Dodd-Frank didn't change the postcrisis status quo of too-big-to-fail banks; it cemented it.

I INITIALLY HELD out some hope that at least some transparency could be brought to what I worried would be the FSOC's feckless execution of its duties. Dodd-Frank had also created a new oversight entity called the Council of Inspectors General on Financial Oversight (CIGFO), which had loosely defined oversight authority over FSOC. As one if its designated members, I thought I might be able to help the group hold FSOC's feet to the fire.

Unfortunately, whatever promise CIGFO might have had was squelched by Congress's choice for its chairman, the quintessential lapdog, Treasury Inspector General Eric Thorson. Even before the first meeting, my worries about Thorson's chairmanship were confirmed when one of the participants at a mid-August 2010 lunch of the regulatory IGs (which I skipped) reported in an e-mail that Thorson had commented that he wanted to talk to Geithner about the new council and assure him that he has nothing to worry about with them.

I figured I still had to at least try to make the council effective. Congress had granted the council the authority to audit FSOC functions, and I thought a couple of well-placed reviews might be an effective counterweight to the influence the banks and their lobbyists would certainly have on the regulators. My efforts, however, were unsuccessful.

The first two CIGFO meetings, in October and November, were disasters. Geithner had said that the FSOC meetings would be one-half private and one-half public, and when I asked Thorson if he or anyone else from our council had observed the private portion of the first meeting, he said no.

"Did you ask?" I pressed.

"I did, but the deputy secretary explained that he didn't want me at the first couple of meetings," Thorson said.

When I asked why, Thorson explained, sympathetically, that the deputy secretary, Neal Wolin, had told him that it was better that Thorson not attend because it was still too "uncertain" what would occur at the meetings. Thorson assured the group that we would get an after-the-fact briefing about what happened at the meetings from FSOC staffers.

I told him that I thought that this wasn't acceptable, and I urged the group to send a letter of protest to Geithner, signed by all of us, insisting that we be permitted to observe the meetings. Thorson objected, and after he told the group that he was "sure" that Wolin would let him attend the next meeting, they followed along. I told Thorson that I also wanted to attend, but I never heard back from him.

I proposed during that same meeting that we could use the powers granted by Congress to pursue audits. When I received the draft of the rules that would govern what we could do, though, I saw that they kept tight control of the group in Thorson's hands. He had unilateral authority to decide who would be the "lead inspector general" for any project initiated, so he could make my auditors and me subordinate to him on anything we did.

Without being able to initiate and conduct independent audits, I saw little opportunity to use the council to do any real good. Much like aspects of Dodd-Frank, the creation of the council contributed to a false sense of security, lulling others who might otherwise be vigilant by the false promise of effective oversight. I tried to get the group to change the rules to make them more democratic, but I was voted down.

IN MY WANING months at SIGTARP, I continued to raise concerns about the too-big-to-fail problem, and I was part of a growing chorus. Many academics and a number of other government officials had also concluded that Dodd-Frank had failed its primary objective. As the Kansas City Fed president stated, "like it or not, these firms remain too big to fail" and are "still in control of our country's economic destiny."[26] Much of the political establishment, however, was instead focused on the ongoing fiscal crisis and the need for deficit reduction.

I argued that the two issues were inextricably linked. While Treasury and Wall Street were trumpeting that the big banks had all paid back their TARP funds, the gaping deficits that became the focus of the fiscal debate were very much the result of the damage wreaked on the economy by the financial crisis. Even as the government spent more and more billions of dollars on stimulus and the bailouts, the recession sapped hundreds of billions in tax revenues out of its coffers. So those concerned with fiscal restraint should have been adamant about solving the too-big-to-fail problem and the fiscal horror that would accompany the next financial crisis that it might cause. Instead, the issue was largely shunted aside.

The fact that the Dodd-Frank provisions alone would be inadequate to prevent another set of massive bailouts in the face of another systemic shock was all but conceded by Geithner in an interview that Geoff did with him in late December 2010 in connection with an audit we were about to publish on the bailout of Citigroup. During the interview, Geoff pressed Geithner on Citi's too-big-to-fail status, and in the ensuing conversation, Geithner acknowledged some of the limitations of the act. Among other things, he admitted that one of the core tasks of FSOC—determining which nonbank financial institutions posed systemic risk and therefore should be subject to enhanced supervision—was virtually impossible. "You won't be able to make a judgment about what's systemic and what's not until you know the nature of the shock," he acknowledged. Most tellingly, he also admitted that while he believed that "we have better tools now thanks to Dodd-Frank," the uncertainty of what the next crisis might bring meant that "in the future we may have to do exceptional things again if we face a shock that large."[27] In other words, as a subsequent *Wall Street Journal* editorial explained, "Dodd-Frank was supposed to reduce the odds of back-pocket rescue decisions, but now even its main promoters are admitting that the law gives them enormous discretion to do it all over again, based on little more than their own ad-hoc judgments."[28]

After Geoff filled me in on the substance of the interview, he paused.

"What?" I asked.

"I asked the other question that you wanted," Geoff said.

When Geithner and Massad had refused to adopt our recommendation to clarify their change in methodology for calculating AIG's losses, Geoff was bewildered by their response. I told him that Karen had once jokingly offered a theory that Geithner suffers from narcissism, and therefore might be psychologically incapable of truly admitting that he had made a mistake. I said that we should ask him what mistakes he might have made in administering TARP, to see if he could come up with any.

"What did he say?" I asked.

"He said, 'The only real mistake that I can think of was that there were times when we were unnecessarily unsure of ourselves. We should have realized at the time just how right each of our decisions were,'" Geoff reported.

I laughed. "So Karen was right."

And so was Geithner, at least about the limits of Dodd-Frank.

BY EARLY 2011, with TARP winding down, I decided that I would give notice on Monday, February 14, 2011, and leave six weeks later on March 30 (Geoff, knowing that I had kept my Yankees season tickets, figured out that I had picked the date because March 31 was opening day at Yankee Stadium). As I organized my thoughts in preparing my letter of resignation, I knew the agency had a strong foundation, and I was proud of our accomplishments. Despite the battles, our reports had helped bring transparency to TARP, and I thought that our recommendations, particularly those on PPIP and TALF, had helped prevent mistakes that might have cost taxpayers tens of billions of dollars. Our investigations division had developed into a sophisticated white-collar law enforcement agency, and I expected that scores of additional defendants would soon be joining those already in jail for their TARP-related crimes. And most important, as even Geithner had acknowledged during our last meeting, we had helped scare away enough bad guys and pushed through enough anti-fraud provisions to keep TARP's fraud losses to historic lows for a program of its size.

I started telling my senior staff of my plans ahead of time, and I asked Lori on the Friday preceding my announcement to see if she could arrange calls with the chairmen and ranking members of the congressional committees to which we reported for the following Monday morning, so that

I could tell them myself that I was leaving. I told her to be cryptic about the purpose of the calls. When I told Kevin about my plan, he cracked up, joking "Are you crazy? Barney Frank is going to think that you're about to indict him if Lori tells him that."

Sure enough, Frank had a memorable reaction. When I told him that I was stepping down, he said, "Thank God. I had a tough weekend. No offense, but nobody likes to get a call from you, especially on a Friday. It reminded me of those Friday calls I used to get from Hank Paulson back in 2008 telling me that the world was about to end."

The rest of the calls went well, with the members thanking me for my service and wishing me luck. Although Congress understandably has a terrible reputation nationwide, I genuinely enjoyed my interactions with the members. So much of Washington is tainted by partisan politics, but for me Congress served as an important bipartisan ally, without which SIGTARP would have accomplished little. I wasn't naive; I understood that many of the members supported us primarily because it served their political interests. The Republicans loved us first and foremost because we were critical of a Democratic administration, and they gleefully used our reports to put political points on the board. But I also think that many, including in particular Senator Grassley and Representative Issa, were truly bothered by the lack of transparency in Treasury's administration of TARP. Certainly neither one held back when we were criticizing the Republicans for their early handling of the program.

I had a particular respect, though, for the Democrats who so strongly supported us even when it wasn't politically palatable to the Obama administration. At times, I had heard, they were under tremendous pressure from Treasury and the White House to back off from their support of us, but whether it was Senator Boxer's staff making sure that Kevin was in the room when the Treasury team tried to sabotage the Ensign-Boxer amendment for PPIP, Barney Frank calling Orzsag and Geithner to make sure that we could go forward with our audit of the banks about their use of TARP funds, Representative Cummings's unsolicited request that we audit Geithner's role in the decision to pay off AIG's counterparties, or Chairman Baucus's unwavering and vocal support for SIGTARP even after Treasury and the White House launched their most virulent attacks on me, that group often put what they believed was right over party politics.

I appreciated the kind statements that our supporters in Congress put out on the day I announced my resignation, and I was particularly grateful when the White House, in a classy gesture, issued a statement noting my "strong oversight" and saying that it was "grateful" for my service. Treasury, on the other hand, was less gracious: they had an anonymous Treasury official describe me to *The Washington Post* as having "scared some needy banks away from participating in" TARP and say that my February 14 resignation "was like a nice Valentine to us."[29] Karen and I could only laugh when we saw that good-bye message in the *Post* the next day.

I had no idea what I was going to do next. I wasn't interested in jumping to a law firm, and a small part of me feared that I might end up renting Neel Kashkari's newly built cabin out in the woods of California that had been the subject of the *Post* profile. I was therefore beyond thrilled when just a few days later I got a call from Richard Revesz, the dean of my alma mater, New York University School of Law, inviting me to come back to New York to teach. Karen and I were going home.

On my final day at SIGTARP, March 30, 2011, *The New York Times* published an op-ed I had written that outlined where I thought TARP had fallen short, and I testified at a House hearing entitled "Has Dodd-Frank Ended Too Big to Fail?" It was the perfect sendoff. Two of our strongest supporters in the House, Representatives Issa and Cummings, came to the hearing just to say good-bye. And as I laid out to the committee the ongoing dangers of too big to fail and jousted one last time with both the Democrats and the Republicans, I had a fleeting hope that if I kept repeating the message, even beyond my time at SIGTARP, perhaps eventually it would get through. Maybe not right away, and maybe not even in time to prevent the next crisis, but perhaps eventually.

I felt transformed that last day as I left the Hill, hopped into the car, and headed back to clean out my office. My only real concern? Karen and I had a train to catch to New York. There was a whole new season of baseball starting the next day.

AFTERWORD

I N T H E Y E A R S I N C E I stepped down from SIGTARP, the sadly predictable consequences resulting from the government's disparate treatment of Wall Street and Main Street have only become worse. As the banks amass even more size and power, Main Street continues to get pummeled.

The economic "recovery" that has been heralded in some quarters pales in comparison to the damage wrought on the economy. Nearly nine million jobs were lost as a result of the financial crisis[1] along with 3.5 million homes,[2] accompanied by a loss of $7 trillion in housing wealth.[3] The poor have suffered the most, with the poverty rate increasing from 12.5 percent to 15.1 percent since 2007.[4] And even these startling numbers don't capture the human toll from long-term unemployment and the stresses involved in the ongoing housing crisis.

Part of the current economic malaise can be traced directly to Treasury's betrayal of its promise to use TARP to "preserve homeownership." For HAMP, there has been little meaningful improvement, with fewer than 800,000 ongoing permanent modifications as of March 31, 2012, a number that is growing at the glacial pace of just 12,000 per month.[5] In June 2011, Treasury appeared to take a tentative step toward holding the servicers accountable for their widespread misconduct by declaring the equivalent of a "time out" in making the incentive payments to three of the largest servicers, Wells Fargo, Bank of America, and JPMorgan Chase. At the time, Treasury pledged that it would withhold HAMP payments until those servicers finally came into compliance with the program's rules. Treasury, though, couldn't even keep this modest commitment to

HAMP accountability. Although Treasury found that Wells Fargo had improved its performance and awarded it all of its withheld incentive payments, JPMorgan Chase and Bank of America continued to fail to meet Treasury's baseline standard. Nonetheless, rather than sticking to its guns and continuing to dock the banks until they were in full compliance, in March 2012, as part of a broader settlement of the so-called robo-signing scandal, Treasury released all of the withheld payments, totaling more than $170 million.[6] As a result, Treasury has not held any servicer responsible in even the slightest way for the widespread abuses of HAMP applicants, nor is it ever likely to do so.

The parties to the broader settlement included the servicers, DOJ, and forty-nine of the states' attorneys general. In return for what was touted as a $25 billion payout, the banks received broad immunity from future civil cases arising out of their widespread use of forged, fraudulent, or completely fabricated documents to foreclose on home owners. Although the headline number sounds impressive, the details behind the number paint a far different picture. The banks only had to cough up $1.5 billion to provide a paltry $2,000 to each borrower wrongfully foreclosed upon, a few billion dollars more in penalties to the states, and a few billion on top of that to provide for borrower refinancing.[7] The remaining $17 billion, however, won't involve actual payouts of money, but will be met in the form of the banks receiving "credits" for certain activities. This includes $7 billion that will be "earned" for routine tasks related to the housing crisis, such as bulldozing worthless houses, donating homes to charity, and agreeing not to pursue deficiency judgments against home owners, whereby banks seek to force a home owner to pay the difference between the balance of the loan at the time of foreclosure and what is recovered by the bank from a foreclosure sale.[8] This sounds good, but it should be noted that these are all part of the normal course of business for the banks. For example, banks reportedly pursue such judgments in just a small minority of cases, in large part due to the unlikelihood of ever actually collecting on the debt.[9]

The remaining $10 billion in credits are supposed to be scraped together through principal reductions on underwater mortgages, but that does not mean that the banks *themselves* will be taking $10 billion in losses. The settlement grants them partial credit for reducing the principal on loans that they service but do not own, such as those contained in mortgage-backed securities.[10] Worse still, they can earn additional "credits" toward the settlement through taxpayer-funded HAMP modifications. For example, if a servicer reduces $100,000 in principal for a mortgage through HAMP and receives a taxpayer incentive check for $40,000, it will still be able to claim $60,000 in credit toward meeting its obligations under the settlement.[11] As a result, it is now possible that in certain circumstances the banks might actually recognize a taxpayer-funded *profit* on a modification done in furtherance of the settlement. In other words, the same settlement that was touted as supposedly punishing the banks will actually involve money flowing, once again, from taxpayers to the banks, not the other way around.

Treasury's actions also represent yet another lost opportunity for Treasury to meaningfully help underwater home owners. If that were Treasury's goal, it would have demanded as a condition of the settlement the recommendation that we made at SIGTARP years ago: make the HAMP principal reduction alternative mandatory for the banks, without "credit," whenever it was in the best interests of the owner of the mortgage under Treasury's NPV test. Had it implemented this requirement, it could have then required the banks to meet their settlement obligations with loans on their own books that were not otherwise eligible for HAMP. While this effort may have still fallen short of what would be necessary to address the problems caused by the more than 31 percent of all mortgages in this country that are underwater,[12] it would have at least widened the scope of relief for home owners.

One other announcement that accompanied the settlement, made by the president during his State of the Union address, was the launching of a new working group under the banner of DOJ's larger Financial Fraud Enforcement Task Force to investigate some of the toxic mortgage practices at the heart of the financial crisis. As a former cochair of one of the other Task Force working groups, I found that it primarily served as a centralized press release repository so that the bureaucrats in Washington could take credit for the work done by prosecutors' offices across the country. There is little reason to think that this new working group will be any different, and indeed it looks far more like an election-year public-relations move than a serious attempt to bring criminal cases against those responsible for the financial crisis.

The announcement arose out of the political fallout from the government's failure to bring any significant criminal cases related to the financial crisis (other than SIGTARP's case against Farkas). With the statute of limitations fast approaching for much of the conduct underlying the crisis, it seems increasingly unlikely that any will. It is a fair question to ask why not. President Obama,[13] Attorney General Eric Holder,[14] and Geithner[15] have all answered this question by suggesting in different public comments that it was greed and bad judgment, not criminal conduct, that contributed to the crisis, and a number of high profile investigations (AIG, Countrywide, and Washington Mutual) have been closed without criminal charges.[16] Although I am loathe to judge prosecutorial decisions made by others without first seeing all of their evidence, I often commented to Kevin that if DOJ approached the financial crisis matters with the same timidity and lack of sophistication that we often saw in our investigations, it would help explain the dearth of cases. I hope that I will be proven wrong, but it seems unlikely to me that an eleventh-hour task force will result in a proliferation of handcuffs on culpable bankers.

One thing that is clear, however, is that the criminal justice system has proven itself ill equipped to address the deep fundamental problems at the heart of the financial crisis. For that, we needed effective regulatory reform. Instead, we got Dodd-Frank.

My fear about the inadequacy of Dodd-Frank has only gotten worse over the past year. The top banks are 23 percent larger than they were before the crisis.[17] They now hold more than $8.5 trillion in assets, the equivalent of 56 percent of our country's annual output, up from 43 percent just five years ago.[18] The risk in our banking system is remarkably concentrated in these banks, which now control 52 percent of all industry assets, up from 17 percent four decades ago.[19] As to Dodd-Frank, there is now broad recognition that it has not solved the problem it was meant to address—the power and influence of banks deemed too big to fail. The Dallas Federal Reserve, for example, declared that "Dodd-Frank does not eradicate TBTF,"[20] and, in fact, "leaves TBTF entrenched."[21] Similar sentiments have been expressed by the current presidents of the Kansas City,[22] St. Louis,[23] and Richmond[24] Federal Reserve banks, as well as by renowned academics like Simon Johnson, Anat Admati, and Joseph

Stiglitz. Senator Sherrod Brown even reintroduced the Brown-Kaufman amendment as a stand-alone bill, seeking once again to cap the size and leverage of the megabanks. The growing consensus is that Dodd-Frank "did not adequately deal with the too-big-to fail banks."[25]

More important than the views of academics and regulators, however, are the financial markets, which continue to bet that the government will once again come to the big banks' rescue. Creditors still give the largest banks more favorable terms than their smaller counterparts—a direct subsidy to those that are already deemed too big to fail, and an incentive for others to try to join the club.[26] Indeed, by some reports, the big banks' funding advantage actually *increased* after Dodd-Frank's passage, with an existing subsidy calculated in the tens of billions of dollars per year.[27] Similarly, the credit rating agencies continue to give the major banks higher credit ratings based on the assumption that they will once again be bailed out.[28] Further, although certainly not scientific, an online poll conducted by the *American Banker* indicated that just 10 percent of its respondents believed that the government would refrain from bailing out the largest banks in the event of another system-wide financial crisis.[29]

As a result, the market distortions that flow from TBTF may have actually gotten worse. With megabanks' continued access to artificially cheap credit, freedom from creditor-imposed market discipline, and incentives that reward large and highly leveraged risks, one of the significant causes and catalysts for the 2008 financial crisis—the presumption of bailout—remains unaddressed. Indeed, by failing to alter this presumption, Dodd-Frank may have inadvertently sowed the seeds for the next financial crisis.[30]

Dodd-Frank did give the regulators the tools to counter these market assumptions, but as the Dallas Fed explained, "words on paper only go so far."[31] Although there has been a growing chorus of voices calling for "breaking up the nation's biggest banks into smaller units,"[32] FSOC and the regulators have, to date, met the lowest of expectations. FSOC has still taken no significant action to limit the size or power of the largest banks, and has only just begun to make noises about bringing nonbank financial institutions (like AIG) under its jurisdiction. Even basic steps such as creating and implementing the new rules under which the banks are supposed to operate have lagged, with two-thirds of Dodd-Frank's rule-making deadlines already blown by May 1, 2012.[33] And where there has been action, in some instances the regulators have taken a step backward.

For example, one of the best protections against future bailouts short of breaking up the largest banks is to make sure that banks have thick capital cushions that can absorb potential losses. More capital means that the banks' shareholders—and not the taxpayer through bailouts—pay if the banks suffer large losses. Although Dodd-Frank called for higher capital levels to be set by the regulators for the largest banks, as of this writing, they have still not formally done so. But instead of trying to make sure that the banks retain as much capital as possible before the new rules are announced and imposed, in March 2012, the Federal Reserve authorized fifteen of the nineteen largest bank holding companies to *drain their capital* through cash payouts in the form of dividends to their shareholders and buybacks of their stocks.[34] Though these actions unquestionably benefit the banks' senior executives, who as owners of large amounts of their banks' stock will personally reap millions of dollars,[35] they also increase the risk to the taxpayer that the banks will once again have to be bailed out. That the Fed is authorizing such actions before even imposing final capital requirements is beyond irresponsible.

The banks have also been hard at work gaming and watering down the rules and regulations set forth in Dodd-Frank. One of the best examples is with respect to the Volcker Rule, which is supposed to prohibit the banks from making risky proprietary bets that could lead to large losses and eventual bailouts. The final version of the rule was left to the regulators to determine, but a number of carve-outs and exceptions that were pushed in the aggressive lobbying before the passage of the bill have left large potential loopholes. For example, in April 2012, *Bloomberg* reported that JPMorgan Chase had apparently moved some of its soon-to-be banned trading operations overseas into its London-based Treasury unit, branding a multi-hundred-billion-dollar trading position in synthetic credit derivatives as a "hedge."[36] Legitimate hedging was one of the hard-fought exemptions to the Volcker Rule won by the banks, intended to permit banks to *minimize* risk to the system by allowing them to offset specific risks from specific positions that may remain in their portfolios. But as *The New York Times* and *Bloomberg* reported, JPMorgan's supposed

Treasury "hedges," which it initially claimed were made against its entire portfolio of assets as opposed to individual positions, appeared profit-driven and were so large that they moved markets.[37]

After the articles warned that JPMorgan's positions were potentially destabilizing and were likely unable to be unwound without potentially "causing a dislocation in the markets,"[38] the bank's outspoken CEO, Jamie Dimon, dismissed the concerns, claiming that they were little more than a "tempest in a teapot."[39] His CFO agreed, saying that positions were careful "hedges" with which the bank was "very comfortable."[40] Dimon has been one of Wall Street's most vocal critics of regulatory reform, attacking those who sought to rein in the megabanks' practices. For example, he claimed that Paul Volcker, the former chairman of the Federal Reserve for whom the rule was named, "doesn't understand capital markets"[41] and reportedly described both Volcker and the president of the Dallas Fed as "infantile."[42]

Just weeks after dismissing concerns about the trade, Dimon disclosed that it had cost his bank $2 billion and counting. Demonstrating the weakness and ambiguity of the proposed Volcker Rule, it remains unclear whether the risky trade undertaken by JPMorgan will even be covered by the rule once it is finally issued.

Hopefully the incident will help embolden regulators to better use Dodd-Frank's tools to clamp down on Wall Street's risk taking. To date, however, the response has been more accommodating. As Geithner told Congress in March 2012 when confronted with arguments similar to those made by the banks: "We're a careful people, and we're going to look at all the concerns expressed by these rules. . . . It is my view that we have the capacity to address those concerns. It's very important we do that."[43]

Words like these presumably led one of the Volcker Rule's legislative authors, Senator Carl Levin, a Democrat, to warn that some at "Treasury are willing to weaken the law."[44] Indeed, words like Geithner's, when accompanied by actions such as the Fed's authorization of the largest banks to release capital, send what should be a clear message to anyone that is carefully listening. The banks are exercising considerable influence over their own reforms and we may be in danger of quickly returning to the pre-crisis status quo of inadequately capitalized banks that take outsized risks while being coddled by their over-accommodating regulators. And if that occurs, a repeat of the financial crisis will soon be upon us.

*   *   *

AS THE NOVEMBER 2012 election approaches, Treasury's triumphant declarations of mission accomplished for TARP have picked up steam, focusing largely on the reduction in expected losses for TARP.[45] While it is unquestionably good news that TARP losses will be far less than originally anticipated, the numbers that Treasury has been publishing are incomplete. For example, Treasury continues to offset expected TARP losses on AIG with gains from the New York Fed's separate pre-TARP bailout by declaring the more than 500 million shares of AIG stock that the New York Fed received in return for its bailout as part of "Treasury's investment."[46] Similarly, Treasury's projections do not include or make reference to the potentially enormous losses in future tax revenue from AIG, Citigroup, GM, and others that Treasury exempted through a change in IRS rules, which allowed the bailed-out entities to "carry forward" prior losses to offset future profits despite a change in ownership. Though this action unquestionably buoyed the common stock price for these entities (thus producing lower TARP losses when Treasury sells off the shares of stock that it received in the companies as part of their bailouts), it may result in the loss of up to tens of billions of dollars in future tax revenues.

Treasury's focus on TARP's financial costs, of course, detracts from its significant non-financial costs detailed in this book, including the worsening of too big to fail and the lost opportunity to help struggling home owners. But a separate cost—the loss of many Americans' faith in their government—may still yield a significant benefit.

One welcome development of the past year has been expanding awareness of the perils presented by the largest banks outside the relatively obscure world of academia and lower-tier banking regulators. First the Tea Party and then the Occupy Wall Street movements have helped raise awareness of these dangers, and at least some politicians appear to be following suit. Even one of the Republican presidential candidates, Jon Huntsman, advocated breaking up the largest banks as part of his short-lived campaign.

Ironically, I repeatedly warned Geithner and his Treasury team of the anger and disillusionment that would follow their bank-centric policies, and publicly stated when I stepped down that the resulting loss of faith might make it politically impossible for the government to take the necessary steps to shore up our financial system when the next crisis strikes.

I now realize, though, that Treasury's dismissal of our warnings has produced a valuable byproduct, the widespread anger that may contain the only hope for meaningful reform of our system. I now realize that the American people *should* lose faith in their government. They *should* deplore the captured politicians and regulators who took their taxpayer dollars and distributed them to the banks without insisting that they be accountable for how the bailout money was spent. They *should* be revolted by a financial system that rewards failure and protects the fortunes of those who drove the system to the point of collapse and will undoubtedly do so again. They *should* be enraged by the broken promises to Main Street and the unending protection of Wall Street. Because only with this appropriate and justified rage can we sow the seeds for the types of reform that will one day break our system free from the corrupting grasp of the megabanks. It is my own anger that compelled me to write this book, and I hope that in some small way it can help put us on that path.

May 2012

ACKNOWLEDGMENTS

S O MANY TO THANK, so little room. First, everyone at Free Press, particularly my amazing editor Emily Loose, who exhibited Job-like patience in walking me through the publishing process and whose wielding of the editorial ax has made this a far better book. Next, words can't express my gratitude to New York University School of Law and its incredibly generous dean, Ricky Revesz. I wouldn't even have considered writing this book but for the remarkable support that Ricky and NYU have provided to me and my family.

I could never have gotten this book done on time without the NYU Law students who somehow balanced the rigors of law school with helping me with research: Zander Li, my primary research assistant; Christina Dahlman and Daniel Koffmann, who provided invaluable assistance; and Chad Harple and Karl Mulloney-Radke, who helped out with spot research assignments. The legal community will be a far better place with the addition of these talented young lawyers. Additional thanks to Josh Rosner, for his valuable advice on some of the more technical aspects of portions of the book.

Thanks to my sister Karen, the true writer in the family, for her input on the manuscript, as well as to Kevin Puvalowski and the others who took time from their busy schedules to review the book and ensure that that my recollections were accurate. I'd also like to thank Mike Garcia for recommending me, President Bush for nominating me, and President Obama, both for keeping me on and for the letter his office sent me after I stepped down. At times, being SIGTARP was a thankless job, but that final thank-you meant a great deal to me. I'd also like to thank Kevin and my other former deputy, Geoff Moulton, for their tireless work at SIG-TARP on behalf of the taxpayers and for the remarkable personal sacrifices that they made. And, of course, thanks to the fine men and women at SIGTARP who joined me in its mission and whose work exemplified the very best of government service.

Thanks also to my agent, David Kuhn, and his associate, Grant Ginder, as well as to those who convinced me, against my better judgment, that I *had* to write this book. I'd also like to thank my mom and dad, who among many other things made countless sacrifices as I was growing up to make sure that I had the very best education, and my sister Vickie, for her unwavering support.

Most important, I'd like to express my eternal gratitude to my wife, Karen, to whom this book is dedicated. As you likely know by now, I have an annoying habit of taking jobs or embarking on projects that all but remove me from her life for extended periods of time, and the four months I spent writing and editing this book were no exception. Without her support and sacrifices, none of this—SIGTARP, the book, my career— would have been possible. She is my rock, my world, and my inspiration. Finally, I'd like to thank my son, Jack, for waiting until I was done with the manuscript before entering the world, and my daughter, Zoe, who is every bit as remarkable and perfect as her mother.

NOTES

Foreword to the Paperback Edition

1 Order Instituting Proceedings Pursuant to Sections 6(c) and 6(d) of the Commodity Exchange Act, as Amended, Making Findings and Imposing Remedial Sanctions at 7–11, 19–25, *In the Matter of Barclays PLC*, CFTC Docket No. 12–25, available at http:// www.cftc.gov/ucm/groups/public/@lrenforcementactions/documents/legalpleading /enfbarclaysorder062712.pdf; Non-Prosecution Agreement Between United States Department of Justice, Criminal Division, Fraud Section, and Barclays Bank PLC Appendix A Statement of Facts at ¶¶ 11–22, 30–33, 39–41, available at http://www .justice.gov/iso/opa/resources/9312012710173426365941.pdf.

2 Hugh Son, "BofA Says Libor Probe Draws U.S. Subpoenas on Submissions," *Bloomberg News*, August 3, 2012, www.bloomberg.com/news/2012-08-02/bofa-says-libor-probe -draws-u-s-subpoenas-on-submissions.html; Azam Ahmed and Ben Protess, "As Libor Fault-Finding Grows, It Is Now Every Bank for Itself," *New York Times*, August 6, 2012, A1.

3 Michael J. De La Merced and Ben Protess, "New York Fed Knew of False Barclays Reports on Rates," *New York Times*, July 14, 2012, A1.

4 FRBNY Markets and Research and Statistics Groups, "Recommendations for Enhancing the Credibility of LIBOR," e-mail message from Timothy Geithner to Mervyn King, June 1, 2008, http://www.bankofengland.co.uk/publications/Documents/news/2012 /nr068.pdf.

5 Jeffrey Sparshott, "Geithner Defends His Reponse to Libor Concerns," *Wall Street Journal*, July 25, 2012, http://online.wsj.com/article/SB100008723963904433437045775490921 22361070.html; Ben Protess, "Facing Congress, Geithner Grilled on Rate-Rigging," *New York Times*, July 24, 2012, http://dealbook.nytimes.com/2012/07/25/facing-congress -geithner-grilled-on-rate-rigging.

6 Ben Protess, "Facing Congress, Geithner Grilled on Rate Rigging," *New York Times*, July 24, 2012, http://dealbook.nytimes.com/2012/07/25/facing-congress-geithner-grilled -on-rate-rigging.

7 Carrick Mollenkamp and Mark Whitehouse, "Study Casts Doubt on Key Rate: WSJ Analysis Suggests Banks May Have Reported Flawed Interest Data for Libor," *Wall Street Journal*, May 29, 2008, A1.

8 Ben Protess and Mark Scott, "U.S. Is Building Criminal Cases in Rate-Fixing," *New York Times*, July 15, 2012, A1.

9 Associated Press, "Report: US banks subject to money-laundering probe," *Daily Finance*, September 16, 2012, http://www.dailyfinance.com/article/report-us-banks-subject-of -money-laundering-probe/2254975; Kate Davidson, "JPMorgan to Pay $88 Million for OFAC Violations," *onwallstreet*, August 26, 2011, http://www.onwallstreet.com/news /jpmorgan-ofac-violations-settlement-2674841-1.html.

10 Staff of S. Permanent Subcomm. on Investigations, 112th Cong., U.S. Vulnerabilities to

Money Laundering, Drugs, and Terrorist Financing: HSBC Case History (Comm. Print 2012), available at http://www.hsgac.senate.gov/download/?id=2a76c00f-7c3a-44c8 -902e-3d9b5dbd0083, at 80-99, 191-203.

11   Complaint, *People v. J.P. Morgan Securities LLC*, No. 451556-2012 (N.Y. Sup. Ct. Oct. 1, 2012), available at http://www.ag.ny.gov/sites/default/files/press-releases/2012/jpm complaint.pdf.

12   Michael Virtanen, "Too Late for NY Prosecution in Securities Meltdown," Associated Press, October 4, 2012, bigstory.ap.org/article/too-late-ny-prosecution-securities -meltdown; Jim Puzzanghera, "Prosecutor: Big Bank Misled Investors," *Los Angeles Times*, October 2, 2012, B2.

13   Financial Fraud Enforcement Task Force, "President Obama Establishes Interagency Financial Fraud Enforcement Task Force," news release, November 17, 2009, http://www .stopfraud.gov/news/news-11172009-01.html.

14   William K. Black, "Geithner Channels Greenspan and Airbrushes Fraud Out of Our Cri- ses," *The Big Picture* (blog), May 3, 2012, http://www.ritholtz.com/blog/2012/05/geithner -channels-greenspan-and-airbrushes-fraud-out-of-our-crises.

15   William K. Black, "2011 Will Bring More de Facto Decriminalization of Elite Financial Fraud," *Huffington Post*, December 28, 2010, http://www.huffingtonpost.com/william -k-black/the-role-of-the-criminal_b_802115.html.

16   U.S. Securities and Exchange Commission, "Citigroup to Pay $285 Million to Settle SEC Charges for Misleading Investors About CDO Tied to Housing Market," news release, October 19, 2011, http://sec.gov/news/press/2011/2011-214.htm.

1: Fraud 101

1   Financial Crisis Inquiry Commission, *The Financial Crisis Inquiry Report*, April 13, 2011 (Washington, D.C.: U.S. Government Printing Office, 2011), 393.

2   "Foreclosure Activity Increases 81 Percent in 2008," January 15, 2009, www.realtytrac .com/content/press-releases/foreclosure-activity-increases-81-percent-in-2008-4551.

3   Human Rights Watch, *"You'll Learn Not to Cry": Child Combatants in Colombia* (New York: Human Rights Watch, 2003), www.hrw.org/reports/2003/colombia0903/colombia 0903.pdf, 7-8.

4   *Narco-Terror: The Worldwide Connection Between Drugs and Terrorism: Hearing Before the Subcommittee on Technology, Terrorism, and Government Information of the Com- mittee on the Judiciary, United States Senate,* March 13, 2002 (Washington, D.C.: U.S. Government Printing Office, 2003), www.gpo.gov/fdsys/pkg/CHRG-107shrg85660 /pdf/CHRG-107shrg85660.pdf, 13 (statement of Asa Hutchinson, Administrator, Drug Enforcement Administration).

5   Binyamin Applebaum, "As Subprime Lending Crisis Unfolded, Watchdog Fed Didn't Bother Barking," *The Washington Post*, September 27, 2009, A1; *The Financial Crisis Inquiry Report*, 76-78.

2: Hank Wants to Make It Work

1   Deborah Solomon, "Paulson to Tap Adviser to Run Rescue Program," *The Wall Street Journal*, October 6, 2008, A3; "Kashkari Appointed Interim Assistant Secretary for Financial Stability," October 6, 2008, www.treasury.gov/press-center/press-releases/Pages /hp1184.aspx.

2   Ben Smith, "Iraq Media Guy Rebuilds Qatar at the Garden," *New York Observer*, Octo-

ber 27, 2003, http://observer.com/2003/10/27/iraq-media-guy-rebuilds-qatar-at-the -garden.

3 Ibid.

4 Ibid.; Michael Massing, *Now They Tell Us: The American Press and Iraq* (New York: New York Review of Books, 2004), 5.

5 "Text of Draft Proposal for Bailout Plan," *The New York Times*, September 20, 2008, www .nytimes.com/2008/09/21/business/21draftcnd.html.

6 Ibid.

7 Henry M. Paulson, Jr., *On the Brink* (New York: Business Plus, 2010), 323–24.

8 Ibid., 337.

9 Ibid., 365.

10 Congressional Oversight Panel, *February Oversight Report: Valuing Treasury's Acquisitions*, February 6, 2009 (Washington, D.C.: U.S. Government Printing Office, 2009), www.gpo.gov/fdsys/pkg/CPRT-111JPRT47178/pdf/CPRT-111JPRT47178.pdf, 4, 34.

11 "Joint Statement by Treasury, Federal Reserve, and FDIC," October 14, 2008, www .treasury.gov/press-center/pages/npl206.aspx.

12 "Statement by Secretary Henry M. Paulson, Jr. on Actions to Protect the U.S. Economy," October 14, 2008, http://www.treasury.gov/press-center/press-releases/Pages/hp1205.aspx.

13 Ibid.

14 "Joint Statement by Treasury, Federal Reserve, and FDIC," October 14, 2008, www .federalreserve.gov/newsevents/press/monetary/20081014a.htm.

15 "Statement by Secretary Henry M. Paulson, Jr. on Actions to Protect the U.S. Economy," October 14, 2008, http://www.treasury.gov/press-center/press-releases/Pages/hp1205 .aspx.

16 Office of the Special Inspector General of the Troubled Asset Relief Program [hereinafter SIGTARP], *Emergency Capital Injections Provided to Support the Viability of Bank of America, Other Major Banks, and the U.S. Financial System*, October 5, 2009, www .sigtarp.gov/reports/audit/2009/Emergency_Capital_Injections_Provided_to_Support _the_Viability_of_Bank_of_America . . . _100509.pdf, 17.

17 For an example, see the letter agreement between the United States Department of the Treasury and Citigroup, Inc., October 26, 2008, www.treasury.gov/initiatives/financial -stability/programs/investment-programs/cpp/Documents_Contracts_Agreements /Citigroup_10262008.pdf, 1.

18 *Is Treasury Using Bailout Funds to Increase Foreclosure Prevention, as Congress Intended?: Hearing Before the Subcommittee on Domestic Policy of the Commission on Oversight and Government Reform, House of Representatives*, November 14, 2008 (Washington, D.C.: U.S. Government Printing Office, 2009), www.gpo.gov/fdsys/pkg/CHRG -110hhrg50097/pdf/CHRG-110hhrg50097.pdf, 24.

19 Ibid., 47.

20 *Oversight Concerns Regarding Treasury Department Conduct of the Troubled Assets Relief Program: Hearing Before the Committee on Financial Services, House of Representatives*, December 10, 2008 (Washington, D.C.: U.S. Government Printing Office, 2009), www .gpo.gov/fdsys/pkg/CHRG-110hhrg46596/pdf/CHRG-110hhrg46596.pdf, 8, 13.

21 Ibid., 16.

22 Amit R. Paley, "Bailout Lacks Oversight Despite Billions Pledged," *The Washington Post*, November 13, 2008, A1.

23 "About Eric Thorson," U.S. Department of the Treasury, last updated November 13, 2010, www.treasury.gov/about/organizational-structure/ig/Pages/thorson-e.aspx.

24 Eric M. Thorson, letter to the editor, *The Washington Post*, November 21, 2008, A22.

25 *Anticipated Nomination of Neil M. Barofsky: Hearing Before the Committee on Finance,*
    United States Senate, November 17, 2008 (Washington, D.C.: U.S. Government Print-
    ing Office, 2008), http://finance.senate.gov/hearings/hearing/download/?id=15c1d16a
    -026b-4320-8ad2-7292f25a47d1, 1–2.

26 Ibid., 6 (Sen. Schumer); ibid., 18 (Sen. Rockefeller); ibid., 19 (Sen. Snowe).

27 Ibid., 13.

28 Ibid., 23–24.

29 *Nomination of Neil M. Barofsky: Hearing Before the Committee on Banking, Housing,*
    and Urban Affairs, United States Senate, November 19, 2008 (Washington, D.C.: U.S.
    Government Printing Office, 2009), www.gpo.gov/fdsys/pkg/CHRG-110shrg50419
    /pdf/CHRG-110shrg50419.pdf, 6–7.

30 Ibid.

31 Chris Isidore, "Big Three Plead for $34B from Congress," December 5, 2008, http://
    money.cnn.com/2008/12/04/news/companies/senate_hearing/.

3: The Lapdog, the Watchdog, and the Junkyard Dog

1 Bess Levin, "Hank Paulson Explains His Disfigurement," March 3, 2010, http://deal
   breaker.com/2010/03/hank-paulson-explains-his-disfigurement/.

2 Stephen Labaton and David M. Herszenhorn, "White House Ready to Offer Aid to Auto
   Industry: Plan for Interim Lending After Senate Loss," *The New York Times,* December
   13, 2008, A1.

3 Associated Press, "GOP Senators Voice Opposition to Auto Bailout," December 10, 2008,
   www.msnbc.msn.com/id/28108346/ns/business-autos/t/gop-senators-voice-opposition
   -auto-bailout/#.T1qp3zc-csI.

4 Alex Koppelman and Mike Madden, "Meet the GOP's Wrecking Crew," December 13,
   2008, www.salon.com/2008/12/13/bailout_8/.

5 12 U.S.C. § 5202(9) (Supp. II, 2009).

6 12 U.S.C. § 5202(5) (Supp. II, 2009).

7 The COP thought that this was a closer call than I did. Congressional Oversight Panel,
   September Oversight Report: The Use of TARP Funds in the Support and Reorganization
   of the Domestic Automotive Industry, September 9, 2009 (Washington, D.C.: U.S. Government Printing Office, 2009), www.gpo.gov/fdsys/pkg/CHRG-111shrg51964/pdf
   /CHRG-111shrg51964.pdf, 57.

8 Inspector General, Department of Defense, *Semiannual Report to the Congress, April 1,*
   2011–September 30, 2011, www.dodig.mil/sar/SAR_OCT_2011.pdf, 4.

9 Neil A. Lewis, "White House Defends Inspector General's Firing," *The New York Times,*
   June 18, 2009, A24.

10 Eric M. Thorson, letter to Barney Frank, November 25, 2008, http://pogoarchives.org/m
   /go/thorson-letter-20081125.pdf.

4: I Won't Lie for You

1 5 U.S.C. app. § 6(e)(3) (2006).

2 David Enrich, Robin Sidel, and Michael R. Crittenden, "Much Bank Aid May Not Go
   to Loans," *The Wall Street Journal,* October 28, 2008, C1; David Enrich and Robin Sidel,
   "Banks Promise to Use Rescue Funds for New Loans," *The Wall Street Journal,* October
   31, 2008, A4; Dan Fitzpatrick and Jason Leow, "BofA, in CCB Play, Stays Course," *The*
   Wall Street Journal, November 18, 2008, C3.

3 Thomas L. Friedman, "Time for (Self) Shock Therapy," *The New York Times*, January 18, 2009, WK13.

4 *Nomination of Neil M. Barofsky: Hearing Before the Committee on Banking, Housing, and Urban Affairs, United States Senate*, November 19, 2008 (Washington, D.C.: U.S. Government Printing Office, 2009), www.gpo.gov/fdsys/pkg/CHRG-110shrg50419/pdf/CHRG-110shrg50419.pdf, 4, 14, 26–27.

5 Ibid., 14.

6 SIGTARP, *Initial Report to the Congress*, February 6, 2009, www.sigtarp.gov/reports/congress/2009/SIGTARP_Initial_Report_to_the_Congress.pdf, 54–55.

7 Ibid., 45.

5: Drinking the Wall Street Kool-Aid

1 Gretchen Morgenson and Louise Story, "Banks Bundled Debt, Bet Against It and Won," *The New York Times*, December 24, 2009, A1.

2 Ben Protess, "Hedge Funds Got Help, Too," December 1, 2010, http://dealbook.nytimes.com/2010/12/01/who-on-wall-street-got-fed-loans/; Federal Reserve Board, "Term Asset-Backed Securities Loan Facility TALF.Borrower Data," December 1, 2010, last modified January 24, 2011, www.federalreserve.gov/newsevents/files/talf.borrower.xls.

3 SIGTARP, *Initial Report to the Congress*, February 6, 2009, www.sigtarp.gov/reports/congress/2009/SIGTARP_Initial_Report_to_the_Congress.pdf, 81.

4 John (Xuefeng) Jiang, Mary Harris Stanford, and Yuan Xie, "Does It Matter Who Pays for Bond Ratings? Historical Evidence," *Journal of Financial Economics*, Author's Accepted Manuscript, doi:10.1016/j.jfineco.2012.04.001, 6–9, 34 (describing the factors that led to the shift from investor-pay to issuer-pay revenue models).

5 Gretchen Morgenson and Joshua A. Rosner, *Reckless Endangerment* (New York: Times Books, 2011), 135–36.

6 United States Senate, Permanent Subcommittee on Investigations, Committee on Homeland Security and Governmental Affairs, *Wall Street and the Financial Crisis: Anatomy of a Financial Collapse*, April 13, 2011, http://hsgac.senate.gov/public/_files/Financial_Crisis/FinancialCrisisReport.pdf (Washington Mutual was on notice in 2005 that 78 percent of loans from two Southern California loan centers were riddled with fraud); Michael Hudson, "The Great Mortgage Cover-up: Countrywide Protected Fraudsters by Silencing Whistleblowers, Say Former Employees," September 22, 2011, www.iwatchnews.org/2011/09/22/6687/countrywide-protected-fraudsters-silencing-whistleblowers-say-former-employees (Countrywide's fraud investigations chief and other employees were fired in retaliation for reporting fraud).

7 Financial Crisis Inquiry Commission, *The Financial Crisis Inquiry Report*, April 13, 2011 (Washington, D.C.: U.S. Government Printing Office, 2011).

8 Ibid., 7.

9 For example, in March 2009, Ford issued asset-backed notes through an entity called Ford Credit Auto Owner Trust 2009-A. Nearly $500 million in Class A-4 notes were issued at an interest rate yield of 6.07%, with a final scheduled payment date of May 15, 2014. At that time, TALF loans were available at 3.0445% (100 basis points over the three-year Libor swap rate). Board of Governors of the Federal Reserve System, "Term Asset-Backed Securities Loan Facility: Frequently Asked Questions," March 3, 2009, www.newyorkfed.org/markets/talf_faq.html.

10 Markit ABX.HE, an index of subprime mortgage bonds, dropped from 87.510 on January 29, 2008, to around 50 in January 2009. It would bottom out at 28.905 on June 16,

2009. Daily price graph for Markit ABX.HE Index, January 1, 2008, to February 15, 2012, via Bloomberg LP, accessed February 16, 2012.

11 Gretchen Morgenson and Louise Story, "Banks Bundled Debt, Bet Against It and Won," *The New York Times,* December 24, 2009, A1.

12 Robert Schmidt, "Geithner Aides Reaped Millions Working for Banks, Hedge Funds," October 14, 2009, www.bloomberg.com/apps/news?pid=newsarchive&sid=abo3Zo0if zJg (reporting that Sachs made $3.4 million in salary alone in 2008).

13 Morgenson and Story, "Banks Bundled Debt, Bet Against It and Won" (describing Tricadia as "[a]mong the most aggressive C.D.O. creators" of all, issuing fourteen mortgage-linked CDOs between 2003 and 2007; two of those deals were among the top ten worst-performing CDOs in 2007).

14 Ibid. (noting that Tricadia's hedge fund made roughly a 50 percent profit in 2007, in part on short bets).

15 Bob Ivry and Jody Shenn, "How Lou Lucido Helped AIG Lose $35 Billion with CDOs Made by Goldman Sachs," March 31, 2010, www.bloomberg.com/news/2010-03-31 /how-lou-lucido-helped-aig-lose-35-billion-with-cdos-made-by-goldman-sachs.html (reporting that Tricadia's TABS 2005-4, "lost almost three-quarters of its value by the time it was bought by the New York Fed for Maiden Lane III").

16 Serena Ng and Carrick Mollenkamp, "Big Funds Also Were Assisted," *The Wall Street Journal,* December 2, 2010, C1.

17 United States Senate, Permanent Subcommittee on Investigations, Committee on Homeland Security and Governmental Affairs, *Wall Street and the Financial Crisis: Anatomy of a Financial Collapse,* 318–20.

18 U.S. Securities and Exchange Commission, "Citigroup to Pay $285 Million to Settle SEC Charges for Misleading Investors About CDO Tied to Housing Market," October 19, 2011, http://sec.gov/news/press/2011/2011-214.htm.

19 U.S. Securities and Exchange Commission, "Goldman Sachs to Pay Record $550 Million to Settle SEC Charges Related to Subprime Mortgage CDO," July 15, 2010, http://sec.gov /news/press/2010/2010-123.htm.

20 U.S. Securities and Exchange Commission, "J.P. Morgan to Pay $153.6 Million to Settle SEC Charges of Misleading Investors in CDO Tied to U.S. Housing Market," June 21, 2011, http://sec.gov/news/press/2011/2011-131.htm.

21 Deborah Solomon, "Sachs, a Top Aide to Geithner, to Exit," *The Wall Street Journal,* March 4, 2010, C3.

22 United States Senate, Permanent Subcommittee on Investigations, Committee on Homeland Security and Governmental Affairs, *Wall Street and the Financial Crisis: Anatomy of a Financial Collapse,* 6, 267.

23 David Barstow, "Treasury's Oversight of Bailout Is Faulted," *The New York Times,* January 9, 2009, B3.

24 J. Taylor Rushing and Molly K. Hooper, "GOP Leaders Take Different Approach to Bailout Funds," The Hill, January 14, 2009, http://thehill.com/homenews/news/17750 -gop-leaders-take-different-approach-to-bailout-funds.

6: The Worst Thing That Happens, We Go Back Home

1 Mike McIntire, "Bailout Is a No-Strings Windfall to Bankers, if Not to Borrowers," *The New York Times,* January 18, 2009, A1.

2 Ibid.

3 Ibid.

4 Rebecca Christie, "Treasury Demands Banks with TARP Funds Report Lending (Update2)," January 20, 2009, www.bloomberg.com/apps/news?pid=newsarchive&sid =auklVwYcgEG0&refer=news# www.siliconinvestor.com/readmsgs.aspx?subjectid=54 034&msgnum=100751&batchsize=10&batchtype=Next].

5 The House bill required Treasury to report quarterly on "use of assistance." TARP Reform and Accountability Act of 2009, H.R. 384, 111th Cong. (2009) (as passed by House of Representatives, January 21, 2009), www.gpo.gov/fdsys/pkg/BILLS-111hr384eh/pdf/ BILLS-111hr384eh.pdf.

6 "Letter from Lawrence H. Summers to Congressional Leaders," January 15, 2009, http://change.gov/newsroom/entry/letter_from_lawrence_h._summers_to _congressional_leaders/.

7 SIGTARP, *Quarterly Report to Congress*, October 21, 2009, www.sigtarp.gov/reports /congress/2009/October2009_Quarterly_Report_to_Congress.pdf, 6, 21.

8 Ibid., 21.

9 Complaint at 60–62, *People v. Bank of America*, No. 450115/2010 (N.Y. Sup. Ct. Feb. 4, 2010).

10 *Bank of America and Merrill Lynch: How Did a Private Deal Turn into a Federal Bailout? Part III: Joint Hearing Before the Committee on Oversight and Government Reform and the Subcommittee on Domestic Policy of the Committee on Oversight and Government Reform, House of Representatives*, July 16, 2009 (Washington, D.C.: U.S. Government Printing Office, 2010), www.gpo.gov/fdsys/pkg/CHRG-111hhrg55765/pdf/CHRG -111hhrg55765.pdf, 2.

11 Business Wire, "Colonial BancGroup Received Preliminary Approval from the U.S. Treasury for $550 Million in Capital," December 2, 2008, www.businesswire.com/news/ home/20081202006381/en/Colonial-BancGroup-Received-Preliminary-Approval -U.S.-Treasury.

12 David Enrich, "Shining a Bright Light Under the TARP," *The Wall Street Journal*, January 29, 2009, C12.

13 Ibid.

14 Jeff Harrington and Robert Trigaux, "Colonial Bank Dodges Bullet: An Ocala Firm's $300 Million Investment Helps Keep the State's Fifth Biggest Bank Afloat," *Tampa Bay Times*, April 2, 2009, B4.

15 U.S. Attorney's Office for the Eastern District of Virginia, "Former Chief Financial Officer of Taylor, Bean & Whitaker Pleads Guilty to Fraud Scheme," March 20, 2012, www .justice.gov/usao/vae/news/2012/03/20120320dearmasnr.html.

16 Michael D. Shear and Peter Slevin, "Obama Names Top Economic Officials," *The Washington Post*, November 25, 2008, A1.

17 Jackie Calmes, "Treasury Nomination Hits Snag over Issue of Past Unpaid Taxes," *The New York Times*, January 14, 2009, A1.

18 *Nomination of Timothy F. Geithner: Hearing Before the Committee on Finance, United States Senate*, January 21, 2009 (Washington, D.C.: U.S. Government Printing Office, 2009), http://finance.senate.gov/hearings/hearing/download/?id=b82761d2 −3fdd-42ab-ab27-c28d3fa0fce2, 216.

19 Ibid., 118.

20 The Internal Revenue Code states that the "amount of any tax . . . shall be assessed within three years after the return was filed." 26 U.S.C. § 6501(a) (2006).

21 *Nomination of Timothy F. Geithner: Hearing Before the Committee on Finance, United States Senate*, January 21, 2009, 115.

22 As a result of the IRS audit, Geithner paid $12,719 in additional taxes for tax year 2003 and $2,128 for tax year 2004, plus interest of $1,885. Ibid., 207.

23 Geithner submitted amended tax returns for tax years 2001 and 2002 to the IRS on November 24, 2008. Ibid., 115. He paid $2,364 in back taxes for tax year 2001 and $16,812 for tax year 2002, plus interest of $6,794. Ibid., 207.

24 Ibid., 116.

25 Congressional Oversight Panel for Economic Stabilization, *Questions about the $700 Billion Emergency Economic Stabilization Funds: The First Report of the Congressional Oversight Panel for Economic Stabilization* (Washington, D.C.: U.S. Government Printing Office, December 10, 2008), www.gpo.gov/fdsys/pkg/CPRT-110JPRT45840/pdf/CPRT -110JPRT45840.pdf, 9–11.

26 Ibid., iv; Congressional Oversight Panel, *Accountability for the Troubled Asset Relief Program: The Second Report of the Congressional Oversight Panel,* January 9, 2009 (Washington, D.C.: U.S. Government Printing Office, 2009), www.gpo.gov/fdsys/pkg /CPRT-111JPRT46500/pdf/CPRT-111JPRT46500.pdf, II, 41–43.

27 "Frank Praises Treasury TARP Inspector General," January 27, 2009, http://democrats .financialservices.house.gov/press/PRArticle.aspx?NewsID=453.

28 *Oversight Concerns Regarding Treasury Department Conduct of the Troubled Assets Relief Program: Hearing Before the Committee on Financial Services, U.S. House of Representatives,* December 10, 2008 (Washington, D.C.: U.S. Government Printing Office, 2009), www.gpo.gov/fdsys/pkg/CHRG-110hhrg46596/pdf/CHRG-110hhrg46596.pdf, 6–7, 40.

29 Kevin Bohn, "The Situation: Wednesday, November 9," November 9, 2005, http://arti cles.cnn.com/2005-11-09/politics/sr.weds_1_grassley-senate-seat-senate-replacement? _s=PM:POLITICS.

30 Chuck Grassley, "Grassley Urges OMB to Get Out of the Way of Special IG for TARP," January 30, 2009, www.grassley.senate.gov/news/Article.cfm?customel_data PageID_1502=19056.

31 Amit R. Paley, "Bailout Fund Letters Are Held Up," *The Washington Post,* January 31, 2009, D3.

32 Ibid.

7: By Wall Street for Wall Street

1 *Pulling Back the TARP: Oversight of the Financial Rescue Program: Hearing Before the Committee on Banking, Housing, and Urban Affairs, United States Senate,* February 5, 2009 (Washington, D.C.: U.S. Government Printing Office, 2009), www.gpo.gov/fdsys /pkg/CHRG-111shrg50577/pdf/CHRG-111shrg50577.pdf, 26.

2 Ibid., 48.

3 Ibid., 2–4 (Sen. Dodd); 8 (Sen. Menendez); 50 (Sen. Johnson); 51 (Sen. Brown).

4 Ibid., 3.

5 Ibid., 18, 41–42.

6 Kevin G. Hall and Greg Gordon, "Watchdogs: Government Overpaid for Wall Street Assets," February 5, 2009, www.mcclatchydc.com/2009/02/05/v-print/61620/watchdogs -government-overpaid.html.

7 Board of Governors of the Federal Reserve System, press release, February 10, 2009, www.federalreserve.gov/monetarypolicy/20090210b.htm; SIGTARP, *Quarterly Report to Congress,* April 21, 2009, www.sigtarp.gov/reports/congress/2009/April2009_Quar terly_Report_to_Congress.pdf, 38, 95, 105.

8 Stephen Labaton and Edmund L. Andrews, "Bailout Plan: $2.5 Trillion and a Strong U.S. Hand: Scant Details, and Wall Street Reacts with a 4.6% Plunge," *The New York Times,* February 11, 2009, A1.

9 Ibid.

10 Walter Hamilton, "Stimulating? Not Exactly: A Vague Speech by the Treasury Chief Sends Investors Fleeing," *Los Angeles Times,* February 11, 2009, C1.

11 "GDP (Current US$)," http://data.worldbank.org/indicator/NY.GDP.MKTP.CD/countries ?order=wbapi_data_value_2009+wbapi_data_value&sort=desc, last accessed April 15, 2012.

12 Ibid.

13 12 U.S.C. §§ 5219–5220 (Supp. II, 2009).

14 "2008 Year-End Foreclosure Market Report," February 5, 2009, www.realtytrac.com/con tent/news-and-opinion/2008-year-end-foreclosure-market-report-4621 (foreclosure filings); "Mortgage Lending Industry Prevented Almost 240,000 Foreclosures in Decem- ber," January 29, 2009, www.hopenow.com/press_release/files/HOPE%20NOW%20 December%202008%20Data%20Release%20.pdf (bank repossessions), 4.

15 "Labor Force Statistics from the Current Population Survey," U.S. Department of Labor, Bureau of Labor Statistics, updated April 16, 2012, http://data.bls.gov/time series/LNS14000000 (August 2008 to February 2009).

16 Barack H. Obama, "Remarks by the President on the Home Mortgage Crisis," Dobson High School, Mesa, Arizona, February 18, 2009, www.whitehouse.gov/the-press-office /remarks-president-mortgage-crisis.

17 Ibid.

18 "Homeowner Affordability and Stability Plan Executive Summary," February 18, 2009, www.treasury.gov/press-center/press-releases/Pages/tg33.aspx; "Homeowner Afford- ability and Stability Plan Fact Sheet," February 18, 2009, www.treasury.gov/press-center /press-releases/Pages/20092181117388144.aspx.

19 Rick Santelli, "Santelli's Tea Party," CNBC, February 19, 2009, video.cnbc.com/gallery /?video=1039849853, 0:42, 1:32.

20 Ibid., 1:10.

21 Ibid., 2:20.

22 SIGTARP, *Selecting Fund Managers for the Legacy Securities Public-Private Invest- ment Program,* October 7, 2010, www.sigtarp.gov/reports/audit/2010/Selecting%20 Fund%20Managers%20for%20the%20Legacy%20Securities%20Public-Private%20 Investment%20Program%2009_07_10.pdf, 4 n. 7.

23 Ibid.

24 SIGTARP, *Quarterly Report to Congress,* April 21, 2009, 147–51.

25 FDIC, "Legacy Loans Program—Test of Funding Mechanism," July 31, 2009, www.fdic .gov/news/news/press/2009/pr09131.html.

26 SIGTARP, *Quarterly Report to Congress,* April 21, 2009, 110.

27 SIGTARP, *Selecting Fund Managers for the Legacy Securities Public-Private Investment Program,* October 7, 2010, 7–9.

28 SIGTARP, *Quarterly Report to Congress,* July 21, 2009, www.sigtarp.gov/reports/con gress/2009/July2009_Quarterly_Report_to_Congress.pdf, 176.

29 Neil M. Barofsky, memorandum to Herbert M. Allison, Jr., July 7, 2009, www.sigtarp .gov/reports/audit/2009/EM_Review_of_Status_and_Challenges_Confronting_the _Home_Affordable_Modification_Program.pdf.

30 SIGTARP, *Factors Affecting Implementation of the Home Affordable Modification Pro-*

gram, March 25, 2010, www.sigtarp.gov/reports/audit/2010/Factors_Affecting_Imple
mentation_of_the_Home_Affordable_Modification_Program.pdf, 21–24.

31 Ibid., 24.

32 Ibid.

33 Ibid., 23.

34 Ibid., 13.

35 Deborah Solomon and Liz Rappaport, "Mr. Barofsky, the TARP Cop, Gets into Role as
Street Tough," *The Wall Street Journal,* March 6, 2009, C1.

36 Ibid.

37 Amit R. Paley, "Shining Light on the Bailout Effort," *The Washington Post,* March 24,
2009, D1.

38 Ibid.

39 *Following the Money: A Quarterly Report by the Special Inspector General for the TARP:
Hearing Before the Joint Economic Committee, Congress of the United States,* April 23,
2009 (Washington, D.C.: U.S. Government Printing Office, 2009), www.gpo.gov/fdsys
/pkg/CHRG-111shrg52273/pdf/CHRG-111shrg52273.pdf, 37.

40 Ibid.

8: Foaming the Runway

1 Martin Kady II, "Grassley on AIG Execs: Quit or Suicide," March 9, 2009, www.politico
.com/news/stories/0309/20083.html.

2 Andrew M. Cuomo to Barney Frank, March 16, 2009, www.foxnews.com/politics/2009
/03/17/raw-data-cuomo-letter-aig-bonuses/.

3 12 U.S.C. § 5221(b)(3)(D)(iii) (Supp. III, 2010).

4 SIGTARP, *The Special Master's Determinations for Executive Compensation of Companies Receiving Exceptional Assistance Under TARP,* January 23, 2012, www.sigtarp.gov
/reports/audit/2012/SIGTARP_ExecComp_Audit.pdf, 31–36.

5 Ibid.

6 James Oliphant, "House OKs Tax on AIG Bonuses as Anger Spreads," *Los Angeles Times,*
March 20, 2009, A1.

7 *Troubled Asset Relief Program: Hearing Before the Subcommittee on Oversight of the
Committee on Ways and Means, House of Representatives,* March 19, 2009 (Washington, D.C.: U.S. Government Printing Office, 2009), www.gpo.gov/fdsys/pkg/CHRG
-111hhrg50333/pdf/CHRG-111hhrg50333.pdf, 47.

8 Tom Raum, "Analysis: CIA Tape Case Evokes Watergate," *USA Today,* December 19,
2007, www.usatoday.com/news/washington/2007-12-19-4236616569_x.htm.

9 Zachary Roth, "Bailout IG: 'Who Knew What, When, and Why' On AIG Bonuses?,"
March 19, 2009, http://tpmmuckraker.talkingpointsmemo.com/2009/03/bailout_ig
_who_knew_what_when_and_why_on_aig_bonus.php.

10 Simon Johnson, "The Quiet Coup," *The Atlantic,* May 2009, www.theatlantic.com/maga
zine/archive/2009/05/the-quiet-coup/7364/?single_page=true.

11 Gretchen Morgenson, "Behind Biggest Insurer's Crisis, a Blind Eye to a Web of Risk," *The
New York Times,* September 28, 2008, A1.

12 Commodity Futures Modernization Act of 2000, Pub. L. No. 106–554, app. E, 114 Stat.
2763, 2763A-365 (codified as amended in scattered sections of 7 U.S.C.); Financial Crisis
Inquiry Commission, *The Financial Crisis Inquiry Report,* April 13, 2011 (Washington,
D.C.: U.S. Government Printing Office, 2011).

13 SIGTARP, *Factors Affecting Efforts to Limit Payments to AIG Counterparties,* November

17, 2009, www.sigtarp.gov/reports/audit/2009/Factors_Affecting_Efforts_to_Limit_Pay ments_to_AIG_Counterparties.pdf, 8.

14 The Financial Crisis Inquiry Commission, *The Financial Crisis Inquiry Commission Report*, 345, 347.

15 5 U.S.C. app. § 8D(a)(1)(D) (2006).

16 Ibid., § (a)(2).

17 *Anticipated Nomination of Neil M. Barofsky: Hearing Before the Committee on Finance, United States Senate,* November 17, 2008 (Washington, D.C.: U.S. Government Printing Office, 2008), http://finance.senate.gov/hearings/hearing/download/?id=15c1d16a -026b-4320-8ad2-7292f25a47d1, 24.

18 Darrell Issa, "AIG Investigation Must Move Forward Without Interference from Treasury," Committee on Oversight and Government Reform, June 19, 2009, http:// oversight.house.gov/release/aig-investigation-must-move-forward-without-interference -from-treasury/.

19 "Abolish the Inspector General," *The Wall Street Journal,* June 25, 2009, A14.

20 155 Cong. Rec. S9096 (2009), www.gpo.gov/fdsys/pkg/CREC-2009-08-07/pdf/CREC -2009-08-07-pt1-PgS9096-5.pdf (Senate adjourned on August 7, 2009); Jim Kuhnhenn, "Treasury Backs Down in Clash with Bailout Watchdog," September 3, 2009, www.huffingtonpost.com/2009/09/03/treasury-backs-down-in-cl_n_276779 .html (Treasury's withdrawal letter was dated August 7, 2009).

21 Laura Blumenfeld, "The $700 Billion Man," *The Washington Post,* December 6, 2009, A1.

22 155 Cong. Rec. S5110 (2009).

23 Ibid., S5109.

24 Timothy L. O'Brien, "A Federal Turf War Over Derivatives Control," *The New York Times,* May 5, 2008, www.nytimes.com/1998/05/08/business/a-federal-turf-war-over -derivatives-control.html.

25 T. W. Farnam, "Ethics Order Affects Aide to Geithner," *The Wall Street Journal,* January 28, 2009, A4; "About Mark A. Patterson," www.treasury.gov/about/organizational -structure/Pages/patterson-m.aspx, last updated March 8, 2011.

26 Lisa Lerer, "Bailout Overseer Draws Fire from Right," April 19, 2009, www.politico.com/ news/stories/0409/21423.html.

27 SIGTARP, *Factors Affecting Implementation of the Home Affordable Modification Program,* March 25, 2010, www.sigtarp.gov/reports/audit/2010/Factors_Affecting_Imple mentation_of_the_Home_Affordable_Modification_Program.pdf, 23; *Foreclosure Prevention: Is The Home Affordable Modification Program Preserving Homeownership?: Hearing Before the Committee on Oversight and Government Reform, House of Representatives,* March 25, 2010 (Washington, D.C.: U.S. Government Printing Office, 2010), www.gpo.gov/fdsys/pkg/CHRG-111hhrg63144/pdf/CHRG-111hhrg63144.pdf, 88 (written testimony of Gene L. Dodaro).

28 SIGTARP, *Factors Affecting Implementation of the Home Affordable Modification Program,* 26.

29 Paul Kiel and Olga Pierce, "Homeowner Questionnaire Shows Banks Violating Gov't Program Rules," August 16, 2010, www.propublica.org/article/homeowner-question naire-shows-banks-violating-govt-program-rules.

30 SIGTARP, *Factors Affecting Implementation of the Home Affordable Modification Program,* 13.

31 Home Affordable Modification Program, "Supplemental Directive 09–01: Introduction of the Home Affordable Modification Program," April 6, 2009, https://www.hmpadmin .com/portal/programs/docs/hamp_servicer/sd0901.pdf, 14.

32 Paul Kiel, "Disorganization at Banks Causing Mistaken Foreclosures," May 4, 2010, www.

propublica.org/article/disorganization-at-banks-causing-mistaken-foreclosures-050410; *The Worsening Foreclosure Crisis: Is It Time to Reconsider Bankruptcy Reform?: Hearing Before the Subcommittee on Administrative Oversight and the Courts of the Committee on the Judiciary, United States Senate,* July 23, 2009 (Washington, D.C.: U.S. Government Printing Office, 2010), www.gpo.gov/fdsys/pkg/CHRG-111shrg55519/pdf/CHRG-111shrg55519.pdf, 77 (written testimony of Alys Cohen, National Consumer Law Center).

33 *Preserving Home Ownership: Progress Needed to Prevent Foreclosures: Hearing Before the Committee on Banking, Housing, and Urban Affairs,* July 16, 2009 (Washington, D.C.: U.S. Government Printing Office, 2010), www.gpo.gov/fdsys/pkg/CHRG-111shrg55032/pdf/CHRG-111shrg55032.pdf, 213–217 (written testimony of Diane E. Thompson, National Consumer Law Center).

34 SIGTARP, *Factors Affecting Implementation of the Home Affordable Modification Program,* 25.

35 SIGTARP, *Quarterly Report to Congress,* October 26, 2010, www.sigtarp.gov/reports /congress/2010/October2010_Quarterly_Report_to_Congress.pdf, 12, 172–175; Shahien Nasiripour and Arthur Delaney, "Michigan Family Says Obama Foreclosure-Prevention Program Cost Them Their Home," May 25, 2011, www.huffingtonpost.com /2011/02/01/michigan-family-says-obam_n_816684.html; Paul Kiel, "Homeowners Say Banks Not Following Rules for Loan Modifications," January 14, 2010, www.propublica .org/article/homeowners-say-banks-not-following-rules-for-loan-modifications.

36 SIGTARP, *Quarterly Report to Congress,* July 21, 2010, www.sigtarp.gov/reports/con gress/2010/July2010_Quarterly_Report_to_Congress.pdf, 19–20; U.S. Attorney for the Southern District of California, "Financial Fraud Enforcement Task Force Announces Regional Results of 'Operation Stolen Dreams' Targeting Mortgage Fraudsters," June 17, 2010, www.justice.gov/usao/cas/press/cas10–0617-USAO_SDCA_SD.pdf.

37 SIGTARP, *Quarterly Report to Congress,* October 26, 2010, 34.

38 U.S. Department of the Treasury, "U.S. Department of the Treasury, U.S. Department of Housing and Urban Development and the Ad Council Unveil National PSA Campaign to Raise Awareness of Making Home Affordable Program," July 28, 2010, www.treasury .gov/press-center/press-releases/Pages/tg795.aspx; SIGTARP, *Factors Affecting Implementation of the Home Affordable Modification Program,* 27.

39 David Dayen, "Portrait of HAMP Failure: The Mother of All HAMP Nightmares," February 9, 2011, http://news.firedoglake.com/2011/02/09/portrait-of-hamp-failure-the-mother-of-all-hamp-nightmares/.

40 Shahien Nasiripour, "Obama Administration Defends Lackluster Foreclosure Programs; Says Interest Rates Will Remain Low to Help Housing Market," August 19, 2010, www .huffingtonpost.com/2010/08/19/obama-foreclosures-tarp_n_688355.html (reporting comments by a "senior Obama administration official," who acknowledged that "one success for the administration has been its role in lengthening the foreclosure process," and calling that "a good thing . . . because it gives the market time to absorb these homes gradually—without leading to a dramatic drop in home prices"); calendar of Secretary Geithner, April–August 2010, http://www.treasury.gov/FOIA/Documents/TFG %20Calendars%20April%20to%20August%202010%20permanently%20redacted%20 OCR%20final.pdf. (showing calendar entry for Geithner on Wednesday, August 18, "Blogger Meeting").

41 SIGTARP, *Factors Affecting Implementation of the Home Affordable Modification Program,* 16.

9: The Audacity of Math

1 SIGTARP, *Quarterly Report to Congress,* April 28, 2011, www.sigtarp.gov/reports/con gress/2011/April2011_Quarterly_Report_to_Congress.pdf, 31.

2 As of December 31, 2007, the five largest bank holding companies held $6.92 trillion in assets, and by December 31, 2010, the number was $8.47 trillion. See Federal Reserve System, National Information Center, "BHCPR Peer Group Average Reports" (report names 2007: Peer 1, 4th Quarter, and 2010: Peer 1, 4th Quarter; accessed April 17, 2012), www.ffiec.gov/nicpubweb/Content/BHCPRRPT/BHCPR_PEER.htm#2007; see also Thomas M. Hoenig, op-ed, "Too Big to Succeed," *The New York Times,* December 2, 2010, A37.

3 Michael Hirsh, "Wall Street Digs In," *Newsweek,* April 9, 2009, www.thedailybeast.com /newsweek/2009/04/09/wall-street-digs-in.html; Simon Johnson, "The Quiet Coup," *The Atlantic,* May 2009, 49; Gretchen Morgenson and Don Van Natta, Jr., "Even in Crisis, Banks Dig In for Battle Against Regulation," *The New York Times,* June 1, 2009, A1.

4 SIGTARP, *Quarterly Report to Congress,* July 21, 2009, www.sigtarp.gov/reports/con gress/2009/July2009_Quarterly_Report_to_Congress.pdf, 152–153.

5 Ibid., 143.

6 Ibid., 140–141.

7 Floyd Norris, "Big Estimate, Worth Little, on Bailout," *The New York Times,* July 21, 2009, B1.

8 SIGTARP, *Quarterly Report to Congress,* July 21, 2009, 138.

9 Matthew Jaffe, "$23.7 Trillion to Fix Financial System?" ABC News, July 20, 2009, http:// abcnews.go.com/Business/Politics/story?id=8127005&page=1#.T0rMKMwzJYQ

10 Floyd Norris, "Big Estimate, Worth Little, on Bailout," *The New York Times,* July 21, 2009, B1.

11 The White House, Office of the Press Secretary, News Conference by the President, July 22, 2009, www.whitehouse.gov/the-press-office/news-conference-president-july-22-2009.

12 Committee on Oversight and Government Reform, "Issa Statement on President's Response to SIGTARP Report Question," July 23, 2009, http://oversight.house.gov/release /issa-statement-on-presidents-response-to-sigtarp-report-question/.

13 SIGTARP, *Quarterly Report to Congress,* January 30, 2010, www.sigtarp.gov/reports /congress/2010/January2010_Quarterly_Report_to_Congress.pdf, 140–141.

14 Ibid., 11, 141.

15 SIGTARP, *SIGTARP Survey Demonstrates that Banks Can Provide Meaningful Informa- tion on Their Use of TARP Funds,* July 20, 2009, www.sigtarp.gov/reports/audit/2009 /SIGTARP_Survey_Demonstrates_That_Banks_Can_Provide_Meaningful_Informa tion_On_Their_Use_Of_TARP_Funds.pdf, 8.

16 Ibid., 11.

17 Ibid., 11–12.

18 Ibid., 5–6.

10: The Essential $7,700 Kitchen Assistant

1 SIGTARP, *Initial Report to the Congress,* February 5, 2009, www.sigtarp.gov/reports /congress/2009/SIGTARP_Initial_Report_to_the_Congress.pdf, 74, 78.

2 SIGTARP, *Factors Affecting the Decisions of General Motors and Chrysler to Reduce Their*

Dealership Networks, July 19, 2010, www.sigtarp.gov/reports/audit/2010/Factors%20 Affecting%20the%20Decisions%20of%20General%20Motors%20and%20Chrysler%20 to%20Reduce%20Their%20Dealership%20Networks%207_19_2010.pdf, 3.

3 Ibid., 3–5.

4 Ibid., 2.

5 U.S. Department of the Treasury, "Chrysler February 17 Plan: Viability Determination," March 30, 2009, www.whitehouse.gov/assets/documents/Chrysler_Viability_Assess ment.pdf, 1; U.S. Department of the Treasury, "GM February 17 Plan: Viability Determination," March 30, 2009, www.whitehouse.gov/assets/documents/GM_Viabil ity_Assessment.pdf, 1; SIGTARP, *Factors Affecting the Decisions of General Motors and Chrysler to Reduce Their Dealership Networks,* 7–8.

6 SIGTARP, *Quarterly Report to Congress,* July 21, 2009, www.sigtarp.gov/reports/con gress/2009/July2009_Quarterly_Report_to_Congress.pdf, 94.

7 Josh Mitchell, "Car Chiefs Grilled on Dealer Closings," *The Wall Street Journal,* June 4, 2009, B1.

8 Mark Tapscott, "Furor Grows over Partisan Car Dealer Closings," *Washington Examiner,* May 26, 2009, http://washingtonexaminer.com/politics/beltway-confidential/2009/05 /furor-grows-over-partisan-car-dealer-closings/135803; Terry Krepel, "Right-Wing Media Won't Concede Obama-Chrysler Dealer Conspiracy Is Bogus," June 4, 2009, www.huffingtonpost.com/terry-krepel/right-wing-media-wont-con_b_211318.html.

9 SIGTARP, *Factors Affecting the Decisions of General Motors and Chrysler to Reduce Their Dealership Networks,* 14–15.

10 Ibid., 13–14.

11 Ibid., 23–24.

12 Ibid., 10–12.

13 Ibid., 16–23, 30–31.

14 "Labor Force Statistics from the Current Population Survey," Bureau of Labor Statistics, http://data.bls.gov/timeseries/LNS14000000, accessed March 21, 2012.

15 The Financial Crisis Inquiry Commission, *The Financial Crisis Inquiry Commission Report* (New York: Public Affairs, 2011), 345, 347.

16 SIGTARP, *Factors Affecting Efforts to Limit Payments to AIG Counterparties,* November 17, 2009, www.sigtarp.gov/reports/audit/2009/Factors_Affecting_Efforts_to_Limit _Payments_to_AIG_Counterparties.pdf, 8, 11.

17 Ibid.; Financial Crisis Inquiry Commission, *The Financial Crisis Inquiry Report,* April 13, 2011 (Washington, D.C.: Government Printing Office, 2011), www.gpo.gov/fdsys /pkg/GPO-FCIC/pdf/GPO-FCIC.pdf, 347–348.

18 SIGTARP, *Factors Affecting Efforts to Limit Payments to AIG Counterparties,* 8, 11.

19 Ibid., 9, 11.

20 Ibid., 8.

21 Ibid., 11.

22 Ibid.

23 Ibid., 11–12.

24 Ibid., 20.

25 SIGTARP, *Extent of Federal Agencies' Oversight of AIG Compensation Varied, and Important Challenges Remain,* October 14, 2009, www.sigtarp.gov/reports/audit/2009 /Extent_of_Federal_Agencies%27_Oversight_of_AIG_Compensation_Varied_and _Important_Challenges_Remain_10_14_09.pdf, 13–14, 22.

26 Ibid., 13; U.S. Department of Treasury, "U.S. Treasury and Federal Reserve Board

Announce Participation in AIG Restructuring Plan," March 2, 2009, http://www.trea sury.gov/press-center/press-releases/Pages/tg44.aspx.

27 SIGTARP, *Extent of Federal Agencies' Oversight of AIG Compensation Varied, and Important Challenges Remain*, 12.

28 SIGTARP, *Emergency Capital Injections Provided to Support the Viability of Bank of America, Other Major Banks, and the U.S. Financial System*, October 5, 2009, www .sigtarp.gov/reports/audit/2009/Emergency_Capital_Injections_Provided_to_Support _the_Viability_of_Bank_of_America . . . _100509.pdf, 18.

29 Ibid., 18.

30 SIGTARP, *Factors Affecting Efforts to Limit Payments to AIG Counterparties*, 29.

31 Christine Richard and Jody Shenn, "Ambac to Pay $850 Million in Citigroup CDO Set tlement (Update7)," August 1, 2008, www.bloomberg.com/apps/news?pid=newsarchive &sid=aiApBWhAOmMM.

32 Reuters, "Ambac Reaches Agreement on $3.5 Billion in Exposure," *The New York Times*, November 20, 2008, B7.

33 SIGTARP, *Factors Affecting Efforts to Limit Payments to AIG Counterparties*, 29.

34 Ibid.

35 David Cho, "N.Y. Fed Pushed AIG on Contracts," *Washington Post*, October 28, 2009, A16.

36 SIGTARP, *Factors Affecting Efforts to Limit Payments to AIG Counterparties*, 30.

37 The Huffington Post, November 17, 2009, http://screenshots.assets.huffingtonpost.com /originals/2009/11/17/2009111706-home.jpg.

38 Robert Schmidt and Lorraine Woellert, "Geithner Resignation Calls May Increase as 2010 Election Nears," November 20, 2009, www.bloomberg.com/apps/news?pid=news archive&sid=awXy12PVV7.0; Noam Scheiber, "Should Geithner Resign?," *The New Republic*, November 24, 2009, www.tnr.com/blog/the-stash/should-geithner-resign.

39 Kara Scannell, "Geithner Strikes Back," *The Wall Street Journal*, November 17, 2009, http://blogs.wsj.com/economics/2009/11/17/geithner-strikes-back/. Attorney General Eric Holder, briefing on the formation of the Financial Fraud Enforcement Task Force, November 17, 2009, C-SPAN video, www.c-spanvideo.org/program/FraudEf.

40 Paul Krugman, "The Big Squander," *The New York Times*, November 20, 2009, A35.

41 Shahien Nasiripour, "Senator to Fed Chair Bernanke: 'You Are the Definition of Moral Hazard,'" December 3, 2009, www.huffingtonpost.com/2009/12/03/senator-to-fed -chair-bern_n_378673.html.

42 *The Federal Bailout of AIG: Hearing Before the Committee on Oversight and Government Reform, House of Representatives*, January 27, 2010, www.gpo.gov/fdsys/pkg/CHRG -111hhrg63136/pdf/CHRG-111hhrg63136.pdf.

43 Ibid., 52–53.

44 Ibid., 47.

45 Stephen Gandel, "Former TARP Official on TARP: A Big Fat Failure, Mostly," *Time*, March 30, 2011, business.time.com/2011/03/30/former-tarp-official-on-tarp-a-big-fat -failure-mostly.

11: Treasury's Backseat Driver

1 SIGTARP, *Quarterly Report to Congress*, January 30, 2010, www.sigtarp.gov/reports /congress/2010/January2010_Quarterly_Report_to_Congress.pdf, 11.

2 Remarks by the President on the Home Mortgage Crisis, Dobson High School, Mesa,

Ariz., February 18, 2009, www.whitehouse.gov/the-press-office/remarks-president
-mortgage-crisis.

3 SIGTARP, *Factors Affecting Implementation of the Home Affordable Modification
Program,* March 25, 2010, www.sigtarp.gov/reports/audit/2010/Factors_Affecting
_Implementation_of_the_Home_Affordable_Modification_Program.pdf, 9.

4 Ibid.

5 Treasury Department, "Making Home Affordable Program: Servicer Performance
Through December 2009," www.treasury.gov/initiatives/financial-stability/results
/MHA-Reports/Documents/report.pdf, 3.

6 Andrew Haughwout, Richard Peach, and Joseph Tracy, "The Homeownership Gap," *Current Issues in Economics and Finance* 116, no. 5 (2010): 9, www.newyorkfed.org/research
/current_issues/ci16-5.pdf.

7 SIGTARP, *Factors Affecting Implementation of the Home Affordable Modification Program,* 34.

8 Ibid., 54.

9 *Hearing with Treasury Secretary Timothy Geithner, Congressional Oversight Panel,*
December 10, 2009 (Washington, D.C.: U.S. Government Printing Office, 2009), www
.gpo.gov/fdsys/pkg/CHRG-111shrg55245/pdf/CHRG-111shrg55245.pdf, 48.

10 *Foreclosure Prevention: Is the Home Affordable Modification Program Preserving Homeownership?: Hearing Before the Committee on Oversight and Government Reform, House
of Representatives,* March 25, 2010 (Washington, D.C.: U.S. Government Printing Office,
2010), www.gpo.gov/fdsys/pkg/CHRG-111hhrg63144/pdf/CHRG-111hhrg63144.pdf,
198–201, 212.

11 U.S. Department of the Treasury, "Housing Program Enhancements Offer Additional
Options for Struggling Homeowners," March 26, 2010, www.treasury.gov/press-center
/press-releases/Pages/tg614.aspx.

12 John Prior, "FHA and the Short Refi Left Behind," October 4, 2011, www.housingwire
.com/2011/10/04/fha-and-the-short-refi-left-behind; U.S. Department of Housing and
Urban Development, "Mortgagee Letter 2010–23," www.hud.gov/offices/adm/hudclips
/letters/mortgagee/files/10–23ml.pdf.

13 SIGTARP, *Quarterly Report to Congress,* July 21, 2010, www.sigtarp.gov/reports/con
gress/2010/July2010_Quarterly_Report_to_Congress.pdf, 265.

14 Ibid., 174–75.

15 SIGTARP, *Quarterly Report to Congress,* July 21, 2010, 175, 265.

16 Binyamin Appelbaum, "Measuring Housing's Drag on the Economy," February 24,
2012, http://economix.blogs.nytimes.com/2012/02/24/measuring-housings-drag-on
-the-economy/.

17 Martin S. Feldstein, "How to Stop the Drop in Home Values," *The New York Times,* October 12, 2011, A29.

18 SIGTARP, *Quarterly Report to Congress,* July 21, 2010, 175–76, 265.

19 U.S. Department of the Treasury, *Troubled Asset Relief Program: Two Year Retrospective,*
October 2010, www.treasury.gov/press-center/news/Documents/TARP%20Two%20
Year%20Retrospective_10%2005%2010_transmittal%20letter.pdf, 75.

20 SIGTARP, *Quarterly Report to Congress,* October 26, 2010, www.sigtarp.gov/reports
/congress/2010/October2010_Quarterly_Report_to_Congress.pdf, 12.

21 Ibid., 165–175.

22 "The President's FY 2012 Budget and Revenue Proposals," http://budget.senate.
gov/democratic/index.cfm/committeehearings?ContentRecord_id=9f8d731e-4313
-4b3b-9e86-23136c18c36f&ContentType_id=14f995b9-dfa5-407a-9d35

-56cc7152a7ed&Group_id=d68d31c2–2e75–49fb-a03a-be915cb4550b&MonthDispl
ay=2&YearDisplay=2011 (statement of Timothy Geithner, Secretary of the United States
Department of the Treasury); Reuters, "Geithner: Mortgage Program Won't Meet Initial
Goals," February 17, 2011, www.reuters.com/article/2011/02/17/usa-housing-geithner-
idUSWAT01487920110217.

23 *Legislative Proposals to End Taxpayer Funding for Ineffective Foreclosure Mitigation
Programs: Hearing Before the Subcommittee on Insurance, Housing, and Community
Opportunity of the Committee on Financial Services, U.S. House of Representatives,* March
2, 2011 (Washington, D.C.: U.S. Government Printing Office, 2011), www.gpo.gov/fdsys
/pkg/CHRG-112hhrg65670/pdf/CHRG-112hhrg65670.pdf, 31 (statement of Neil Barofsky, special inspector general for the Troubled Asset Relief Program) (citing RealtyTrac
data).

24 Jon Prior, "Treasury Makes Adjustments to Give HAMP a Chance," February 24,
2011, www.housingwire.com/2011/02/24/treasury-makes-adjustments-to-give-hamp
-a-chance.

25 U.S. Department of the Treasury, "Obama Administration Kicks Off Mortgage Modification Conversion Drive," November 30, 2009, www.treasury.gov/press-center/press-
releases/Pages/tg421.aspx.

26 Congressional Oversight Panel, *December Oversight Report: A Review of Treasury's
Foreclosure Prevention Programs,* December 14, 2010 (Washington, D.C.: U.S. Government Printing Office, December 14, 2010), http://www.gpo.gov/fdsys/pkg/CPRT
-111JPRT62622/pdf/CPRT-111JPRT62622.pdf, 41.

27 *Bailouts and the Foreclosure Crisis: Report of the Special Inspector General for the Troubled
Asset Relief Program: Hearing Before the Committee on Oversight and Government
Reform, House of Representatives,* January 26, 2011 (Washington, D.C.: U.S. Government Printing Office, 2011), www.gpo.gov/fdsys/pkg/CHRG-112hhrg67062/pdf/CHRG
-112hhrg67062.pdf, 35.

28 SIGTARP, *Quarterly Report to Congress,* January 26, 2012, http://www.sigtarp.gov/Quar
terly%20Reports/January_26_2012_Report_to_Congress.pdf, 59.

29 *President's Proposed Fee on Financial Institutions Regarding TARP: Hearings Before the
Committee on Finance, United States Senate,* April 20, May 4, and May 11, 2010 (Washington, D.C.: U.S. Government Printing Office, 2010), http://finance.senate.gov/hear
ings/hearing/download/?id=f316e952–30b0–46e3–97be-e27f66654de8, 27.

30 Ibid.

31 Mark Knoller, "White House Exults in General Motors Repayment," April 21, 2010,
www.cbsnews.com/8301–503544_162–20003116–503544.html.

32 Briefing by White House Press Secretary Robert Gibbs, April 21, 2010, www.whitehouse
.gov/the-press-office/briefing-white-house-press-secretary-robert-gibbs-42110.

33 "Statement from Treasury Secretary Geithner on the Presidential Task Force on the Auto
Industry," July 13, 2009, www.treasury.gov/press-center/press-releases/Pages/tg207.aspx

34 General Motors, "GM Pays Back Government Loans in Full, Announces Investment in
Fairfax, Detroit Hamtramck," April 21, 2010, http://media.gm.com/content/media/us/en
/news/news_detail.brand_gm.html/content/Pages/news/us/en/2010/Apr/0421_fairfax.

35 Ibid.

36 "Grassley asks about GM repaying TARP loans with other TARP funds," April 22, 2010,
www.grassley.senate.gov/news/Article.cfm?customel_dataPageID_1502=26293.

37 Herbert M. Allison, Jr., letter to Charles E. Grassley, April 27, 2010, www.grassley.senate
.gov/about/upload/2010-04-27-Letter-from-Treasury-Dept.pdf.

38 Gretchen Morgenson, "Repaying Taxpayers with Their Own Cash," *New York Times*, May 1, 2010, B1.

39 SIGTARP, *Factors Affecting the Decisions of General Motors and Chrysler to Reduce Their Dealership Networks*, July 19, 2010, www.sigtarp.gov/reports/audit/2010/Factors%20 Affecting%20the%20Decisions%20of%20General%20Motors%20and%20Chrysler%20 to%20Reduce%20Their%20Dealership%20Networks%207_19_2010.pdf, 11–12.

40 Ibid., 13.

41 Ibid.

42 Ibid., 8.

43 Ibid., 28.

44 Ibid., 10–11.

45 SIGTARP, *Factors Affecting the Decisions of General Motors and Chrysler to Reduce Their Dealership Network*, 4, 39.

46 Ibid., 12.

47 Ibid., 9.

48 Ibid., 13–14.

49 Ibid., 33.

50 SIGTARP, *Quarterly Report to Congress*, October 26, 2010, 21.

51 Ibid., 25.

52 Bureau of Labor Statistics, "Labor Force Statistics from the Current Population Survey," http://data.bls.gov/timeseries/LNS14000000, accessed March 24, 2012.

53 Darrell Issa, "SIGTARP Audit Examining Auto Bailout Finds Obama Administration 'Accelerated' Job Losses," July 18, 2010, http://oversight.house.gov/sigtarp-audit-examining-auto-bailout-finds-obama-administration-qaccelerated-job-losses.

54 Christine Tierney, "Report: U.S. Ignored Impact of Shutting Auto Dealerships," *Detroit News*, July 19, 2010, A8; Jerry Hirsch, "Treasury Slammed Over Dealer Cuts," *Los Angeles Times*, July 19, 2010, A15.

55 Editorial, "Treasury's Back-Seat Driver," *The Washington Post*, July 20, 2010, A20.

56 "Troubled TARP," July 24, 2010, web.utsandiego.com/news/2010/jul/24/troubled-tarp/; "Engineered by Obama Motors," August 10, 2010, www.washingtontimes.com/news/2010/aug/10/engineered-by-obama-motors/.

57 Brady Dennis, "Battle Looms over New Financial Watchdog," *The Washington Post*, July 20, 2010, A17; Neil Irwin, "Is Elizabeth Warren Really the Best Pick to Run the New Consumer Finance Agency?" *The Washington Post*, July 20, 2010, http://voices.washingtonpost.com/political-economy/2010/07/is_elizabeth_warren_really_the.html.

58 Shahien Nasiripour, "Tim Geithner Opposes Nominating Elizabeth Warren to Lead New Consumer Agency," July 15, 2010, www.huffingtonpost.com/2010/07/15/tim-geithner-opposes-nomi_n_647691.html; Brady Dennis, "Battle Looms over New Financial Watchdog," *The Washington Post*, July 20, 2010, A17.

59 *Hearing with Secretary Timothy Geithner Before the Congressional Oversight Panel, United States Senate*, June 22, 2010 (Washington, D.C.: U.S. Government Printing Office, 2010), www.gpo.gov/fdsys/pkg/CHRG-111shrg62218/pdf/CHRG-111shrg62218.pdf, 54–56 (statements of Elizabeth Warren, chair of the Congressional Oversight Panel, and Timothy Geithner, secretary of the U.S. Department of the Treasury).

60 *An Update on the TARP Program: Hearing Before the Committee on Finance, United States Senate*, July 21, 2010 (Washington, D.C.: U.S. Government Printing Office, 2010), http://finance.senate.gov/hearings/hearing/download/?id=279a74b5-0845-4012-96c7-dcbc3de6af93, 2.

61 Ibid., 29.

12: Happy Endings

1 *Has Dodd-Frank Ended Too Big to Fail?: Hearing Before the Subcommittee on TARP, Financial Services and Bailouts of Public and Private Programs of the Committee on Oversight and Government Reform, House of Representatives,* March 30, 2011 (Washington, D.C.: U.S. Government Printing Office, 2011), www.gpo.gov/fdsys/pkg/CHRG -112hhrg67620/pdf/CHRG-112hhrg67620.pdf, 17 (statement of Neil Barofsky, special inspector general for the Troubled Asset Relief Program).

2 Al Kamen, "Small Towns' Loss Could Be Bipartisanship's Gain," *The Washington Post,* February 16, 2011, A17; Al Kamen, "Drop the Pencil and Keep Your Assets in Plain View," *The Washington Post,* March 9, 2011, A21.

3 Louise Story and Mary Williams Walsh, "U.S. Is Said to Seek Way to Sever Ties with A.I.G.," *The New York Times,* September 29, 2010, B1 (posted online on September 28, 2010 http://www.nytimes.com/2010/09/29/business/29aig.html); David Lawder and Paritosh Bansal, "AIG Exit Plan Announcement Possible in Days-Source," Reuters, September 29, 2010, http://www.reuters.com/article/2010/09/29/aig-exit-idUS WAT01466920100929; Hugh Son and James Sterngold, "Treasury Said to Prepare AIG Exit, Repayment Plan," September 27, 2010, www.bloomberg.com/news/2010–09–26/ treasury-said-to-ready-plan-to-sell-aig-stake-recoup-taxpayer-investment.html; Serena Ng et al., "AIG to U.S.: Keep the Change," *The Wall Street Journal,* September 30, 2010, C1.

4 SIGTARP, *Quarterly Report to Congress,* October 26, 2010, www.sigtarp.gov/reports/con gress/2010/October2010_Quarterly_Report_to_Congress.pdf, 7, 121–26.

5 U.S. Department of the Treasury, *Troubled Asset Relief Program: Two Year Retrospective,* October 2010, www.treasury.gov/press-center/news/Documents/TARP%20Two%20 Year%20Retrospective_10%2005%2010_transmittal%20letter.pdf, 4.

6 U.S. Department of the Treasury, "Summary Tables of Trouble [*sic*] Asset Relief Program (TARP) Investments as of March 31, 2010," www.treasury.gov/initiatives /financial-stability/briefing-room/reports/Documents/TARP%20Cost%20Estimates% 20-%20March%2031%202010.pdf, 1.

7 U.S. Department of Treasury, *Troubled Asset Relief Program, Two Year Retrospective,* 4.

8 Timothy Geithner, "5 Myths About TARP," *The Washington Post,* October 10, 2010, B3.

9 SIGTARP, *Quarterly Report to Congress,* January 30, 2010, http://www.sigtarp.gov/Quar terly%20Reports/January2010_Quarterly_Report_to_Congress.pdf, 20–21.

10 SIGTARP, *Quarterly Report to Congress,* October 26, 2010, 332.

11 Mary Williams Walsh, "Treasury Hid A.I.G. Losses, Report Says," *New York Times,* October 26, 2010, B1; Daniel Indiviglio, "So Much for Treasury's [REDACTED] Transparency?," *The Atlantic,* October 26, 2010, www.theatlantic.com/business/archive/2010/10 /so-much-for-treasurys-redacted-transparency/65209.

12 Jen Psaki, "The Facts on AIG," October 27, 2010, www.whitehouse.gov/blog/2010/ 10/27/facts-aig.

13 Jim McTague, "Running Afoul of Obama's Adding Machine," *Barron's,* November 1, 2010, 40; Alain Sherter, "Why the Obama White House Is Feuding with TARP Watchdog Neil Barofsky," October 28, 2010, www.cbsnews.com/8301–505123_162–43548482 /why-the-obama-administration-is-feuding-with-tarp-watchdog-neil-barofsky/.

14 *Bailouts and the Foreclosure Crisis: Report of the Special Inspector General for the Troubled Asset Relief Program: Hearing Before the Committee on Oversight and Government Reform, House of Representatives,* January 26, 2011 (Washington, D.C.: U.S. Government Printing Office, 2011), www.gpo.gov/fdsys/pkg/CHRG-112hhrg67062/pdf/CHRG-112hhrg67062.pdf, 4.

15 Federal Reserve System National Information Center BHCPR Peer Group Average Reports (report names 2007: Peer 1, 4th Quarter, and 2010: Pier 1, 4th Quarter; accessed April 17, 2012), www.ffiec.gov/nicpubweb/Content/BHCPRRPT/BHCPR_PEER .htm#2007.

16 Thomas M. Hoenig, *Keynote Address: Pew Financial Reform Project and New York University Stern School of Business Forum on Regulating "Too Big to Fail" Companies,* video, June 27, 2011, www.c-spanvideo.org/program/300236–4, 48:41.

17 Thomas M. Hoenig, "Too Big to Succeed," *The New York Times,* December 2, 2010, A37.

18 Aaron Lucchetti and Stephen Grocer, "On Street, Pay Vaults to Record Altitude," *The Wall Street Journal,* February 2, 2011, C1.

19 SIGTARP, *Quarterly Report to Congress,* January 30, 2010, www.sigtarp.gov/reports /congress/2010/January2010_Quarterly_Report_to_Congress.pdf, 6.

20 Ibid.

21 John Heilemann, "Obama Is from Mars, Wall Street Is from Venus," *New York Magazine,* May 22, 2010, http://nymag.com/news/politics/66188/index6.html.

22 Dodd-Frank Wall Street Reform and Consumer Protection Act § 121(a), 12 U.S.C.A. § 5331(a) (West 2011).

23 Jeremy W. Peters and Edmund L. Andrews, "Reassurance by Fed Chief on Loan Ills," *The New York Times,* March 29, 2007, C1.

24 Timothy Geithner, "Liquidity Risk and the Global Economy," May 15, 2007, www .newyorkfed.org/newsevents/speeches/2007/gei070515.html.

25 Dodd-Frank Wall Street Reform and Consumer Protection Act §§ 121(a), 203(b), 12 U.S.C.A. §§ 5331(a), 5383(b) (West 2011).

26 Hoenig, "Too Big to Succeed."

27 SIGTARP, *Extraordinary Assistance Provided to Citigroup, Inc.*, January 13, 2011, http:// www.sigtarp.gov/Audit%20Reports/Extraordinary%20Financial%20Assistance%20 Provided%20to%20Citigroup,%20Inc.pdf, 43–44.

28 Editorial, "The Ruling Ad-Hocracy," *The Wall Street Journal,* January 21, 2011, A12.

29 Brady Dennis, "Bank-Bailout Overseer Barofsky Will Resign," *The Washington Post,* February 15, 2011, A17.

Afterword

1 Federal Reserve Bank of Dallas, *2011 Annual Report,* www.dallasfed.org/assets/documents /fed/annual/2011/ar11.pdf, 12.

2 CoreLogic, *National Foreclosure Report—March 2012,* www.corelogic.com/about-us /researchtrends/asset_upload_file347_14980.pdf, 1.

3 Edward J. DeMarco, Acting Director, Federal Housing Finance Agency, "Addressing the Weak Housing Market: Is Principal Reduction the Answer?" (speech, The Brookings Institution, Washington, D.C., April 10, 2012), www.fhfa.gov/webfiles/23876/Brook ings_Institution_-_Principal_Forgiveness_v11R-_final.pdf, 3.

4 Carmen DeNavas-Walt, Bernadette D. Proctor, and Jessica C. Smith, U.S. Census Bureau, Current Population Reports, P60-239, *Income, Poverty, and Health Insurance Coverage in the United States: 2010* (Washington, D.C.: U.S. Government Printing Office, 2011), www.census.gov/prod/2011pubs/p60-239.pdf, 14.

5 Compare U.S. Department of the Treasury, *Making Home Affordable Program Performance Report Through March 2012,* www.treasury.gov/initiatives/financial-stability /results/MHA-Reports/Documents/Mar%202012%20MHA%20Report%20Final.pdf, 3 (794,748 active permanent modifications in March 2012), with U.S. Department of

the Treasury, *Making Home Affordable Program Performance Report Through February 2012*, www.treasury.gov/initiatives/financial-stability/results/MHA-Reports/Documents/Feb%202012%20MHA%20Report%20FINAL.pdf, 3 (782, 609 active permanent modifications in February 2012).

6   Arthur Delaney, "HAMP: Obama Administration Lets Banks Out of Doghouse for Bad Mortgage Servicing," March 2, 2012, www.huffingtonpost.com/2012/03/02/hamp -mortgage-barack-obama_n_1316873.html.

7   U.S. Department of Justice, "Federal Government and State Attorneys General Reach $25 Billion Agreement with Five Largest Mortgage Servicers to Address Mortgage Loan Servicing and Foreclosure Abuses," news release, February 9, 2012, www.justice .gov/opa/pr/2012/February/12-ag-186.html.

8   Shaila Dawan and Jessica Silver-Greenberg, "Foreclosure Deal Credits Banks for Routine Efforts," *New York Times*, March 28, 2012, B1.

9   Jessica Silver-Greenberg, "House Is Gone but Debt Lives On," *Wall Street Journal*, October 1–2, 2011, A1.

10 Consent Judgment as to Residential Capital, LLC, Ally Financial, Inc., and GMAC Mortgage, LLC, United States of America et al. v. Bank of America Corporation et al., Docket No. 1:12-cv-00361-RMC, April 4, 2012, www.justice.gov/opa/documents/residential -consent-judgement.pdf, D1–2 ($1.00 write-down = $0.45 credit for first lien principal forgiveness modification on investor loans [forgiveness by investor]).

11 HUD Public Affairs, "Myth vs. Fact: Setting the Record Straight about Historic Mortgage Servicing Settlement," *The HUDdle* (U.S. Department of Housing and Urban Development's official blog), March 12, 2012, http://blog.hud.gov/index.php/2012/03/12/myth -vs-fact-setting-the-record-straight-about-historic-mortgage-servicing-settlement/. ("If a servicer receives a HAMP investor incentive payment of 20 cents for every dollar of principal reduction, it can receive credit at the applicable rate on the remaining 80 cents.")

12 Stan Humphries and Svenja Gudell, "Zillow Negative Equity Research Report March 2012," May 24, 2012, www.zillow.com/blog/research/2012/05/24/despite-home-value- gains-underwater-homeowners-owe-1-2-trillion-more-than-homes-worth.

13 Barack Obama, interview by Steve Kroft, *60 Minutes*, CBS, December 11, 2011, www.cbsnews.com/8301-504803_162-57341009-10391709/president-obama-the-full -60-minutes-interview. ("I can't, as President of the United States, comment on the decisions about particular prosecutions.... I can tell you, just from 40,000 feet, that some of the most damaging behavior on Wall Street, in some cases, some of the least ethical behavior on Wall Street, wasn't illegal.")

14 Eric Holder, "Preventing and Combating Financial Fraud" (speech, Columbia University Law School, New York, NY, February 23, 2012), www.justice.gov/iso/opa/ag /speeches/2012/ag-speech-120223.html. ("... we've found that much of the conduct that led to the financial crisis was unethical and irresponsible. But we also have discovered that some of this behavior—while morally reprehensible—may not necessarily have been criminal.")

15 "Financial Crises Caused by 'Stupidity and Greed': Geithner," *Reuters*, April 25, 2012, www.reuters.com/article/2012/04/26/us-usa-economy-geithner-idUS BRE83P01P20120426. ("Most financial crises are caused by a mix of stupidity and greed and recklessness and risk-taking and hope.... You can't legislate away stupidity and risk-taking and greed and recklessness.")

16 Gretchen Morgenson and Louise Story, "A Financial Crisis with Little Guilt," *New York Times*, April 14, 2011, A1; Jean Eaglesham, "Criminal Mortgage Probes Fizzle Out," *Wall Street Journal*, August 6, 2011, B1.

17 At the end of 2010, the five largest bank holding companies had combined consolidated assets of $8,469,312,377, up from $6,921,561,423 at the end of 2007. Compare *BHCPR Peer Group 01 Data, 4th Quarter 2010*, www.ffiec.gov/nicpubweb/Content/BHCPRRPT /REPORTS/BHCPR_PEER/Dec2010/PeerGroup_1_december2010.pdf, 27–28, with *BHCPR Peer Group 01 Data, 4th Quarter 2007*, www.ffiec.gov/nicpubweb/Content /BHCPRRPT/REPORTS/BHCPR_PEER/Dec2007/PeerGroup_1_December2007. pdf, 27–28.

18 David J. Lynch, "Banks Seen Dangerous Defying Obama's Too-Big-to-Fail Move," *Bloomberg*, April 16, 2012, www.bloomberg.com/news/2012-04-16/obama-bid-to-end -too-big-to-fail-undercut-as-banks-grow.html.

19 Federal Reserve Bank of Dallas, *2011 Annual Report*, 6.

20 Ibid., 1.

21 Ibid., 21.

22 Esther L. George, President and Chief Executive Officer, Federal Reserve Bank of Kansas City, "Looking Ahead: Financial Stability and Microprudential Supervision" (remarks presented at the 21st Annual Hyman P. Minsky Conference, Levy Economics Institute of Bard College, New York, NY, April 11, 2012), www.kc.frb.org/publicat/speeches/2012 -george-ny-levyeconinstitute-04-11.pdf.

23 Steve Matthews, "Fed's Bullard Says Largest U.S. Banks Should Be Split," *Bloomberg*, May 17, 2012, www.bloomberg.com/news/2012-05-17/fed-s-bullard-says-largest-u-s-banks -should-be-split.html.

24 Jeffrey M. Lacker, President, Federal Reserve Bank of Richmond, "A Program for Financial Stability" (speech, The Banking Institute, UNC School of Law, Charlotte, NC, March 29, 2012), www.richmondfed.org/press_room/speeches/president_jeff_lacker/2012/ lacker_speech_20120329.cfm.

25 *An Overall Assessment of Tarp and Financial Stability: Hearing Before the Congressional Oversight Panel*, March 4, 2011 (Washington, D.C.: U.S. Government Printing Office, 2011) (written testimony of Joseph Stiglitz), www.gpo.gov/fdsys/pkg/CHRG -112shrg65276/pdf/CHRG-112shrg65276.pdf, 116.

26 Victoria McGrane, "Avoiding Next Big Bailout," *The Wall Street Journal*, May 10, 2012, C1. The Dallas Fed estimates that this advantage is "perhaps a percentage point or more." Federal Reserve Bank of Dallas, *2011 Annual Report*, 17.

27 Review & Outlook, "Still Too Big, Still Can't Fail," *The Wall Street Journal*, March 5–6, 2011, A14. ("The funding advantage enjoyed by banks with more than $100 billion in assets over those in the $10-$100 billion range rose from 71 basis points in the first quarter to 78 basis points in the third quarter, which began with President Obama signing the bill and proclaiming an end to too-big-to-fail. The advantage increased to 81 in the fourth quarter.") For other attempts to value the subsidy, see David J. Lynch, "Banks Seen Dangerous Defying Obama's Too-Big-to-Fail Move," *Bloomberg*, April 16, 2012, www.bloomberg.com/news/2012-04-16/obama-bid-to-end-too-big-to-fail-undercut- as-banks-grow.html ("In 2011, funding costs for banks with more than $10 billion in assets were about one-third less than for the smallest banks, according to the FDIC. That gap was only slightly narrower than the 37 percent advantage the largest banks enjoyed when Dodd-Frank was signed."); Dean Baker and Travis MacArthur, "The Value of the 'Too Big to Fail' Big Bank Subsidy," Center for Economic and Policy Research, September 2009, www.cepr.net/documents/publications/too-big-to-fail-2009-09.pdf, 4 (calculating "a government subsidy of $34.1 billion a year to the 18 bank holding companies with more than $100 billion in assets in the first quarter of 2009"); A. Joseph Warburton

and Deniz Anginer, "The End of Market Discipline? Investor Expectations of Implicit State Guarantees," November 18, 2011, http://ssrn.com/abstract=1961656 ("The total value of the subsidy amounted to about $4 billion per year before the crisis, increasing to $60 billion during the crisis, topping $84 billion in 2008."); Andrew G. Haldane, Executive Director, Financial Stability, Bank of England, "The $100 Billion Question," Comments at the Institute of Regulation & Risk, Hong Kong, March 30, 2010, www .bis.org/review/r100406d.pdf?frames=0, 3. ("For the sample of global banks, the average annual subsidy for the top five banks was just less than $60 billion per year.")

28 Standard & Poor's, "The U.S. Government Says Support For Banks Will Be Different 'Next Time'—But Will It?" July 12, 2011, www.politico.com/pdf/PPM223 _7-12-11_-_the_us_government_says_support_for_banks_will_be_different_next time_but_will_it_071211.pdf, 9–10. Moody's Investors Service, "Rating Action: Moody's downgrades Citigroup Inc to P-2; Citibank Prime-1 affirmed; all long-term senior ratings confirmed," September 21, 2011, www.moodys.com/research/Moodys -downgrades-Citigroup-Inc-to-P-2-Citibank-Prime-1--PR_226520; Moody's Investors Service, "Moody's downgrades Bank of America Corp. to Baa1/P-2; Bank of America N.A. to A2, P-1 affirmed," September 21, 2011, www.moodys.com/research /Moodys-downgrades-Bank-of-America-Corp-to-Baa1P-2-Bank--PR_226511.

29 "Poll Results: Do Regulators Really Have the Power to Let Banks Fail?" *American Banker*, April 5, 2012, www.americanbanker.com/issues/177_67/poll-results-ber nanke-dodd-frank-regulators-too-big-to-fail-1048201-1.html.

30 Federal Reserve Bank of Dallas, *2011 Annual Report*, 20.

31 Ibid., 20.

32 Ibid., 21.

33 Davis Polk & Wardwell LLP, "Dodd-Frank Progress Report," May 2012, www.davispolk .com/files/Publication/5f006bb2-86f9-4318-874c-7b26cc0e0625/Presentation/ PublicationAttachment/c57275f5-a41e-4759-9a24-7d11f9160705/May2012_Dodd. Frank.Progress.Report.pdf, 2.

34 J.B. Silver-Greenberg, "Questions As Banks Increase Dividends," *The New York Times*, March 15, 2012, B1.

35 Jesse Eisinger, "Fed Shrugged Off Warnings, Let Banks Pay Shareholders Billions," March 2, 2012, www.propublica.org/article/fed-shrugged-off-warning-let-banks-pay- shareholders-billions.

36 Erik Schatzker, Christine Harper, and Mary Childs, "JPMorgan Said to Transform Treasury to Prop Trading," *Bloomberg*, April 13, 2012, www.bloomberg.com/news/2012- 04-13/jpmorgan-said-to-transform-treasury-to-prop-trading.html; Jesse Eisinger, "Volcker Rule Gets Murky Treatment," *The New York Times*, April 18, 2012, http:// dealbook.nytimes.com/2012/04/18/interpretation-of-volcker-rule-that-muddies-the -intent-of-congress/.

37 Ibid.

38 Erik Schatzker, Christine Harper, and Mary Childs, "JPMorgan Said to Transform Treasury to Prop Trading."

39 William D. Cohan, "The One Thing Jamie Dimon Got Right This Week," *Bloomberg*, www. bloomberg.com/news/2012-05-11/the-one-thing-jamie-dimon-got-right-this-week.html.

40 Ibid.

41 Peter Coy, "JPMorgan's Big Loss: Volcker's Not So Dumb After All," *Bloomberg Business- week*, May 11, 2012, www.businessweek.com/articles/2012-05-11/jpmorgans-big-loss -volckers-not-so-dumb-after-all.

42 Gretchen Morgenson, "At JPMorgan, the Ghost of Dinner Parties Past," *The New York Times*, May 12, 2012, B1.

43 Donna Borak, "Geithner Seeks to Allay Fears on 'Volcker Rule,' European Bailout," *American Banker*, March 20, 2012, www.americanbanker.com/issues/177_55/geithner-volcker-rule-bailout-1047698-1.html.

44 Transcript, *Meet the Press*, May 13, 2012, www.msnbc.msn.com/id/47403362/ns/meet_the_press-transcripts/t/may-reince-priebus-martin-omalley-gavin-newsom-al-cardenas-kathleen-parker-jonathan-capehart-chris-matthews-jamie-dimon/#.T7FomlIdzTo.

45 "The Financial Crisis Response in Charts," April 13, 2012, www.treasury.gov/resource-center/data-chart-center/Documents/20120413_FinancialCrisisResponse.pdf.

46 U.S. Department of the Treasury, "Treasury Announces Pricing of $5.0 Billion of AIG Common Stock," May 6, 2012, www.treasury.gov/press-center/press-releases/Pages/tg1571.aspx.

INDEX

"advance-fee" schemes, 16–17, 126, 210
AIG: bailout commitments to, 43, 64;
bank consortium plan for, 179, 180–81;
CDOs/CDS and, 141–42, 176, 180–81,
183–87, 213–14; Congress and, 143,
179, 182, 186, 189–90, 214; credit-rating agencies and, 141–42, 180; criminal
investigation of, 229; executive bonuses
at, 60, 138–39, 140, 143, 144, 176, 179,
181–82, 183; Federal Reserve and, 143,
187, 212; financial crisis of 2008 and, 4;
French bank and, 184, 186–87; FSOC
and, 230; losses for TARP investment
in, 213–14, 223, 233; media and, 146,
186, 188–89, 212, 214; New York Fed
and, 142, 179–80, 181, 183, 184–87,
213–14, 233; Psaki comments about,
214–15; public assessment of bailouts
and, 183; restructuring of bailout of,
212–13; SIGTARP audit/investigation
of, 60, 137, 143–46, 174, 178–81, 182,
183, 185, 186, 187–91, 224; SIGTARP
recommendations to Treasury and,
76; SIGTARP-Treasury relations and,
137, 139, 143–46, 186, 187–91, 212–13;
too-big-to-fail argument and, 178–81,
197–98; transparency about, 213–14;
Treasury's double standard and,
175–76, 182; Tricadia and, 91; *Two
Year Retrospective* account of, 213–14
Alix, Cathy, 110–11
Allison, Herb: AIG executive compensation and, 140; auto industry bailout
and, 201; Barofsky-Geithner meetings
and, 171–72; Barofsky influence on
TARP decisions at Treasury and, 215;

and Barofsky's future plans, xiii-xvi,
205; Barofsky's meetings with, xi,
xii-xvi, 147, 149, 150, 212; Colonial
Bank case and, 105; at congressional
hearings, xii, 207; credibility of, 167;
Ensign-Boxer Amendment and, 149;
ethical walls and, 167, 168, 169; as
Fannie Mae CEO, xi, 147; HAMP and,
157, 193, 194, 195, 197, 198; PPIP and,
167–68; professional background of,
xi, 147; resignation of, 211; Senate confirmation of, 149; SIGTARP-Treasury
relations and, xiv-xv, 147, 168, 173–74,
208, 212; TARP appointment of, xi,
147; transparency issue and, 171–72;
Warren-Barofsky conversation about,
207
Alvarez, Scott, 117, 187–88
Angell, John, 69, 191, 207
Antonucci, Charles, 192, 210
audit(s): Burke-Barofsky conversation
about, 62; by CIGFO of FSOC functions, 220, 221; executive compensation and, 139–40; Frank-Barofsky
meeting about, 116–17; Frank call
about, 117; Frank endorsement of, 114;
as primary function of inspectors general, 53, 54; results of SIGTARP, 174;
and Rymer suggestion of joint audit of
banking regulators, 58, 59–60; as SIG-
TARP function/focus, 2, 54; SIGTARP
letters to banks about, 98–101, 115–17,
118–20; SIGTARP status as independent agency and, 143–46; SIGTARP-
Treasury relations and, 96–97, 99–101,
116, 119, 143–46; Treasury's double

ABOUT THE AUTHOR

NEIL BAROFSKY is currently a Senior Fellow at NYU Law School. From December 2008 until March 2011, he was the special inspector general in charge of oversight of the Troubled Asset Relief Program (TARP). Before that he was an assistant U.S. attorney for the Southern District of New York. This is his first book.

Aurova 2⁰⁸ 353 1394
Schmidt